JUDITH JAMISON

ASPECTS OF A DANCER

OLGA MAYNARD

·

JUDITH
JAMISON

·

ASPECTS
OF A DANCER

DOUBLEDAY & COMPANY, INC., GARDEN CITY, NEW YORK
1982

For Kathy Ayeh and Sandra Foster-King

because, like Judith Jamison,

they are dancers who happen to be black.

Library of Congress Cataloging in Publication Data
Maynard, Olga.   Judith Jamison, aspects of a dancer.   Includes index.
1. Jamison, Judith.   2. Dancers—Biography.   I. Title.
GV1785.J26M38   793.3'2'0924   [B]
AACR2
ISBN: 0-385-12985-8   Library of Congress Catalog Card Number 78–1245

Design by Beverley Vawter Gallegos

CONTENTS

ACKNOWLEDGMENTS

The genesis of this book, as I have acknowledged in "Author's Note," lies in my work at the University of California at Irvine and Berkeley. I must also acknowledge the help of several people, personally unknown to me, in shaping the book.

While the manuscript was in its successive drafts it was read by a number of people, of varied interests: in dancing; in women; in the artist in contemporary American society. Many queries were made, by readers of the manuscript, for elucidation of statements, and for definition of some theatrical terminology. These I have tried to answer, in the text and in footnotes, with the intent to make this a book not only for dancers but also for the public, as general theatregoers and as general readers.

It has been exceedingly gratifying that many artists have encouraged me to write the book. I am grateful for the confidences of black dancers, on their hopes and fears. Through these confidences I was able to expand the book from a study of one dancer to many, and I was moved to write of the environment for the black and the white dancer.

Alvin Ailey, from the start, showed the keenest interest in my "Jamison book," with as much generosity and good will as he would have shown me for an "Ailey book," which it has become, in good part.

Granted anonymity, friends and enemies can be articulate. Miss Jamison's compeers have spoken freely of her and none more authoritatively and eloquently than Dudley Williams. Paul Szilard, Miss Jamison's and Mr. Ailey's agent, has, as none other could, kept me informed on their professional activities and, very often, their whereabouts. Many of the anecdotes related here are culled from Mr. Szilard's reminiscences, of his travels with the Alvin Ailey American Dance Theater, and with Judith Jamison.

When John Neumeier choreographed *Josephslegende* for the Vienna State Opera Ballet, in which Judith Jamison created the role of Potiphar's Wife, I was invited to the premiere in Vienna—and, in 1977, to observe the filming, by UNITEL of Munich, of the ballet. I am grateful to Mr. Neumeier for giving me the opportunity of seeing Jamison at work in new media (the ballet and the cinema), in circumstances pitilessly revealing of Jamison and other dancers—and in conditions that bred unparalleled intimacy, and confidences.

Statistical data was compiled from the archives of the Alvin Ailey Dance Theater Foundation, to which I was allowed free access by Mr. Ailey, and by Lois Franheim, executive director of the Foundation. In 1977, after I had compiled the major part of my research, Mr. Ailey was good enough to suggest as reference his biographical study, compiled (as a doctoral dissertation) by Jacqueline Quinn Moore Latham in 1974.[1] I have used Miss Latham's dissertation chiefly as a check on dates for performances of the Alvin Ailey American Dance Theater and my gratitude to Miss Latham for the painstaking compilation of her study is assuredly shared by all writers on the Ailey company.

I have had the good fortune to hear the clear recollections of persons who knew Alvin Ailey and his mother, Mrs. Lula E. Cooper, during Ailey's childhood, adolescence, and his early years as a dancer, when Ailey lived in Los Angeles. Here Ailey first danced, first choreographed, and began to direct a company of dancers.

My chief gratitude, of course, is to Judith Jamison, who consented to interrogations with such good humor as has earned my affection. Her almost total recall of her childhood, and the emotions she described of her life as a performer, have given the narrative a substance and an immediacy it would otherwise have lacked. I thank her for the respect she has paid me as the writer of this book, which is about and not by, or for, Judith Jamison.

Throughout the slow and lengthy process of research and writing I have been encouraged and supported by Louise Gault, my editor at Doubleday & Company, Inc., who, like Jamison, studied ballet as a girl in Pennsylvania. Equally sustaining has been the saintly patience of my literary agent, Julie Fallowfield of McIntosh & Otis, Inc.,

---

[1] Submitted, in partial fulfillment of the doctoral degree, to the College of Health, Physical Education, and Recreation, at Texas Woman's University, Denton, Texas.

William Como, Editor-in-Chief of *Dance Magazine,* and Edna Moore of the Alvin Ailey American Dance Center generously assisted in gathering photographs, from which Doubleday's art director, Alex Gotfryd, made the selection that vividly represents Jamison as dancer and as person, and forms a pictorial record of her career. The manuscript was thoughtfully copy-edited by Glenn Rounds.

AUTHOR'S NOTE

I have been asked why I chose Judith Jamison as the pivot of a book on black dancers in contemporary America. The choice of the subject was made because Jamison is a woman and because she is a black dancer.

In 1968, when I began conducting courses in dance history for the University of California at Irvine, I was made aware of the sparseness of literature on American dance. At the time, the Civil Rights movement and the feminist movement were attempting to win recognition for two so-called "minority" strata in American society. Students in the courses I conducted, and audiences who attended my public lectures, asked questions that this book attempts to answer, about black dancers, and about women dancers, in the United States.

In the late 1960s I was asked to write a book on black dancers and I began work on biographical studies of two men, Alvin Ailey in modern dance and Arthur Mitchell in ballet. A considerable amount of work was completed on that book (from which were drawn two articles on Mitchell, published in *Dance Magazine*) before I realized that, in their very beings, these men obscured the view that I wished to open on black dance in America. Reluctantly, I gave up the book.

Meanwhile, I had inaugurated a course (within the larger studies of Dance in America) as "Black Dance: Its African Origins and Its Western Evolutions."[1] And, for the Graduate Program in Dance, I was conducting a research project into "Women Dancers Throughout History." The book on Judith Jamison became organic to the two courses of study, the more so as students expressed the wish to

[1] "Black Dance: Its African Origins and Its Western Evolutions" investigates the influences of African dance and music on jazz in the United States, calypso in Trinidad, samba in Brazil, and more.

explore not only the techniques and aesthetics of American dance, but also its social and philosophical aspects as these relate to the dancer.

In 1972, when Jamison was recipient of the Dance Magazine Award, I was asked to write an article on her for *Dance Magazine.* Almost from our first meeting, Miss Jamison and I agreed that I would write a book about her and her work.

I did not want to write the biography of Judith Jamison, where the focus of the subject would obscure all on its periphery. I wished to describe an American dancer in her time and place.

I had done so, on a modest scale, in *Bird of Fire,* the story of Maria Tallchief,[2] presenting an American ballerina of the epoch— the 1940s and 1950s—in which the Franco-Russo-American ballet gave way to the valid American ballet.

Tallchief, half white and half Indian (her father was a full-blooded Osage from Oklahoma), had an irrefragable American ancestry. Jamison, a "black" American, could trace her roots only for two generations. They were utterly unlike, as artists and as personalities. Yet, there were interesting similarities between them.

Tallchief is a child of the upper middle class; Jamison, of the lower, or "blue collar" class. Both came from disciplined but not repressive environments, in which certain verities were instilled in the children. Their lives were dedicated, we may say, from childhood, to an ethic of work, in the pursuit of excellence. The wonder is that from a prosaic environment the artist of imagination and talent flowers into a Tallchief, and a Jamison. Is a spiritual stamina drawn from this source?

My primary interest in Judith Jamison was as a woman who dances. The interest was extended to Jamison as a dancer who happens to be black. It is not my inclination to segregate dancers by their shades of skin. That such segregation has occurred is a fact, and a factor, in American dance. This study of Jamison, in its precise form, was undertaken only after I had been convinced that it was of value, as perspective on the larger subject of American dance.

I gave up my book on Alvin Ailey and Arthur Mitchell because they are brilliant men who altered their environments. Each was

[2] *Bird of Fire,* published by Dodd, Mead & Company, New York, in 1961.

successful, to a degree unequaled for their compeers, as a performer. Each man founded a school and a company, thereby freeing themselves of the domination of white theatre. Ailey and Mitchell could then exert power over other dancers and they ceased, then, to be representative of the black dancer in America.

Judith Jamison remains vulnerable as the artist, because she is dependent on choreographers and companies. At the height of her success, she is the most vulnerable. This is the point, the pitch, at which I have described her, and her way to becoming Judith Jamison.

The intention is to show the aspects of a dancer. The woman dancer in history, into our time, is a barometer of society as much as she is the instrument of dance. More and more, urgent questions are being asked about women who dance: *How and why do they become dancers? By what impulse and toward what ends? When and where do they dance? And for whom, by whose wish and whim, other than their own will and desire?* It is my hope that this book will lead to much larger discussion on American dance, and on women who dance.

Judith Jamison: Aspects of a Dancer is as accurate an account of the dancer's life as I could make within the bounds of good taste, and it is as honest and as intimate a statement as Jamison herself chose to make, about dancing and about living. The book has been drawn from several sources but, in its final phase, it has assumed a shape and substance of its own.

STATISTICS

Judith Jamison was born in Philadelphia, Pennsylvania, on May 10, 1944. She was educated in the primary and secondary Pennsylvania school systems, from which she graduated at seventeen. She went, on a Physical Education scholarship, and as a Psychology major, to Fisk University in Nashville, Tennessee, where she studied for three semesters. Her education was completed at the Philadelphia Dance Academy.

Jamison's dance education began at the age of six, under Marian Cuyjet and teachers of the Judimar School of Dance in Philadelphia, and continued there for eleven years. During that period Jamison also studied with other teachers, among them Antony Tudor and Maria Swoboda. Her training was principally in the classical dance, ballet.

She made her debut at age six, at Town Hall in Philadelphia; and, in 1959, made another, formal debut as Myrtha in *Giselle*. In 1964, while studying at the Philadelphia Dance Academy, she was discovered by Agnes de Mille, who took her to New York and cast her (with three other black dancers) in the ballet *The Four Marys*. Jamison's services were engaged by American Ballet Theatre for the spring season, 1965, at the New York State Theater, after which she was dismissed from the company.

That same year Jamison joined the Alvin Ailey American Dance Theater and appeared with it in the United States and on overseas tours, in Europe and Africa. When the company was disbanded by Ailey, Jamison joined the Harkness Ballet, with which Ailey and a few members of his company were affiliated, in Europe. Jamison was a member of the Harkness Ballet in 1966–67, leaving it to rejoin Ailey when he reactivated his company.

Thereafter, except for leaves of absence, Judith Jamison has been a member of the Ailey company, in which, since 1971, she has occupied a position comparable to that of a prima ballerina in a classical company.

She has danced an extensive range of the Ailey company's repertory and in many works choreographed for her, of which the most famous is Ailey's great solo, *Cry*. She was with the Ailey company on all its foreign tours (into 1979, when, because of an injury, she was obliged to take leave from the European tour) and, in 1980, assumed the position of co-director (to Alvin Ailey) of the company, in its seventeenth New York City Center season and for a Japanese tour. These tours have included Russia, where the Ailey company was the first modern dance company to appear, and Asia, India, Africa, Australia, the Near and the Far East, Europe, and North and South America.

In the 1970s Jamison achieved international "star" status, in part through her appearances with the Ailey company and in large part through her appearances as a guest artist with European ballet companies. She was cast in the leading female role of Potiphar's Wife in a production of *Josephslegende* (choreographed by John Neumeier) for the ballet of the Vienna State Opera, and later performed the role with the Hamburg Ballet, in Hamburg and Munich. The film of *Josephslegende,* produced by Munich's UNITEL Film and Television Production Company, made Jamison known to the European audience en masse and increased her popularity in Europe, where she is called the Black Venus of twentieth-century dance, as well as the *monstre sacre* of American dance.

In 1978 Maurice Béjart choreographed a modern version of *Le Spectre de la Rose* for Jamison, who appeared in the pas de deux with the Brussels-based Ballet of the 20th Century, on a tour of capital European cities. She danced her role in Béjart's *Rose* again, when the Ballet of the 20th Century staged a spring 1979 season in New York, at the Minskoff Theater.

In 1972 Judith Jamison, with The Royal Ballet's premier danseur Anthony Dowell, were recipients of the Dance Magazine Award. Presenting the award to Jamison was the illustrious black dancer Katherine Dunham. In 1978, Jamison was chosen to present the Dance Magazine Award to Mikhail Baryshnikov, the Russian danseur, with whom she appeared, earlier, in Alvin Ailey's *Pas de "Duke,"* to the music of Duke Ellington, dancing the pas de deux for the Ailey company and American Ballet Theatre in New York and, later, at the State Opera House, Vienna.

In 1972 Jamison was selected by President Richard M. Nixon for the board of the National Endowment for the Arts, on which she served into 1976. Also in 1972 Jamison and the dancer-choreographer Miguel Godreau were married in Stockholm; the marriage was annulled in 1974.

In 1980 Jamison took a leave of absence from the Ailey company to appear in the 1981 Broadway musical, *Sophisticated Ladies.* The aspects of her career are examined into autumn 1980.

PREFACE

This is a book about a woman named Judith Jamison, whose surname is pronounced with emphasis on the first syllable, *Jam,* as in the sweet stuff found in a jar. It is the story of a dancer, but it is not a conventional biography. It should be read, as it is written, for the perspectives it opens onto some aspects of the life of an American artist in contemporary society.

Preferably, a dancer should be viewed as a jewel is best viewed, admired for itself without concern for its history. Jamison is not viewed in this way because of her singularity in the theatre where she occupies a prominent position. Jamison is a famous dancer and she is a dancer who happens to be black. Equally by reason of her art and her color, she is extolled as a symbol in America. Her career, and to great extent her life, has been formed by the conventions of our society.

The worth of the dancer is technical and aesthetic, it is not assessed by the pigmentation of the dancer's skin. Were Jamison's skin (which is the color of dark amber) a different shade, she would still dance as she dances, in a style as uniquely hers as her thumbprint. Yet, Jamison's development as an artist has been dominated by her color as much as by her technical skill and her artistry. In the perspectives on Jamison's story some aspects will be seen as sociological, some as theatrical.

The English writer Graham Greene describes himself as "an author who is a Catholic," and he asks his readers, and the literary critics, to accept him in this view, and not as a Catholic author. Important though Greene acknowledges his religion to be to him, and despite the fact that much of his work is based on themes from Roman Catholicism, Greene's paramount claim to an identity is as a writer.

Judith Jamison is of African ancestry and her "black" lineage is intrinsic to her psyche. She often dances in works choreographed on "the black experience," the experience of being black in white society. Jamison, like Greene, would like her distinction to rest on her identity as the dancer, and so would part of her audience. It does not and it cannot lie there alone, for Jamison can no more extricate her image from its color than she can divide it from its shape and substance.

The existence of an artist in contemporary society is as complicated as that of any other member of the community. It is made the more complex for the dancer by the laborious processes through which he or she is trained to perform and the erratic methods by which the dance theatre is operated. Sentimental accounts of the theatre are spurious romances, far from the truth of the exacting and often murderously enervating ways by which a dancer like Judith Jamison achieves renown. The American dancer inhabits a fragile structure as theatre; the rise and the fall of companies alternately offer opportunities and deprive the dancer of them. Without opportunities to perform, the dancer perishes. The dancer is utterly dependent on the choreographer, whom he must first attract and then inspire, in order to have works made on and for him. There are forces that bear the dancer to fulfillment of his potential, and other forces that work toward his annihilation. Against these unpredictable forces, the dancer is often helpless; he is formed as much by outward pressures as by inward motives.

In the free, autonomous, and competitive American theatre the artist's recognition comes about not only by talent and training but also by luck. Every dancer's career is to some extent affected by chance, in America more so than elsewhere.

Judith Jamison was trained for ballet but she did not become a classical dancer. At a height of five feet, ten inches, Jamison, in *pointe* shoes, is taller than the height considered ideal for a female ballet dancer. And Jamison is not white. In the opinion of purists, her height and her color make Jamison aesthetically unsuitable for ballet.

Nevertheless, Jamison has danced in ballet companies as well as in the "modern" dance company of the Alvin Ailey American Dance Theater. She has defied conventions but only because she is a "superstar." The conditions and circumstances by which Jamison achieved stardom are related here, within their scenes. I have set

Judith Jamison in her time and place, as an American dancer. Passages that relate to other dancers are not idle digressions but integral parts of the Jamison story. The story of Marie Antoinette, Queen of the French, would be meaningless unless it were related within the larger drama of European history.

I chose to arrange the narrative in two connective parts, as "Dancing" and as "Living."

In "Dancing," Jamison is seen as one in a large cast of characters, all of them belonging to the story of American dance. Preeminent in the cast is Alvin Ailey. As it is manifestly impossible to relate the story of Jamison's career without relating Ailey's, this book pertains almost as much to Ailey as to Jamison.

In "Living," Jamison, verbatim, describes the events and emotions that, in her belief, have most strongly affected her life and her work. This is Jamison's account of herself and her world.

It is in these two perspectives, as "Dancing" and "Living," that I propose to open the view onto some aspects of the dancer's life. In one perspective she is viewed externally; in the other, internally.

It is Judith Jamison's triumph, as it is her curse, to be a black dancer in America. The view of the dance in American theatre is not my invention but the record as history is obliged to report it.

OLGA MAYNARD

DANCING

Women, and artists, have phases, like the moon. Phase, in astronomy, is the apparent shape of the moon at a given moment; it is its aspect, the side or part turned to our view.

ONE

It was Thursday, July 29, 1976. American Ballet Theatre was having a season at the New York State Theater and on the program that evening was a new work by Alvin Ailey. *Pas de "Duke,"* a pas de deux in jazz idiom, was set to Duke Ellington's music, "Such Sweet Thunder," "Sonnet to Caesar," "Hank Cinq," "Clothed Woman," with scenery and costumes by Rouben Ter-Arutunian.

Pas de "Duke" had received its world premiere several weeks earlier, on May 11, at the New York City Center. On that Tuesday evening it was featured on a gala bill, a benefit program for the Alvin Ailey Dance Theater. The ballet was a success. Critics agreed that it was one of the best of Ailey's works, and that he had been challenged and stimulated by the talents of the two dancers for whom he had choreographed *Pas de "Duke."*

One was Judith Jamison, a principal dancer of the Ailey company. The other was Mikhail Baryshnikov, an ex-member of the Kirov Ballet of Leningrad and, currently, the star of American Ballet Theatre. They presented, in themselves, a classic study in contrast: male and female, short and tall, white and black. Jamison was categorized as a "modern" dancer, Baryshnikov as a ballet danseur.

Ailey brought these two dancers together as the protagonists in his *Pas de "Duke,"* a ballet that might more readily have been called *Ailey's Agon.*[1] The work was constructed with a solo for each of the dancers, and in the solos Ailey deliberately played on the dancers' aptitudes. He as adroitly emphasized their characteristics: Jamison's elegance, Baryshnikov's perennial boyishness.

Ter-Arutunian's costumes exaggerated the contrasts of the two performers; he dressed Jamison in a sleeveless shiny black satin

[1] *Agon*, from the Greek, meaning contest or struggle (hence: agony), is the title of a famous Balanchine work, premiered in 1957, the third ballet in the choreographer's celebrated collaboration with Igor Stravinsky.

jumpsuit and Baryshnikov in a white replica. Jamison was elongated and Baryshnikov foreshortened as they moved against the cyclorama. The piece began with a duet and ended with another, in the approved mode of the grand pas de deux in ballet. In between, in separate variations, the dancers made individual statements, about dancing, about themselves. When they came together, in Ailey's choreography, they became a swirling abstraction in dance, a living chiaroscuro. The effect was sensational.

Pas de "Duke" scored a double triumph, providing the dancers with a tour de force and the choreographer with a coup. Critics praised Baryshnikov for mastering certain elements of the modern dance and Ailey for having worked, successfully, in the modern idiom with a ballet danseur. Jamison they took for granted; she had long before this proved her talent as a dancer; her contribution seemed to lie in the lending of her presence to the piece, for the contrast it gave to Baryshnikov's, and the piece itself was chiefly significant for being a friendly contest between two artists of widely varying styles, and sizes, and shapes. This was not the first time that Jamison had been used to illustrate a choreographic point, nor the only time she was required to cause a sensation.

Pas de "Duke," premiered as a novelty, for the Ailey gala, was to be revived many times. Two months after its first performance it was staged by American Ballet Theatre at the New York State Theater. The dancers had to adjust their dancing to a larger stage than the one at City Center; having accommodated themselves to the expanded space, they projected to the audience with a greater dynamism than they had at City Center. Baryshnikov had overcome his initial nervousness at appearing in the piece and Jamison was less protective of her partner than she had been; the contest was more intense, the reconciliation far more exciting than at the first performance.

There was a natural exultation in the moment for Jamison. The second performance of *Pas de "Duke"* did not tax as much as the first and the overwhelming success of the piece, with the large audience at the New York State Theater, kindled a euphoric mood. Jamison found herself, that night, looking back to another time when she had danced with American Ballet Theatre.

TWO

American Ballet Theatre celebrated its twenty-fifth anniversary with a season at the New York State Theater. The four-week engagement, begun on March 16, 1965, was a historic event, for which the company summoned all its resources.

Organized, as Ballet Theatre, in 1939, this company staged its inaugural season the following year, at the Rockefeller Center Theater in Radio City. Within a quarter of a century it had become the peer of ballet companies whose traditions had been developed over two and three hundred years.

Ballet Theatre toured widely, in and outside the United States, and for its foreign appearances it appended "American" to its title, eventually adopting the full name of American Ballet Theatre.

Its large and eclectic repertoire, from nineteenth- and twentieth-century choreographers, was the company's greatest attribute. At its inception Ballet Theatre established "wings," within which certain works were maintained, as in the "American" wing, for the ballets of Agnes de Mille and Eugene Loring; the "Russian" wing, for the works of Russian choreographers; and the "English" wing, in which the choreographer Antony Tudor was the presiding genius.

The name Ballet Theatre was chosen to accentuate the character of the company, one similar to that of a great museum. Ballet Theatre intended to mount ballets, old and new, in much the way a museum exhibits art works from the past and the present.

The theatrical character of Ballet Theatre was emphasized, in the content of the repertoire and the mode of production. Ballet Theatre was like a big opera company, except that, instead of singers, it had dancers.

Ballet Theatre was formed out of another company, the Mordkin Ballet. Its founder, Mikhail Mordkin, was one of the many Russian émigré dance artists who came to the United States after the Russian Revolution and following the disbandment of the Paris-based

company, Ballets Russes de Serge Diaghilev. Among the other artists was Michel Fokine, "the father of modern ballet," who spent his
last years working with American Ballet Theatre. Another was
George Balanchine, the choreographer-director of the New York
City Ballet, American Ballet Theatre's arch rival.

One of Mordkin's pupils was a rich young widow, Lucia Chase,
who danced in the Mordkin Ballet. When this company was expanded into Ballet Theatre, Chase became its chief financial support
and, eventually, its artistic director. Chase was one of the American
balletomanes who invested their wealth in the hopes of founding a
great national American ballet.

The term "national ballet" was applicable to the schools and companies of countries with state-subsidized theatres. The European and
Russian ballets had been founded under monarchal patronage and,
even when monarchies fell, the national ballets were supported by
the state. In the United States, however, where there was no official
recognition of theatre, dance companies were obliged to operate,
like ordinary business organizations, as autonomous competitors in
the commercial theatre.

American dance had had a precarious course of development, in
large part because of an impoverished economy. No single fortune,
like that of Lucia Chase, was sufficient to wholly maintain a big
ballet company.

Shortly after its founding, Ballet Theatre was forced to disband,
because of lack of funds. Popular though the company was with the
audience, the box office receipts could not defray the expenses of its
maintenance. Ballet Theatre would have been declared bankrupt,
and its organization brought to an end, but for the intervention of
Lucia Chase. Thereafter, this intrepid woman devoted all her energy, her considerable tact, and most of her money, to achieving her
aim for American Ballet Theatre. This was no less than to make it
one of the great ballet companies of the international theatre.

Chase was aided in her goal by some admirers of American Ballet
Theatre, benefactors who gave the company monetary support, and
by the dedicated dancers who, in good times and in bad, placed their
faith in American Ballet Theatre.

The lack of a home theatre was thought by many to be the
severest handicap imposed on the company, especially in its rivalry
with the New York City Ballet. American Ballet Theatre had toured
the Western world, and performed in forty-eight states of the United

States of America, but it had so far failed to find a home theatre, as a base of operations. When, in 1962, Chase was invited to move her company from New York to Washington, she acceded, in the belief that American Ballet Theatre would thus become the resident ballet of the nation's capital. (The John F. Kennedy Center for the Performing Arts, not yet in operation, was to become the national capital's opera house.)

In Washington, American Ballet Theatre was sponsored by the Washington Ballet Guild, but this body soon discovered that it could not raise sufficient funds to maintain the company. American Ballet Theatre refused to alter its policies or to curtail its scope of operations. In this impasse, the company again disbanded.

As American Ballet Theatre reached its nadir, the New York City Ballet ascended to its zenith. A company of modest beginnings, drawn from the School of American Ballet, the New York City Ballet was now a great classical company. The New York State Theater was designed and built for it and, in 1964, it became the first American dance company to give its dancers fully paid employment, fifty-two weeks of a year.

The School of American Ballet, although an autonomous organization, was the parent school of the New York City Ballet. Both had been founded by Lincoln Kirstein and George Balanchine.

Kirstein, the heir to a department store fortune, and a graduate of Harvard College, was a romantic who conceived the notion of founding a great ballet school in the United States which would be a replica of the Imperial Russian Ballet School in St. Petersburg. George Balanchine was a product of that school (which was to become the Leningrad Choreographic Institute after the Russian Revolution in 1917). Out of the school had come Pavlova and Nijinsky, in one generation—as, in another generation, would emerge Natalia Makarova, Rudolf Nureyev, and Mikhail Baryshnikov.

Balanchine, with his wife Tamara Geva and another young dancer, named Alexandra Danilova, left Russia and joined the company organized by Serge Diaghilev, in Paris, as the Ballets Russes. When Diaghilev died in 1929, the company shattered, to reform in splinter groups of "ballets russes." Balanchine was associated only briefly with one of those groups. He later worked as ballet master with the Royal Danish Ballet, and in the London muscial theatre. In 1933 Balanchine formed a company, which he called Les Ballets 1933, as though pessimistic of its future. It did not survive the year but Kirstein met Balanchine in London and persuaded him to come to America, to direct the School of American Ballet. It was to become the academic fount of ballet in America.[1]

Out of the school, in 1934, Balanchine drew a performing unit, named The American Ballet. Two years later, Kirstein formed a second company, Ballet Caravan. Both companies were short-lived but, after his return from service in the U. S. Army, Kirstein joined Balanchine in 1946 to found yet another company, Ballet Society. It was defined as a lyric, rather than as a dramatic, dance company and its development, within the Balanchine *oeuvre,* was to be in the genre classified as neoclassical ballet.

In 1948, Ballet Society was invited to appear at the City Center in New York. The success of its season established it as City Center's resident ballet. Ballet Society's name was altered to the New York City Ballet.

Under George Balanchine, the New York City Ballet became world famous. Balanchine, the undisputed ballet genius of his era, developed the quintessential Balanchine dancer, through the School of American Ballet. The Balanchine dancer was, typically, of a certain physique and temperament, readily recognizable as a type, in international ballet. As the School trained far more dancers than could be absorbed by the New York City Ballet, its graduates pursued careers in many other companies, in and outside the United States.

Inevitably, factions formed in the audience, partisans of the New York City Ballet and of the American Ballet Theatre. The New York City Ballet cultivated a "balletomane" audience—one somewhat different from the audience en masse. For many years, the New York City Ballet was obliged to maintain an austere economy. The dancers performed in simple practice dress, against bare cyclorama. Far from detracting from Balanchine's ballets, the austerity served to emphasize the nobility and elegance of his choreography, and the phenomenal technique of his dancers. The New York City Ballet possessed a magnificent orchestra and Balanchine's musicality was paramount to his choreography.

---

[1] There is no official "American" ballet school, as there is no official *national* American ballet company. The School of American Ballet, however, by merit of its reputation, is accepted as the academic fount of classical dance in the United States and has been so designated by the National Endowment for the Arts.

In Balanchine's company, the artists assumed a chaste anonymity, as instruments of the dance. The dancers in this company were listed alphabetically, a surprisingly democratic procedure for a director-choreographer who had emerged from the Imperial Russian theatre.

These attitudes and characteristics were in strong contrast to those at American Ballet Theatre. The company's eclectic repertoire required dancers of very wide range. It employed numbers of foreign dancers, and observed the conventional ranking of artists, from *primas* and *premiers,* through soloists into the corps de ballet.

American Ballet Theatre was sometimes accused of abrogating its "American" character but its supporters contended that, in all that it did, the company was veritably a "national" company. The conglomeration of artists, from foreign and native schools, was in itself representative of polyglot America. It was argued that the New York City Ballet, with its repertoire largely formed on the Balanchine *oeuvre,* was in actuality the creation (and the company) of one man, while American Ballet Theatre, with its comprehensive repertoire (drawn from several choreographers, some foreign, some native), was more truly representative of a "national" ballet company.

The strongest contention in favor of American Ballet Theatre's claim to being the "national" ballet lay in its wide renown. The New York City Ballet (although it sometimes appeared abroad) seldom performed outside Manhattan; it was, as its name signified, a New York civic ballet. American Ballet Theatre, however, belonged to the whole country. It existed by touring, sometimes in one-night stands, in cities and towns across the continent. For most of the United States, American Ballet Theatre provided the only knowledge of professional classical dancing.

American Ballet Theatre inherited the audience en masse that had previously belonged to Ballet Russe de Monte Carlo, the first big ballet company to tour America in the twentieth century. The fans of Ballet Russe de Monte Carlo, by now accumulated over several generations, were far more responsive to American Ballet Theatre than they were to the New York City Ballet. And it was this national acclaim, and the warmth of the regard in which American Ballet Theatre was held throughout the United States, that, in the 1960s, saved the company from extinction. Just as American Ballet Theatre reached its nadir, the American government belatedly recognized the national theatre—and the usefulness of dance companies—as a cultural ambassador, for political propaganda.

The enduring argument over the respective merits of the New York City Ballet and the American Ballet Theatre had been exacerbated in the early 1960s by the Ford Foundation's gifts, of millions of dollars, to the School of American Ballet and the New York City Ballet.

Long before the American government recognized dance as art, dance in the United States had been the recipient of funds from private patrons and from industry. In the late 1950s the Ford Foundation initiated a study of ballet in America, with the intent of assisting in the development of a national ballet. In a series of pilot programs (referred to as "The Tutu and the Model-T") the Ford Foundation awarded scholarships, through the School of American Ballet, to students who were believed to have potential for professional ballet.

In 1963 the Ford Foundation made a grant of $7.7 million to the ballet, the largest ever given to dance in America. Substantial amounts of the grant went to the School of American Ballet and to the New York City Ballet, and, over succeeding years, these two organizations were the beneficiaries of other generous Ford Foundation grants of monies. The 1963 grant also benefited some other companies, one of them being the San Francisco Ballet, whose director, Lew Christensen, was a former member of the New York City Ballet. Those antagonistic to the New York City Ballet grumbled that this company and its "satellites" had been grossly favored over American Ballet Theatre, which was not named as a beneficiary of the Ford Foundation grant.

Yet another reason for indignation, on the part of the partisans of American Ballet Theatre, was the favoritism shown the New York City Ballet, as the resident ballet for the New York State Theater at Lincoln Center.

When the complex of theatres was planned for Lincoln Center, the New York State Theater was designated the new home of the New York City Ballet, and, later, the School of American Ballet was moved to a commodious building in the adjacent block, sharing the premises with the Juilliard School. A smaller company, founded by Robert Joffrey, replaced the New York City Ballet at City Center. These two companies, the New York City Ballet at the New York

State Theater and the City Center Joffrey Ballet, enjoyed a status rare in the American dance: they occupied "home" theatres.[2]

The apparent stability of the New York City Ballet was in strong contrast to the perpetual state of crisis in which American Ballet Theatre dwelled. After the debacle of the Washington residence, American Ballet Theatre was destitute. Its supporters hoped that it would be invited to share, with the New York City Ballet, a residence at the New York State Theater. A New York base of operations was as necessary as funding for the company to survive. And residence, for at least part of each year, in a New York theatre would permit American Ballet Theatre to develop its repertoire and to attract patronage, from the industrial foundations and from private donors, for its work. Above all, residence at the New York State Theater—or in some other theatre in the city—would equalize for American Ballet Theatre the conditions in which it operated in competition with the New York City Ballet.

In the 1960s the matter of a "national" ballet preoccupied a great number of people, many of them in the government and in industry, from which grants were disbursed to the arts in America. The assumption of the title "American Ballet Theatre" gave this company tacit claim to being the "national" ballet. The old contention over the respective merits of "Lucia Chase's company" and "George Balanchine's company" suddenly assumed greater import when these merits had to be determined by the Congress of the United States, as funding of the arts. Suddenly the "American" character of a dance company began to outweigh considerations of its aesthetics. Decisions might be guided not so much by artistic merit as by the worth of a company for political propaganda.

Ballet in America, in the 1960s, burgeoned. In the 1970s it would exceed all expectations, in its popularity with the audience en masse and in box office receipts. The unprecedented "ballet boom" occurred, in part, through the awakening of federal and civic bureaucrats to "cultural" assets of the dance. Monies from government and industry were about to be poured into the development of a great American dance theatre. Until then, the weight of supporting the

2 Dancers of the Metropolitan Opera House, New York, perform for opera productions. They do not have identity in their own right as a ballet company. By 1981, only the New York City Ballet could claim a "home" theatre, entrenched as it is at the New York State Theater. Robert Joffrey's company had ceased to be resident at the New York City Center.

dance in America had been borne by a few, among whom were Lucia Chase, at American Ballet Theatre, and Lincoln Kirstein, at the New York City Ballet. These two, at greater personal cost than any others, had devoted their respective fortunes to a single ideal: the establishment of a great ballet company in America.

Early in their histories, Kirstein had proposed the merger of Balanchine's company with that of Chase's. He had been rebuffed, and, thereafter, the two companies remained separate, and rivals— for the same grants of monies, and, to a great extent, for the same public. There were a few other professional ballet troupes but none of the size and repertorial substance of these two. Dancers entered the New York City Ballet, usually, by graduation from the School of American Ballet. American Ballet Theatre, however, engaged dancers on seasonal contracts, to satisfy repertorial requirements.

Lucia Chase is now legendary, for her optimism and her pluck. She had never gambled more boldly than she did in 1963, when, having renounced the Washington residency, she returned to New York and negotiated a four-week lease at the New York State Theater for the celebration of her company's twenty-fifth anniversary.

In August 1964, Chase reactivated American Ballet Theatre for a tour of South America and Mexico, under auspices of the U. S. State Department. The company also went on a tour of the American Southwest where, on November 11, 1964, it premiered *La Sylphide,* the first of the full-length nineteenth-century classics on which American Ballet Theatre would base its claim to being the foremost *traditionally* classical company in America. Up to then, ballet in the United States had been developed in the Diaghilevian principle: three or four short works to a program. Chase favored a more operatic mode, grand ballet, with costly decor, after the style of the European and Russian opera houses. She engaged Harald Lander, from the Royal Danish Ballet and the Paris Opéra Ballet, to mount *La Sylphide,* in an adaptation of the Bournonville version of 1836, with the Danish ballerina Toni Lander as the Sylphide.[3]

[3] Chase, in this decade, engaged the Italian ballerina Carla Fracci for *Coppélia.* She also engaged David Blair of The Royal Ballet to mount the full-length *Swan Lake* (he also set *Giselle* on ABT), initiating a policy for producing large-scale ballets which led to Nureyev's *Raymonda,* Baryshnikov's *Don Quixote* and *The Nutcracker,* and Makarova's *La Bayadère.* With these, ABT has kept its status as a *traditionally* classical company.

The American veterans were not neglected. Chase called on the choreographers Antony Tudor, Agnes de Mille, and Jerome Robbins. Tudor reset his works, on which Ballet Theatre had founded a substantial part of its first renown. De Mille choreographed two new works and Jerome Robbins, who had meanwhile had a lucrative and highly praised career on Broadway, contributed a daringly innovative ballet, *Les Noces,* to a score by Stravinsky.

The company, taking up residence at the New York State Theater, marveled at the gracious appointments of studios and dressing rooms, far removed from the bleak and often dirty quarters in which dancers worked and dressed on tour. The nucleus of the company was in the dancers who had steadfastly placed their trust in American Ballet Theatre's ability to survive its crises. To these were added some dancers, of temporary status in the company, for Agnes de Mille's ballet *The Four Marys.*

In 1940, Ballet Theatre's first year, de Mille choreographed *Black Ritual* (or *Obeah*), based on ceremonies of *obeah,* religious rites practiced in the Caribbean and brought there from Africa, to be used for "black" (evil) and "white" (beneficent) magic. De Mille set *Black Ritual* to Darius Milhaud's *Création du Monde* and (as there were no black dancers in the company) brought in a troupe of itinerant artists. De Mille later wrote that this engagement of black dancers by Ballet Theatre was an act without precedent and one without parallel for a company of the status of Ballet Theatre. The black dancers remained in the company until *Black Ritual* was dropped from the repertoire, at which time they became "an unwarranted luxury." In 1965 de Mille again required black dancers, for *The Four Marys.*

This ballet was drawn from an old Scottish ballad, brought to America by immigrants and absorbed into American music. The ballad commemorates, it is said, an episode that occurred in the time of Mary, Queen of Scots. It relates a drama that reflects the manners and mores of a society in which there is inequitable privilege for the upper class over the lower.

The mistress of a mansion has in her service four pretty young maids: Mary Seaton, Mary Beaton, Mary Carmichael, and Mary Hamilton, of whom the fourth is the gentlest and the loveliest. The mistress' suitor, a handsome young gentleman, becomes enamored of Mary Hamilton. She falls in love with him, yields to him, and in time bears his child. In an attempt to hide her shame and disgrace, Mary Hamilton drowns the infant. The crime is discovered, Mary Hamilton is tried for murder, is condemned and hanged. The gentleman goes free of punishment or blame for Mary Hamilton's sins. The mistress and the three Marys enter into a conspiracy of polite silence, playing their roles with exquisite etiquette, so that all goes as it went before.

De Mille kept the drama intact but transferred the scene, setting it in the antebellum South. Judith Lerner and Paul Sutherland, two white dancers, were cast as the mistress and her suitor. For the four Marys, de Mille engaged Carmen de Lavallade, Glory van Scott, Cleo Quitman, and Judith Jamison, all of whom were black dancers. Their tenure in the company would be temporary but, for the time being, they would be part of American Ballet Theatre's gala celebration of its twenty-fifth season. In the weeks preceding the opening of that season, the atmosphere was charged with electricity and tinged by hysteria. American Ballet Theatre, despite its apparent gaiety, was still in dire straits. In truth, the company was fighting for its life.

The choreographers, on whom a great deal depended for the success of the season, were on their mettle. Impervious to administrative worries, they were concerned with casting and rehearsal, vying, as is usual, for the dancers they most wanted, and for studio time and space. Robbins, known as a meticulous taskmaster, was treated with reverence; de Mille, with almost the same.

This remarkable woman, a pioneer of American ballet, had contributed in large measure to her national theatre, in her *ballet Americana* (of which *Rodeo* and *Fall River Legend* are two masterworks) and on Broadway, where she helped to revolutionize the American musical theatre in *Oklahoma!* De Mille had a catholic dance education and, at her command, a stylistic range from folk dance to contemporary ballet. Next to making dances, de Mille seemed to like nothing better than discovering fresh talent. She could pride herself on an ability to discern the potentiality for greatness, and her protégées were already numerous when she discovered Judith Jamison in a Philadelphia studio.

De Mille was conducting a master class when she first saw Jamison, at once noticeable for her height (over six feet, in *pointe* shoes), and, more enduringly, for the distinctive quality of her movement. Jamison did not wear *pointe* shoes in *The Four Marys*. She danced, as did the other three Marys, in bare feet. The ballet, an admirable work in its genre, was eclipsed, with much of the rest of the repertoire, by *Les Noces* (which premiered March 30, seven days after *The Four Marys*). *Les Noces* was treated as an artistic milestone in American dance. Extravagantly praised by critics, it was as much a triumph for Jerome Robbins as for American Ballet Theatre.

Sentiment played a part in the success of *Les Noces*. By it, Robbins was welcomed back into the fold. He choreographed his first ballet, *Fancy Free* (1944), for Ballet Theatre, before going to the New York City Ballet. Later, he formed a company, Ballets: U.S.A. Then, forsaking the "legitimate" ballet, Robbins went to work on Broadway, where he had a phenomenal success, culminated by *West Side Story* (1962) and *Fiddler on the Roof* (1964). *Les Noces* was seen as the choreographer's crowning achievement. It was especially appropriate that it was produced by his alma mater.

With *Les Noces,* and some other works, American Ballet Theatre reinstated its artistic reputation, which had been in decline during its desperate struggle for survival. Critical approbation may have been instrumental in attracting the attention of the National Council on the Arts, a federal organization, which, in December 1965, made a gift of $100,000 to the company. Lucia Chase's gamble on the New York State Theater season had been played for high stakes, higher by far than the gift from the government. She had bought for American Ballet Theatre a new lease on life.

Robbins returned to the New York City Ballet, and *Les Noces* was only fitfully revived in ensuing years. *The Four Marys* vanished from the repertoire. At the close of that season, the veteran dancers de Lavallade, Scott, and Quitman went their separate ways. The tyro, Jamison, was brought abruptly to a cruel realization. She had been trained, for fourteen years, in ballet, and she was an accomplished technician. In 1965, in America, there was no ballet company that would employ her.

THREE

Judith Jamison was born and brought up in Philadelphia, where she began studying ballet at the age of six, with Marian Cuyjet at the Judimar School of Dance. There she had an eclectic education, with classes in jazz and "primitive" dance, in tap-dancing, and in acrobatics. The primary instruction was in ballet. Cuyjet's students were frequently taught by distinguished guest teachers and Cuyjet sent her prize pupils to take master classes with famous personalities in the dance. The year she was twelve Jamison worked under Antony Tudor, who came weekly to Philadelphia from New York.

Jamison came from a family of modest financial means. Her father was a sheet-metal worker, her mother a housewife. With her parents and a brother, John, Judith Jamison lived in a section of Philadelphia called Germantown, next door to her maternal grandparents. Jamison's training in dance, from an early age, was the natural evolution of her home culture.

Her father was a trained musician, a singer, whose main interest was music. Her mother was well read, and appreciative of theatre and the graphic arts. Jamison says: "My brother John and I lived with two human encyclopedias. Whatever we needed to know about music, from opera on, we got from our father. When it was something to do with history and literature, we turned to our mother. We were the best-informed children in our schools because if we asked a question at home for which one or the other parent did not have an answer, our parents helped us find out—they researched the subject with us. Growing up in my home was a constant learning process. Books and music were like food and drink. I spent all the spare time of my childhood in my room, with the record player going and me, on the bed, with a book. I was the best customer at the local library."

Jamison was taught by her father to play the piano and later studied the violin. She sang in the children's choir of the family's church.

Mrs. Jamison sent her daughter to dancing school, as thousands of other American mothers were sending their little girls. From the 1930s, ballet had been a popular theatrical entertainment and it was now, after lengthy argument, approved as a course of study for girls. Learning to place the feet in positions one through five, at the barre, was as commonplace as learning to play scales on the piano in the parlor.

Judith Jamison took to dancing as a duck to water. Though shy, she enjoyed performing, making her debut at six in a dance choreographed for her by Cuyjet to "I'm an Old Cowhand." Dance studies came easily to Jamison. She was intelligent, had a good memory, and was of a serious and obedient nature. She performed in Cuyjet's concerts and at the cotillions Cuyjet staged in Philadelphia, where prizes were awarded the best dancers by visiting celebrities, sometimes by glamorous screen stars, like Joan Crawford.

Judith Jamison was taken to the theatre by her parents and she remembers the first ballet performance she attended, soon after she had begun studying ballet. It was by the Ballet Russe de Monte Carlo. The dancer who most impressed her was ballerina Alicia Alonso. Jamison begged to be taken backstage, to ask for Alonso's autograph.

It was a surprising request from a child almost pathologically shy of strangers. "I suffered agonies, when my mother forced me to overcome my shyness, by talking to people I didn't know. It was torture for me to go up to an ice cream stand and ask for two chocolate cones, two vanillas, when Johnnie and I were driving around with our parents." On her boldness in seeking Alonso's autograph: "If I had become a psychologist that incident might have told me something about myself. It was an omen, because in 1976 [and again in 1978] Alicia Alonso asked me to dance in Havana."

Jamison might have become a psychologist. She enrolled in psychology courses during the three semesters she attended Fisk University, at Nashville, Tennessee, before deciding that her vocation lay more in dancing than in earning a college degree.

Three years later, when Jamison met Agnes de Mille, she was little changed from the seventeen-year-old girl who graduated from high school, without any plans for a career. She had spent a secure and sheltered adolescence, one little different from the environment of her childhood, making a normal progression through the Germantown educational system, where, as Jamison declares, she received an excellent schooling. Eleven years of studies at the Judimar School of Dance completed her education.

Jamison could not have been described as ambitious. Indeed, she showed no initiative for taking her life into her own hands. She had gone to college because her mother proposed it or, as an alternative, training for a secretarial job. The work ethic was strongly supported in the Jamison household. Jamison had thought, in her early adolescence, of training to be a neurosurgeon because she was fascinated by medicine, to which she was introduced as a member of an organization called Future Nurses of America. A little earlier, she had believed that her greatest bliss would be found in driving an enormous train across the country, or piloting a fast plane. All these notions, like the idea of studying psychology ("to explain myself to me; to explain other people"), were discarded. Only dance remained.

Jamison was an accomplished dancer and a ballet freak, in that she could execute, with ease, the pyrotechnical feats more often observed in the danseur than the danseuse. Strong, supple, and very tall, she was capable of superb extensions; she had a breathtaking arabesque. For a dancer of her height, she had a tremendous jump. Above all, Jamison possessed an elegance without which classicism is unattainable. It lay as much in her physique as in her technique— the small, neat head and long, slender neck, the lyrical arms and powerful legs. These were great assets in the ballet dancer.

Jamison had yet another attribute for the classical dance: an innate dignity and a regal authority. In 1959, when Jamison was fifteen, she danced the role of Myrtha, Queen of the Wilis, in *Giselle*. The title role of this ballet is said to be as great a test for a ballerina as is the role of Hamlet for the actor, but Myrtha is also a taxing role and some of the great exponents of the Queen of the Wilis have danced the Giselles into second place.

Had Jamison been a member of a company, when she was twenty, she would in all probability have been dancing solo roles. The dancer's training for ballet usually begins at eight and is extended into an apprenticeship in a company, between sixteen and eighteen. But Jamison had not joined a company.

There were only a few professional dance companies in America. There were, however, hundreds of accomplished ballet dancers. Only a very few of them could hope to be taken into a major ballet company. Fewer still would rise to ballerina rank. Jamison had more than one count against her.

It was accepted that the "ideal" height for the female ballet dancer did not exceed five feet, five inches, that she should be of certain physical proportions, and, even, a certain appearance. The aesthetics of the nineteenth-century ballet repertoire required certain types of dancers, male and female.

A tall dancer was usually cast as Myrtha—not in the title role—in *Giselle*. For *The Sleeping Beauty*, traditionally, a tall dancer took the role of the Lilac Fairy, while the role of Princess Aurora was delegated to the more "ideal" dancer. Seldom did a régisseur choose a tall girl as Swanilda in *Coppélia*, or as the Sugar Plum Fairy in *The Nutcracker*. An unspoken rule existed in ballet by which a taller-than-average woman dancer was given supporting roles rather than principal roles in the classical repertoire. American ballet aesthetics were largely formed on those of foreign companies. The English ballerina Margot Fonteyn was an "ideal" classical dancer in every respect, including size and deportment.

Many of these traditional rules were about to be broken. The above-normal height of a dancer would cease to be a handicap as American ballet developed ballerinas of the grace and elegance of Suzanne Farrell at the New York City Ballet and Cynthia Gregory at American Ballet Theatre. Modern ballet, ballet of neoclassical rather than traditional classicism (the aesthetics of nineteenth-century ballet), freed the choreographer and the dancer from the old regulations, by which dancers had been typed and categorized.

Judith Jamison might have been taken into a ballet company, regardless of her above-average height, on her merits as a dancer. She was, however, barred from American ballet because of another reason: the color of her skin—and the formation of her features—characterized Jamison as black. Only very, very few black dancers had ever been accepted into the American ballet.

Balanchine liked tall, lean dancers. Jamison was tall and slender, but the New York City Ballet did not make a place for her. In its corps, Jamison would have seemed an incongruity.

The male black dancer fared better than the female black dancer in American ballet, possibly because of the dearth of good danseurs. At New York City Ballet, a black danseur, Arthur Mitchell, was already famous, with American and European audiences. There had never been a black leading dancer, of female gender, in any major American ballet troupe. The epoch into which Jamison came, in the 1960s, was that of "white" ballet. White choreographers worked with white dancers in classical dance. Black and white dancers and dancers of Asiatic antecedents had mingled before then, as members of modern dance troupes. The most celebrated of these integrated companies was that of Alvin Ailey, a black dancer and choreographer.

If and when black dancers appeared with white ballet companies they did so as novelties; or, as de Mille remarked, as unwarranted luxuries in a white company, and for a specific reason: to dance, as black dancers in "black" works, of the type of de Mille's *Black Ritual* and *The Four Marys*.

Jamison's brief tenure with American Ballet Theatre happened by chance, and by de Mille's design.

In 1964, while Jamison was studying at the Philadelphia Dance Academy (a school she describes as "the Philadelphia Juilliard"), she took a master class with de Mille. Fourteen years later, de Mille recalled the meeting: "It was one of those impossible situations, in which the guest teacher is faced with the task of teaching a very large class, of students of various degrees of technical proficiency. You do the best you can, in the circumstances. I saw this girl, quite wonderful, and she and I had a wordless dialogue. I taught the whole class for *her,* the others went along as best they could." By the end of the class, de Mille had determined that the tall girl who had caught her eye would be one of the four Marys in her new ballet.

Jamison has asked the questions, without being able to answer them: "How long would it have taken me to reach a decision about the future? When, at what point of *that* year, or the *next,* would I have faced the necessity of doing something? Would I have picked up myself and gone to New York without any encouragement? Or would I have stayed on in Philadelphia, perhaps to teach?"

Jamison could have made a career in dance in Philadelphia, a city that may well be considered the cradle of American ballet.[1] Marian

---

[1] Philadelphia has an extraordinarily rich ballet tradition, from the Colonial era. In the post-Revolutionary period, when numbers of French dancers settled in America, Philadelphia became the center of academic ballet. In the early 1800s the school of Paul Hazard in Philadelphia produced Augusta Maywood,

Cuyjet had not been the only teacher to perceive Jamison's gifts for dancing. When the Pennsylvania Ballet was formed, and its school, under Barbara Weisberger, was auditioning student dancers, Judith Jamison was among the first to be offered a scholarship. She did not accept it, preferring to stay at the Judimar School, but the Pennsylvania Ballet School's scholarship "subconsciously helped" her to make up her mind to become a dancer.

The chief factor of Cuyjet's training lay in the emphasis on dance as performance. "Marian did not speak to us," says Jamison, "of 'projection' and 'dynamics,' she told us to dance. She made us aware of ourselves *as dancers,* that regardless of where we were onstage— no matter if you were the last kid in the back row—you danced, just as you danced when you were front, stage center. At Judimar, we did not just execute exercises in the studio; we danced, at the barre and center. Everything you did in class, and at rehearsal, was for the stage." Of herself, as the student, Jamison says: "I wanted to dance well because I was brought up to do everything well, as perfectly as possible. That was Mom's way. And I wanted to dance because I loved dancing. It was what I did best because it was what I liked most to do." Agnes de Mille's invitation to Jamison, to come to New York and work in *The Four Marys,* was accepted without hesitation. Jamison had scarcely ever taken an action that was not dictated by someone she respected, and loved.

She recalls that she was very happy in New York, forgetting, or not choosing to remember, any fears she may have felt away from home, and in a city where the current was far swifter and wilder than any she had known in Philadelphia. She was thrilled to be dancing with American Ballet Theatre, one of the two great American dance companies. Jamison looked at all the works in rehearsal

---

the first internationally renowned American ballerina. Another Hazard pupil, Mary Ann Lee, staged the first American *Giselle.* George Washington Smith, the compeer of Maywood and Lee (he was the first American Albrecht), also trained in Philadelphia and was the leading American danseur of his day. The Littlefield School in Philadelphia provided the nuclei of Balanchine's The American Ballet in 1934, and of Ballet Theatre in 1939. Catherine Littlefield, trained in her mother's school, formed the first classical ballet company, in 1936, entirely organized on American dancers. She choreographed the first full-length American *Sleeping Beauty* (1937) and toured her company through Europe. The Pennsylvania Ballet, formed in Philadelphia by Barbara Weisberger in 1963, maintains the city's proud traditions. It is considered to be the most important ballet troupe outside New York.

that she was allowed to see, and, when the season began at the New York State Theater, she saw every program she could attend, between the rehearsals of *The Four Marys.*

It was as though she had become part of an enchanted world, the world that, until now, she had viewed from the other side of the proscenium. "Funny, I had been dancing most of my life, but it took going onstage with Ballet Theatre—one season at the State Theater —to make me *feel* like a dancer." The realization came, perhaps, because Jamison was accepted as a dancer by other dancers.

With her instinctive hero worship, she found an idol: Carmen de Lavallade. De Lavallade was a beautiful woman with long black hair, large, beaming eyes, and the fabled charm of the quadroon. She was a dancer of gracious and radiant lyricism, and of impeccable technique.

Carmen de Lavallade and her sister Yvonne were children of a middle-class family. Born in New Orleans, they were reared in Los Angeles, where they studied dance. In her teens, de Lavallade joined the company of Lester Horton and became its star. She made a New York debut, with Alvin Ailey, in 1954, in a Broadway musical, *House of Flowers,* from which both she and Ailey rose to fame.

In the mid-1950s, de Lavallade was the ballerina of the Metropolitan Opera Ballet, having her greatest success there in *Aïda.* She then joined the company of John Butler and, next, that of Geoffrey Holder, whom she married in 1955. De Lavallade danced in the Ailey company as well and won her widest renown in concert performances, and on television, in works specifically choreographed for her. In 1965, de Lavallade occupied a unique place in the American theatre, appearing with equal success in ballet and in modern dance works.

She brought to the role of Mary Hamilton a seductive power and a poignant melancholy. Judith Jamison was spellbound by de Lavallade's performance. "I drank her up, I ate her up. Carmen is the dancer I put on a pedestal." Jamison was a dancer of different temperament than de Lavallade, but she had valuable lessons to learn from her senior. Jamison's ease, and her prodigious capacities for dancing, had given her a boyish insouciance. De Lavallade taught her something new. She opened up to Jamison as yet undreamed of sources of expression as a woman dancer.

With an insatiable appetite for knowledge, Jamison took every class she could get, amused, as she now recalls, that in the white company of American Ballet Theatre she was "the only chocolate child," the only dancer with dark skin. Jamison did not feel alienated; her school days had been spent among white classmates. Instead, she reveled in an innocent exhibitionism. Jamison, says a former member of American Ballet Theatre, had more strength and vigor than she knew what to do with. "She was a big, raw hunk of talent, waiting to be used. Judi was fine in *The Four Marys,* but it did not ask much of her, technically. It was what she did in the studio that astounded us. If Judi had gone onstage at the State Theater and done some of the things we saw her do in class, the audience would have been shouting for her."

Obedient to the choreography, Jamison danced Mary Seaton as a neat young maidservant, demurely coiffed, the long skirt swirling about her bare ankles. The season ended, and with it American Ballet Theatre's lease of the New York State Theater. So did the contract the company had with de Mille's four black dancers.

Jamison lingered in New York, hoping to get another dancing job. She had had a revelation, the revelation that illumines a life. Jamison had seen the nature of her desire, and the image of its satisfaction.

FOUR

American Ballet Theatre, despite its fine showing in the spring season, was not invited to share the New York State Theater with the New York City Ballet. It returned to its mountebank existence, performing in rented auditoriums and some makeshift theatres on its perennial tours. Judith Jamison, unlike Carmen de Lavallade, did not become a star in her first season of dancing in New York. For a time it seemed that she had made a debut and a farewell appearance in *The Four Marys*.

There ensued a period of waiting, and of doubting herself. Nevertheless, she stayed in New York, having perceived that it was in that city, the center of the American dance world, that she must make her mark as a dancer. In New York the dancer would rise or fall.

Jamison had saved very little money and would take none from her family. "At Fisk, my parents helped, but that was a different proposition—I was getting an education. In New York, I felt that if I was going to make it as a dancer I would have to do it on my own. My family could not afford to support me." The Jamisons lived comfortably on her father's earnings but extra expenditure would have strained the family budget.

Although Jamison was often homesick she resisted giving way to despondency, and she did not go home. She feared that if she went home she would break the tension, the taut thread of hope that connected her to the New York theatre. Philadelphia seemed far removed from New York and to go back to it, to the comfort and the softness of a familiar place, might break her self-imposed spell. For Jamison was spellbound by New York. "I wanted to be a part of the scene I had discovered in that one season at the State Theater. I belonged to it. I was ready and willing to earn my right to share the scene but I felt that I was beating my head against a stone wall."

Her hope of being taken into a company was nourished by the encouragement of those she respected: Agnes de Mille, and Carmen de Lavallade and Geoffrey Holder. "Things will be all right," said de Lavallade. "You are a very special kind of dancer. It takes time to find the right place." De Lavallade did more than offer consoling platitudes. She took her friend home, where, says Jamison, "I about wore out the living room couch!" And de Lavallade introduced Jamison to Holder, and the son she had borne him: "Léo, with an accent on the *e*." Holder came from a Creole culture and the Holder ménage was more exotic than the Jamisons' in Philadelphia. Everywhere, from the paintings on the walls, to the arrangement of flowers in a vase, the apartment bore the emphatic imprint of Holder's gifted hand.

Geoffrey Holder dwarfed the rest of the human race. Tall as a Tusi, with a slender, mobile body and a hieratic head, he had a countenance of lively intelligence, touched by a sardonic humor. He was the supreme sophisticate. Holder looked like no one else. No one moved as he did. Jamison once again enjoyed looking *up* at a man, having previously stood eye to eye with male colleagues or, more often, looked down at them. Male ballet dancers were seldom of more than average height.

But had he been undersized and insignificant of build, Holder would still have been regarded with awe for his accomplishments. He was a reincarnated Renaissance man.

Holder was a dancer and a choreographer; an actor; a painter, and a theatrical designer, of sets and of costumes; a musician; and a writer. He did more than one thing at a time, conducting a radio interview program while immersed in other activities; founding and directing a company for which he choreographed and in which he was the principal male dancer. And everything that Holder did, he did surpassingly well. In 1957 he was awarded a Guggenheim Grant for painting.

Holder danced, choreographed, and directed in the musical theatre (commencing his career in America as Baron Samedi in *House of Flowers*) and also danced in opera (appearing with the Metropolitan Opera Ballet in 1955). Holder was to appear on television in a variety of ways, as choreographer and director (notably, of performances by Carmen de Lavallade) and as the raucous singer (with an exaggerated Trinidadian accent) for commercial jingles advertising sponsors' products. Holder would be depicted in advertisements, where his photographed image offered guarantee of the excellence of the thing on sale, and he was himself an excellent photographer, bringing to this facet of his multitudinous professional activities the same unerring skill and imagination that he brought to everything he did.

Geoffrey Holder could not have been a fictitious character. As such, he would have been incredible. Holder was an elemental truth. Incidentally, he was black.

Born in Trinidad, while it was still part of the British West Indies, Holder and his older brother, Boscoe, were children of a middle-class "coloured" family. There is an apocryphal story that the Holders' papa, given the money to pay a month's rent by the Holders' mama, took the money and made a down payment on a used piano, so that the boys could learn to make music.

Mr. Holder did not have to spend money to teach his children to dance. Like every other boy and girl in Trinidad the Holders danced as soon as they could stand up without falling down. What made the Holders exceptional was that, having mastered the dance forms of their island culture (a mélange from African, Asiatic, and European sources), they began making up their own dances, and displaying them, with an ensemble of dancers, for a paying audience.

Boscoe Holder formed a second company in London, where he settled with his family, and from where his son, Christian, came, years later, to dance in the City Center Joffrey Ballet. At eighteen, Geoffrey Holder inherited his brother's first company, on which he set several musical revues, before leaving Trinidad to work in America. There, Holder had an immediate and enormous success.

Geoffrey Holder and Judith Jamison had in common their size, larger than that of average male and female dancer, and the categorization as black dancers. And they were visibly black dancers. Carmen de Lavallade and her cousin Janet Collins were light in complexion, with long glossy hair; they were more the Caucasian than the African ideal of beauty.

The light-skinned black woman had always been more admired in American theatre than her dark-skinned sister. On the evidence of success, it could be deduced that the lighter the shade of the black entertainer's skin, the greater the popularity. Bill "Bojangles" Robinson was admired for his tap dancing but Robinson did not become the object of romantic adulation as did the light-skinned singers Harry Belafonte and Johnny Mathis. Among popular women singers, Lena Horne and Dorothy Dandridge owed their success as much to their good fortune in looking more "white" than "black" as they did to their artistry.

The protean Holder capitalized on his size and his blackness; Jamison could not capitalize on hers. She was a dancer, dependent on choreographers to make dances for her, dependent on companies in which to dance. At that phase of her career, Jamison was as helpless as an infant. Her sole and total claim to an identity was as a dancer, and she was not the kind of dancer who forms a company in which to shine as the star. So improbable an idea never occurred to her.

Jamison trusted someone to help her. Agnes de Mille had been encouraging and Holder was friendly but neither could provide a place onstage for Jamison. Carmen de Lavallade campaigned for her friend, talking to Alvin Ailey about her. To Jamison, de Lavallade said that Ailey was the best choreographer that Jamison could hope to work with. Ailey had a company, already well known, and he was a gifted choreographer.

Ailey had not seen *The Four Marys,* and he was less than eager to take a neophyte into his company. The Ailey company was much smaller than that of American Ballet Theatre and it was no less plagued than American Ballet Theatre by a precarious economy. The Ailey dancers were versatile, more like a family than a dance company, and Ailey chose every member with care. De Lavallade and Ailey were friends of long standing. She and Ailey were pupils of Lester Horton, had danced in the Lester Horton Dance Theater in California, and had shared an East Coast triumph at their debut. Ailey and Holder had been rivals for the lovely Carmen, who, even after her marriage to Holder, and her work in the Butler and Holder companies, occasionally still danced for Ailey. Nevertheless, de Lavallade was unable to persuade Ailey to engage Jamison.

Jamison was urged to attend auditions and shrank from "showing her wares" to callous entrepreneurs. Their patent boredom, their callous indifference, were "crucifying" to her ego. "Nothing in my life, up to then, had prepared me for rejection. Each time I was turned down I took it as a personal slight. I wasn't good enough. Nobody liked me." Jamison was wrong. Almost everyone who knew her liked her; she was very easy to love. "She was this big, big girl," a colleague reminisces, "bigger than life except when she was dancing, then she stopped being an awkward, overgrown kid and became an artist. She could do everything and do it better than most other dancers, and she had this way of seeming to throw it away—it was easy for her. She was very friendly. Judi laughed a lot, not just because she had a sense of humor but also because she liked to make you feel good—you felt your small jokes were big jokes when you told them to Judi. She wanted to dance but you wondered if she would make it. She was very naïve, much, much younger than her age. And ladylike, nothing like a Broadway gypsy. Judi needed someone to take care of her. She was not tough enough to make it alone."

The Jamisons in Philadelphia felt some anxiety about their daughter. In her long distance calls Jamison cheerfully assured them that she was confident of finding a job, soon. She offered her mother the placebo de Lavallade offered *her:* "It takes time . . . things will be all right." And Jamison was able to tell her parents that friends were taking good care of her. "People I hardly knew opened their doors to me. Someone would take me in for a week; the next week, I would be passed on to someone else." Jamison was to learn that the performer with a pay check helps to support the performer on the dole. On tour when one dancer registered in a hotel room the room might be occupied by "ghosts," who slept on the carpeted floor, rolled up in the extra blankets, and used the free soap, towels, and hot water in the bathroom.

Jamison, new to the rules that summer of 1965, cringed at her dependency and considered herself "a charity case." Never before had she been so conscious of her height; she would gladly have shrunk to the size of a pigmy, in the homes where she was an unwilling guest. Jamison was so apologetic that the equally tempered de Lavallade became exasperated. "Look, girl! You are welcome here!"

Jamison realized that, in the circumstances, she had a great deal to be thankful for but her dependency went against the grain of the Jamisons' daughter. She wanted friends, not benefactors.

"The worst part of that time," says Jamison, "was having to go without class. At Marian Cuyjet's school, in a big brownstone building in downtown Philadelphia, something was happening all the time. There was dancing on every floor: ballet, tap, primitive, acrobatics. And everywhere you heard music. Pianos, drums, flutes, violins. In New York, I was lost without a studio to go to every day."

Temporarily giving up the hope of getting a dance job, Jamison took one at the 1964–65 New York World's Fair, operating the Log Flume Ride "with one hundred Floridians, none of whom talked English that I could understand." She would have died of the ennui except that she made a game of the job, pretending she was the pilot of a wondrous machine, a sort of science fiction wizard who could send the passengers, with a flick of her wrist, into outer space on the flume of water. Just as her imagery was wearing thin, and just before she gave way to panic, she was told of a dance audition at Choreographer's Workshop, on East Fifty-first Street. There was a chance that she might be hired. The choreographer was Donald McKayle. He was a noted dancer-choreographer and he had already benefited the careers of several dancers, among them Alvin Ailey and Arthur Mitchell, the "black princes" of American dance.

FIVE

For a dancer who happened to be black there could not be a more sympathetic reception than in an audition for Donald McKayle. It was this artist's fate to advance the careers of other dancers more than he advanced his own. McKayle narrowly missed being famous, as Ailey and Mitchell were famous, and in the way in which Holder was known.

Born in New York in 1930, McKayle belonged to another generation than that of Ailey and Mitchell, not so much in terms of chronological age as in the chronology of the American dance. Ailey moved from the Horton company onto Broadway after he had begun to choreograph, and to direct a troupe of dancers; Ailey had the instinct for authority and it was inevitable that he would form his own company. Mitchell graduated from the New York High School of Performing Arts and, upon being offered a scholarship to the School of American Ballet, came under the influences of George Balanchine and the faculty of that school. Taken into the New York City Ballet, Mitchell became one of its stars; he was the highest-ranking black danseur in the world.

Donald McKayle was black and in his last year of high school when he saw a performance by a black dancer, Pearl Primus. The event was to affect the course of the rest of his life.

Pearl Primus and her contemporary Katherine Dunham were pioneers among black dancers in the United States. Though unlike each other in technique and in personality, they shared some aspects of their careers. Both women were in the vanguard of "educational" dance, studies in dancing undertaken in colleges and universities. Both women based their ideas of choreography on anthropological research, and on the inspiration of African dance movement and rhythms.

Dunham was the lighter complexioned of the two, and the more beautiful, in the "white" aesthetic of feminine beauty. She had a success different from that earned by Primus, who, though beautiful, was more in the "black" than the "white" aesthetic. Dunham and Primus were the leaders of the "black dance" movement of the 1940s. They helped to elevate the black dancer into concert dance, away from musical revues, the relics of minstrel shows, where the black dancer's "blackness" had been utilized as part and parcel of "Negro dance acts."

Primus did not restrict her work to the college theatre circuit, nor to the concert hall; she had successful Broadway presentations and one, in October 1944, at the Belasco Theatre, is still looked upon as a historic evening for black dance. Dunham's repertoire assumed a sleek, glossy, and preeminently "theatrical" style in production. Primus would be remembered for the passion of her "dances of protest," and the "message" they conveyed, about the black experience in America. In Primus' repertoire, the "black experience" was not only one of suffering and outraged human decency, it was for the most part testimony to the massive capacity of endurance, and the nobility, of the "Negro." Her dances of Africa qualified the African as a person of dignity, not—as in the popular notion—as a savage.

Katherine Dunham made an invaluable contribution to the American dance theatre, and not a little of the influence she exerted was through her own beautiful person. But John Martin, for a very long time the chief arbiter of the dance in the United States, called Pearl Primus "the greatest Negro dancer of them all."

An artist's initial inspiration, like first love, makes an indelible impression. McKayle, although a talented dancer, was to become noted as a choreographer. Other circumstances, perhaps not of his choice, made him into a "show biz" figure, in the musical theatre and on television. At the inception of his career, McKayle was powerfully affected by his teachers and associates at the New Dance Group, whose history is as interesting as that of the dancers it developed, among whom several were black.

In 1932, in the throes of the Depression, some dancers formed the Workers' Dance League. This resoundingly proletarian coalition was drawn largely from modern dance, which, in that era, had its "pink" period, an ideological—and highly idealized—conception of arts and politics, with the "workers" of paramount concern. After the Depression, the League gradually dispersed, leaving the New Dance Group, in a wholly different character, as a school. Its concert wing, although it was able to offer only periodic performances, was established on some of the most gifted artists of the "new" generation of modern dance—the generation, frankly independent of their forebears Martha Graham and Doris Humphrey, who struck out in various directions.

McKayle got another scholarship, to the Graham school, and was, for a time, a member of the Graham company; he was with the troupe in its Far Eastern tour of 1955–56. And McKayle danced in the companies of Jean Erdman and Anna Sokolow, with the company of Merce Cunningham, and was a soloist with the New York City Opera. In January 1962 he joined with Sokolow and Sophie Maslow in a presentation of choreographic works at the YMHA. In association with Daniel Nagrin, another dancer-choreographer from the New Dance Group, McKayle formed the Contemporary Dance Group. At least one McKayle work, *Rainbow 'Round My Shoulder* (1959), in which McKayle, with another notable black modern dancer, Mary Hinkson, created the leading roles, became a classic of its genre.[1]

McKayle was in the cast of *House of Flowers* and was the dance captain in *West Side Story.* He was billed as assistant choreographer for some other Broadway shows and, increasingly, found himself in demand for the musical theatre and for television. By these turns and twists, typical of some American dancers' careers, McKayle had arrived at his current post, choreographer for a television musical spectacular, a Harry Belafonte "Special" called "The Strolling '20s." It was for this show that Judith Jamison auditioned at the Choreographer's Workshop.

A motley crowd of dancers answered the "dance call" for a Broadway or a television show. Ballet and modern dancers vied, at auditions, with seasoned troupers, to whom the term "Broadway gypsies" was applied. Ten years earlier, a modern dancer was likely to cross the street to avoid walking on the same sidewalk as a ballet dancer; now, ballet and modern dancers were not so wary of each other. At auditions for Broadway shows they became allies against the "show biz" entertainers, whom they considered a lower species of dance artist.

---

[1] *Rainbow 'Round My Shoulder* is set to prison songs of the American South. The dancing is accompanied by solo guitar and voice. Hinkson created the role of the woman (mother/sweetheart) of the prisoners' dreams.

An old, puritanical prejudice in American society prompted disdain for the "song-and-dance" performer, the itinerant entertainer who lived from show to show, and, often, on the road (in "road shows" of Broadway musicals). In truth, by the mid-1960s, the "dance gypsy" was an American artist of spectacular virtuosity, the possessor of some attributes unknown to dancers in the "legitimate" theatre.

Donald McKayle understood well the conditions in which dancers danced in the United States. He knew that the ballet and modern dancers at auditions secretly despised the "musical," as commercial theatre but, nevertheless, respected the money to be earned dancing in shows.

McKayle knew that modern dancers depended on occasional, not regular seasons of performance. Unless they belonged to the few stable groups (among which Martha Graham's was perhaps the most secure), they worked free-lance, with choreographers who assembled a troupe for some performances—often, for a single performance. Most modern dancers worked without rehearsal pay.

Ballet dancers, if they belonged to a company, were better off. The ballet had a wider audience and a richer box office, and most ballet troupes were engaged, at least seasonally, on contracts that included pay for rehearsal (and per diem, on tour).

Other than the New York City Ballet, no ballet company contracted its artists for fifty-two weeks of a year, so that there was little security for the majority, over twelve months of work. To compound the problem, there were hundreds of out-of-work dancers in New York, hanging on—with unemployment checks—in hopes of getting a permanent job.

It was not uncommon to come on dancers, of soloist rank in the ballet, auditioning for Broadway shows. More than a few ballerinas (Alexandra Danilova, for one, in *Oh Captain!* in 1958) and several danseurs (the New York City Ballet's Jacques d'Amboise in *Seven Brides for Seven Brothers;* Edward Villella in *Brigadoon*) had been eager to appear in musicals, on Broadway and in films. Television, chiefly through the variety shows, had also proved a fruitful field for dancing, with higher wages than could be earned in the theatre. "Media" and Broadway dancing, however, made specific requirements of the performers. The musical "routines," performed with deceptive ease and ebullience by Broadway gypsies, dazzled and tempted classical dancers—into the 1980s, when Baryshnikov essayed the genre.[2]

Earlier in the history of the American musical theatre, the "chorine" had been purely decorative, chosen for the degree of her comeliness rather than for her talent. A bevy of beauties, who could be trained to perform the simple "step-kick" chorus routine, adorned a show for the effect it was warranted to exert on tired businessmen in the front row.

Great changes had been effected in the American musical. The "chorus boys and girls" were now selected for their ability to sing, dance, and act, as integral aspects of a show. Agnes de Mille, as much as anyone else, had brought this change about, in *Oklahoma!* For that show de Mille, as choreographer, required dancers who danced. Jerome Robbins advanced the principle, in *West Side Story,* a show in which all the elements (of dance, drama, and music) were fully integrated.

"Legitimate" theatre dancers, sequestered in the hothouse atmosphere of "art" dancing, were naïvely arrogant in their assumption of superiority over Broadway dance gypsies. The gypsies were by now of enviable technical virtuosity. They were trained dancers, whose wide range could accommodate the choreography of any dance idiom.

The ladies of the musical chorus had manners and mores no less traditional than those of ballet. Jamison arrived for the McKayle audition dressed, properly, as she thought, in demure tights and leotard. She had on leg warmers, the knitted woolly hose that ballet dancers pull over their tights to keep leg muscles warm so that they will not cramp. Broadway gypsies, however, were not so attired.

"If I had been stark, staring naked," says Jamison, "I would not have been more out of place at the audition. Every girl but me was ready for the ball. I looked around and saw girls in the shortest leotards in creation, showing more leg than I had ever seen onstage. Instead of nylon tights, they were wearing black fishnet stockings— sexier than a black nightgown. They had on, each, two sets of long false eyelashes. And they had on more makeup, for the audition, than I wore when I was *performing.*"

---

[2] Baryshnikov was featured, with Liza Minnelli, in a television "special," "Baryshnikov on Broadway." (Nureyev also appeared in one, with Julie Andrews.)

The audition was run along the usual lines. McKayle and his dance captain (chief assistant) were there to select from hundreds of auditioning dancers the required number. Judgment would be quickly made, on the merits of the auditioning dancers; a judgment predicated not only by the dancer's talent but by the specific requirements of choreography for the show.

The popularity of the musical *A Chorus Line* has greatly enhanced the audience's knowledge of life in a Broadway show. As in *A Chorus Line,* McKayle's audition was primarily to separate the "sheep" from the "goats." In first auditions for shows, the larger group is discarded. The smaller group—in which hope soars temporarily—is auditioned again, for the eventual selection of the chosen few who will be hired for the show. Tests—impromptu routines —are given the auditioning dancers. They must perform on the spot and as these routines are demonstrated by the choreographer's dance captain. McKayle's assistant, for this audition, was the dancer Paula Kelly.

Says Jamison: "I said that I had not seen a dancer like Carmen de Lavallade until I danced with Ballet Theatre. I meant by that: I had never seen a dancer, a woman dancer, of Carmen's style. But when I saw Paula Kelly, that day, I went into total shock. I had never imagined that someone could move like that. Paula was fantastic.

"I don't think I've ever been so at sea, then and since, as I was that day, looking at Paula Kelly doing the routines. I knew I couldn't dance the way she was dancing. I could not imitate her because I just couldn't understand the way she moved.

"The thoughts that ran through my head that day were something like these: At Judimar, I had had all sorts of dance classes. I could perform any combination that was given me in ballet. I was good in 'primitive' dance. I could tap. Although I did not have training in any one particular system of modern dance—Graham or whatever— at the Judimar School, we had 'modern' classes, and I was familiar with the type of movement that is characteristic of modern dance.

"What Paula Kelly was performing was 'show dancing.' It was not so much a technical form as it was a style—but the style was so strong that it looked to me like an entirely new and entirely different kind of dance.

"It took more courage than I knew I had to try to dance like Paula at that audition. I wasn't in the least surprised that I got turned down. Donald McKayle was more than just polite, he was kind. But I writhed. I was embarrassed and humiliated, furious with myself. All I wanted was to fly from the scene and forget the disaster."

She fled so precipitously that she stumbled and almost fell over a man sitting on the steps of the stage. That night, calling home (where fingers had been kept crossed, to wish her good luck at the audition), Jamison for the first time broke down and wept. "I felt so inadequate." It was Mrs. Jamison who now mouthed the worn-out formula: *"It takes time . . ."*

When Jamison hung up the telephone she asked herself if the time had come to give up hope of working in New York. "It was not that I was disillusioned. I was facing reality. I knew there was no hope of getting into Ballet Theatre. I had been thinking in terms of working in a company. Then, I had been willing to settle for working in a show—though, when the show closed, I would have to start all over again, looking for the next show. But I had overestimated the possibilities. I couldn't even get into one show! How much longer could I psych myself into believing that I could make it in New York? At the audition I saw that I was competing with veterans, experienced Broadway dancers—girls choreographers already knew and liked to work with. Against that sort of competition, what chance did I have?"

Yet Jamison postponed the move that now seemed inevitable, back to Philadelphia. Three days later, languishing in New York, she got a call from Ailey, inviting her to join his company. The man over whom she had almost fallen, at McKayle's audition, had been Alvin Ailey.

SIX

Judith Jamison first saw the Ailey dance troupe in 1963, in Philadelphia. It was a memorable experience, from which she took away an impression of exciting dance, but Jamison barely knew, by name, the company she joined in 1965. Of its founder-director, Alvin Ailey, she knew nothing.

Ailey, in his way, was unique in the American dance theatre, to which he had come from an environment far different from Jamison's. Born in 1931, in Rogers, Texas, Ailey's early years were spent in grinding poverty. His seventeen-year-old mother was too undernourished to nurse him when he was born. She lived at her husband's father's house, where there was scarcely enough food to keep body and soul together for thirteen persons, of whom eight were the children of Alvin Ailey's aunt. Under the unbearable pressures of their existence, the father abandoned his wife and child when Alvin Ailey was six months old. Thereafter, Lula Elizabeth Ailey, née Cliff, was the sole support of herself and her son.

She picked cotton and lived in a run-down cabin, with a little bean garden she planted for sustenance. To augment her wages in the cotton fields, Lula Ailey washed and ironed the clothes of white residents in Rogers. Later, she improved living conditions for herself and her child by becoming a domestic in the houses of whites, and of prosperous blacks, with all of whom the little boy, Alvin, was a favorite. He was a handsome and intelligent child, with a compactly muscled body, whose only lovable fault seemed to be his inordinate attachment to his mother. She, for her part, was devoted to her son. When he was two, he became ill one night and Mrs. Ailey put him on her back and carried him eight miles into town, to a doctor.

With the indulgence that very young mothers show their children, Mrs. Ailey sometimes allowed the little boy to act as the head of their household. A year later, they were walking in some woods when they came on an empty, derelict house, which young Alvin instantly appropriated for their home. Mrs. Ailey was then living with a kind black woman, for whom she worked, but she at once acceded to her child's wishes and they moved into the vacant house. It stood on a hill overlooking the Brazos River and in the cellar beneath the high pilings the boy kept a pet, with whom he shared his meals. It was a large chicken snake, which terrorized his mother.

No black child in rural Texas could escape the tensions of living in an inimical white society. As a small boy Alvin Ailey concluded that all adult black males sooner or later went to serve time in the penitentiary, for breaking the laws of the white folks. The child heard of dreadful things, the more terrifying because they were always discussed in a low, ominous mutter by his elders: white-hooded figures, more malevolent than devils; fiery crosses, spelling greater doom than any promised in the Bible; and something called lynching.

Alvin Ailey very early knew of the appalling inequities visited on black people, and of their helplessness against the oppression of whites. He lacked proper food, clothing, and shelter; sometimes, he went to sleep with an empty, aching belly. Yet, Ailey was particularly fortunate in other ways. His mother, who had not had milk enough to suckle him, passed on to her son an indomitable will to survive, and an enormous optimism. More, Lula Ailey provided her child with an almost idyllic awakening to the living world, the natural world of which the country-bred child becomes a part.

When she picked cotton in the fields, Lula Ailey took her child with her; when she worked on farms, he was taught to care for animals. Even if they lived in a town, they were always near woodlands, and there they liked to stroll together, ostensibly to gather nuts and berries but really for the joy of walking in the woods. There were indications that young Alvin might be of a scientific turn of mind: he was fascinated by insects and would observe them for hours. When he went to school, he filled notebooks with drawings of insect life, under which he made notes. His adoption of a snake for a pet showed the keen interest he took in living things, and it showed his fearlessness.

Lula Ailey now says that the chief qualities she noticed in her son as a small boy were his loving thoughtfulness and his ingenuity. He seldom returned home without bringing her a bouquet of flowers and sweet grasses; and from a very young age he showed a creative instinct. When he was three he gave his mother, as a Christmas gift, a little figurine made from a forked stick. The child peeled off the bark, spit-polished the naked wood until it looked like old ivory, and named it "Cottee."

Another factor of his personality, Lula Ailey relates, was his independence. He was self-reliant and could be trusted with small responsibilities; he learned to entertain himself without toys, and without companions. Lula Ailey moved about continually, always to secure better living conditions for herself and her child, and in 1936 she went to Navasota, a town in southeast Texas with a population of about five thousand. Here she made history of a sort, becoming the first black patient admitted to the Navasota Hospital (for an emergency appendectomy). Soon after, she became the first black employee of the hospital, earning $12.50 a week, her highest wages to that time.

The Aileys lived at Navasota for six years and Alvin Ailey went to school at the Navasota Colored School, where, in the fourth grade, he began to study the tuba. His interest in music originated in church and was encouraged by the school principal, who thought that the boy might be trained to play in the school band. Alvin Ailey, meanwhile, was also drawing, and writing verse, some of it so imaginative as to be obscure—indeed, unintelligible, to everyone but himself.

Church was both the religious and the social center of the Aileys' lives. In Navasota they became members of the True Vine Baptist Church. Mrs. Ailey sang in the choir and her son attended Sunday School classes and, when services and religious instruction were finished, they participated in the social activities arranged by the church.

In the custom of Southern Baptists, this church practiced baptism by total immersion. As the celebrants in their snowy white robes were marched to and from the river, or the pond, a choir accompanied them, with music and song and shouts of rejoicing. In late summer, there was public renewal of the faith, in the "revivals," where singing, music, and "speaking in tongues" testified to the worshipers' union with the Divine Being. This uninhibited demonstration of worship, in its rapturous communion with God, had predictable effects on a sensitive child. Equally stimulating were the periodic appearances of traveling musicians who sang and played dolorous "western" folk songs and of comic minstrel shows that stopped off at the small towns in or near which the Aileys lived. If Sunday was the day for praising the Lord, then Saturday night was the time set aside for indulging in dressing up in one's best clothes and prancing about town, the tall boys and men and the emancipated women frequenting the cafés and dance halls.

Ailey left Texas when he was twelve but not before he had assimilated its sights and sounds, sacred and profane. He recalls a place called the Dew Drop Inn, a honky-tonk bar and dance hall with an atmosphere of sensuality accompanied by fear, and of impending trouble. There were fights. Sometimes there were killings. The more desirable a woman, the more dangerous she became to the men who were attracted to her—and to herself, when the men fought over her.

It was also at Navasota that Ailey spent some of his happiest years. There he was given the first dog he ever owned, rode his first horse, and, perhaps most importantly, attached himself to a father figure in the person of his mother's landlord, a kind man named Amos Alexander. It was also at Navasota that Ailey's feelings crystalized as a sense of his alienation. Perhaps it was because the boy had so great a capacity for loving and living that he nurtured so strong a grief at loss and deprivation. He grew up without a father and his association with Mr. Alexander only exacerbated his longing for a father of his own. He felt jealous, and left out, when Mr. Alexander's sister brought her small children on visits. He was reminded, Ailey says, that he was existing in a make-believe world and that Mr. Alexander, despite his kindness, was not a "real" father.

The feeling of "not belonging," which was to haunt the boy, could not help but be strengthened as he grew old enough to recognize the sharp division drawn between black and white children. At Navasota he used to look up at the white students' school, atop a hill. Like a fortress it was impregnable to him, and when the sun shone on its walls it looked like a tower of light. Yet, when Lula Ailey went to Los Angeles in 1942, and her son was enrolled in an integrated school, he begged to be sent to a school that was predominantly black. Ailey had begun to think and to speak, as he still does, of "my people."

In Los Angeles, at the George Washington Carver Junior High School, Ailey received more than a formal education. Los Angeles provided a great deal more than southeastern Texas as stimulus to the imagination. Ailey went on writing his obscure poems and he also enrolled in a creative writing class, where he read classic literature and the works of the major poets. He went on field trips organized by the school, one of which was to the Los Angeles Philharmonic Hall where he attended a performance by the Ballet Russe de Monte Carlo. The bill included *L'Après-Midi d'un Faune* (*The Afternoon of a Faun*) and *Schéhérazade* and although Ailey says now that he was disappointed because the dances seemed tame—instead of "sexy"—he was sufficiently impressed to remember the ballets, even their titles. This ballet matinee introduced Ailey to theatre and opened a new world to him. He thereafter spent his Saturdays in downtown Los Angeles prowling about the theatre district, reading the advertisements. Through them, he found an announcement of performances by a black troupe at the Biltmore Theatre. Here, in 1945, Ailey saw Katherine Dunham's *Tropical Revue* and was fascinated, perhaps more by the costumes than by the dancing.

That year he entered the Thomas Jefferson Senior High School, where he sang in the Glee Club, was active in sports, took gymnastics, and earned A grades in every course except mathematics. He had grown to a strength and size that made the coaches try to persuade him to play football. Ailey disliked the game, as he did all systemized competition. He would work with intensity only for his own interests and never in contests with others.

In Navasota he had made friends with the children of a Spanish-speaking family and had learned a little of their language. In high school he found that he had a marked ability for French and Spanish and he became so fluent in these that he was often required to take over classes in the absence of regular teachers. His proficiency in Spanish led him into reading Spanish literature and poetry.

Mrs. Ailey was employed, for very long hours, by an aircraft corporation and her son was left much on his own. He did not make many friends, nor make friends readily, but those who attached themselves to him became very fond of him and remained protective of the moody, gifted boy. He was essentially a loner and yet he had a mesmeric quality that drew people to him.

Ailey began spending his spare time at the movies. Los Angeles' Central Avenue was the hub of the black community and it was full of theatres that showed films and presented popular singers and bands. The Lincoln Theatre had a chorus line, backing the vaudeville acts. There Ailey heard Pearl Bailey, Lena Horne, and Billie Holiday, and listened to the music of Duke Ellington and his band. The era was one of dance films, of which Ailey liked best the movies of Gene Kelly.

Ailey most admired dancing that seemed free and powerful, in the uninhibited style of one of his schoolmates, Ronald Gaffney. Gaffney, a gifted, self-taught dancer, performed at a school assembly with another pupil, Carmen de Lavallade, in their own version of *Schéhérazade*. The de Lavallade sisters, their glossy, dark hair in neat braids, were so prim and proper that Ailey was astonished to see the younger, Carmen, dancing with such fire, in a red costume. He was even more impressed by her beauty when de Lavallade, in *pointe* slippers and a tutu, danced a classical piece to music by Mozart. The image was to remain forever in his mind's eye.

Ailey was persuaded by another friend Ted Crumb to take class from a Dunham company dancer, Thelma Robinson. Miss Robinson taught the classes in a nightclub and Ailey was "put off," he says, by the sleazy nightclub atmosphere and even more so by what he has called "all that hip-shaking." He refused to take more dance classes until he saw Crumb demonstrating some new steps, in a way of dancing that, according to Ailey, "blew" his mind. Crumb had learned them from Bella Lewitzky, the principal dancer of the Lester Horton Dance Theater. Ailey went with Crumb to the Horton studios, where he was "stunned" by the elegance and the power of the Horton dancers. Ailey was equally thrilled by the bold, vivid colors of Horton's theatre and the unconventional use of design. Ailey intended to earn a university degree in Romance languages. He was to make two abortive attempts at college study before he devoted himself entirely to dance.

Alvin Ailey had by now explored several means of self-expression. At three, he had been the sculptor of "Cottee." A little later, he was the painstaking draftsman, drawing his world of insects. He had written poetry; he had played music; he had sung. Now, almost unwillingly, he was brought to dance. With it, he would communicate to the world what it meant to be Alvin Ailey. For this communication he needed dancers. Judith Jamison was to be one. In 1965, and for ten years after, Ailey was the paramount influence on

Jamison's career. These two, Ailey and Jamison, brought together by chance, were to learn, sometimes with painful but always with productive acumen, how much they were alike, and how much they differed from each other.

SEVEN

Few choreographers have been as overtly autobiographical as Alvin Ailey. His *oeuvre* is the record of a personal history; his works are *rites de passage*. Almost all of his creative activity may be traced to events in his past.

Ailey became a choreographer in 1953 when, at the death of Lester Horton, he took over the company in Los Angeles. It was the second of Horton's troupes, and the principal dancers were Carmen de Lavallade and James Truitte; they, like another notable member of the troupe, Clive Thompson, were black.

Two white men, Karel Shook in ballet and Lester Horton in modern dance, strongly influenced black American dancers.

Horton came from Indiana and began his dance studies in Chicago, under Russian ballet teachers. He worked as a theatrical designer and stage manager and, in Los Angeles, he mounted large-scale works with great flair. His dancing, and his principles of teaching dance, were unconventional. He directed his multiple talents and skills into an innovative approach to theatre dance.

Horton was eclectic in his approach, drawing on his work in Japanese theatre and his studies of American Indian dancing. He believed, like the Southern Baptists, in total immersion for the baptism of his dancers. They formed a close association in and outside the Horton studios, in part to pool their financial resources for food and housing but chiefly to establish Horton's preferred climate for an absolute and entire affinity. Conditions that might have repelled others appealed to the lonely young man Alvin Ailey.

Lula Ailey married for the second time and her son found it difficult to accept a stepfather. The possessive love which was a factor of Ailey's character caused him to look upon his mother's remarriage as heresy. Once again he was the alienated one, this time in his own home. Still intent on a university education, and trying to wean himself of a growing dependence on Horton, Ailey went to San

Francisco, where a double load of classes, and working to support himself, so exhausted Ailey that he fell ill and almost died. He returned to Los Angeles and the Horton company.

Horton is now acknowledged as one of the chief innovators of American modern dance but in his lifetime he was denied the recognition given to his peers. Martha Graham, Doris Humphrey and Charles Weidman, and Hanya Holm worked in New York, where they were encouraged and championed by metropolitan critics and audiences. Lester Horton worked in Los Angeles, in a bywater of the American dance stream, and his theatricality was suspect to the rather solemn progenitors of East Coast modern dance. Yet, Horton was to offer his dancers the widest range of expression of any of the modern dance pedagogues. When Ailey and Truitte, and Carmen de Lavallade and her cousin Janet Collins appeared in New York, they were greeted with enthusiastic admiration, for their technical elegance, and for the dynamism of their dancing.

And Horton had even more merit: his students were not in the least like him, nor were they carbon copies of each other. Bella Lewitzky and Alvin Ailey, the two major choreographers emergent from the Horton school, were wholly individual in style and in their approaches to dance. They lovingly acknowledged their debt to Horton, but they, separately, pursued trains of thought and forms of choreography widely different from Horton's *oeuvre*—and from each other's.

On his assumption of the post of choreographer and director, Ailey loyally attempted to preserve the Horton company. His talent was too powerful, his and the dancers' needs too pressing, for him to nurture for long the Horton phase of dance. It passed or, really, dissolved in the burgeoning of Ailey's talent as choreographer.

Ailey's triumph came first as a dancer, in partnership with Carmen de Lavallade. The "chemical" elements of a perfect partnership lie in the sensuality and the contrasting styles of the two dancers and these elements were pronounced in the lyrical de Lavallade and the dynamic Ailey. No two such dancers have again been seen, as partners, in modern dance.

Hailed as a beautiful and magnetic dancer, Ailey was far more interested in making himself known as a choreographer. He formed a company, which was conceived in 1960, at the demise of the old Horton troupe. As company director he assumed the patriarchal character for which he was born, and for which he had been trained in the long, lonely years when he was thrown back on his own resources, as the only child of a hardworking mother. The syndrome of the only child in a one-parent home, commonplace in twentieth-century American society, was to manifest itself sometimes in self-pity and loneliness. These, in Alvin Ailey, were turned into the searching awareness of self and a quest for identity, the solving of the riddle of who, and what, is Alvin Ailey.

Seldom has an artist so assiduously employed raw life as grist for his mill. And to do so, Ailey found it necessary to pursue a single-minded course, in which the Horton theories and principles of theatre dance supported Ailey's choreographic invention.

Ailey, the young choreographer, was, as some of his compeers recall, a brash young man. Like an American Lochinvar, he came out of the West, and, in the rarefied atmosphere of the East Coast pedants, rode roughshod over some of the most precious tenets of modern dance. At first, Ailey planned a studious investigation of East Coast modern dance, with the intent to improve his technique and to broaden his range. By then, Ailey had danced for Horton and also for Jack Cole, and Cole's choreographic talent had made a lasting impression on Ailey, the more so as Horton called Cole the greatest living male dancer in America.[1] Working with Cole in Hollywood, where Cole choreographed for himself, Carmen de Lavallade, Ailey, and Clive Thompson, was yet another experience that "blew" Ailey's mind.

In New York, Ailey was, in the beginning, wide open and wholly receptive, eager to learn. He had, so far, made only tentative attempts at choreography, not always successful and sometimes almost physically impossible for the dancers. Ailey's great and good friend James Truitte, dancing without pause for thirty-four minutes of a thirty-seven-minute work, *According to Saint Francis,* dropped

[1] Horton's and Ailey's admiration of Cole was as well founded as Balanchine's and Baryshnikov's publicized admiration of Fred Astaire. Cole was both a great dancer and a gifted choreographer. A pupil of Denishawn, he successfully combined careers in live theatre and films, maintaining a company in Hollywood while working in the movies. From the 1940s the Cole style was the standard for Broadway and film musicals, a style that freely drew on ballet, modern dance, Oriental dance forms, and jazz. Indeed, into the current epoch (of Michael Bennett, the late Gower Champion, Bob Fosse, and their compeers) the Cole influence still permeates the American musical theatre, more than is generally recognized—or admitted.

abruptly from 168 to 154 pounds. In this phase of his work, Ailey was being strongly influenced by his emotions; *According to Saint Francis* was in homage to Lester Horton and was premiered seven months after Horton's death.

In his second work, *Mourning, Mourning,* Ailey drew on Tennessee Williams' works (of which Ailey was a voracious reader) for a Southern scene and atmosphere in which to set Carmen de Lavallade at her best. The role he choreographed for her exemplified her dramatic ability and her beauty. Ailey made her dance with her hair loose, because "Carmen was so lovely with her hair down."

His early works were well received in Los Angeles, but Ailey quickly perceived that he could not indulge his personal feelings, however pure and intense they might be. Choreography was more than self-expression; if it remained only that, then it was therapeutic instead of artistic. Ailey's move to New York was well timed, for his career as a dancer and even more so for his career as a choreographer.

In New York he was taken aback by the numbers of fine black dancers, most of them in the cast—with Ailey and de Lavallade—of *House of Flowers.* Louis Johnson and Arthur Mitchell were trained ballet danseurs, who moved with an elegance and authority that Ailey secretly envied. He determined to hone his own technical skills and set off in search of a dance teacher who would give him the same encouragement he had received from Horton. Ailey was unprepared for the cool and distant manners of the New York dance world, in which there was often a wary reticence. Ailey, easily rebuffed, touchily proud, became overly critical.

At Hanya Holm's celebrated school, Ailey thought, the technique seemed more like quasi-ballet than like modern dance. Martha Graham's dance he found "finicky and strange." He thoroughly disliked the kind of dance taught at the studios of Doris Humphrey and her protégé, José Limón. Around all these major figures of modern dance, on the East Coast, cults had formed, of student devotees and members of a growing audience. Horton dancers had, too, been a coalition but, as individuals, they would have denied that their fusion into a company had taken on the character of a cult. Horton did not encourage idolatry, he "created a climate."

Ailey went looking for such a climate in New York, and for a group of dancers who related to each other, freely but closely, as do individuals who belong to an African *sib*. Ailey needed a brotherly and sisterly relationship, not a perpetual *agon,* a struggle for prowess in dancing, one dancer in competition with another. His longing for the Horton "climate," and his own idealized concepts, were expressed in a proposal he made, some years later, for the establishment of a school: "When I was a very young man in California I encountered a place so creative, so free, so marvelous that it . . . left an indelible stamp on my life as an artist and as a human being. This place was called the Lester Horton Dance Theater School and it was created, run, stimulated by the man whose name it bore. Its environment was electric. Its walls held the excitement of all that was organic and creative and positive. Its environment was a celebration of man in his highest state." Horton was dead, the Horton Dance Theater, as school and company, was gone, but Ailey wanted to preserve them as his legacy, to re-create the environment for other dancers. Though he did not quite succeed in summoning the same spirit that had transfigured Horton's organization, Ailey tried to provide a congenial atmosphere for his dancers. In New York, modern dancers struggled for recognition, of their systems of teaching, of their choreographic principles, and for stages on which to perform their works. The major dancers almost always became choreographers, personalizing the genre of modern dance to the extent of schism. The Horton dancers, on the contrary, had subscribed to a prevailing ethic, out of which they had pursued individual themes.

Horton's success came out of various factors, of which the primary one was Horton himself. A man of evangelistic zeal, he had the temperament and the inclination for paternalism, though it was never tyrannical. Horton delighted in nothing so much as the burgeoning of individual talent, and he was patient and sympathetic enough to draw it from the shy and suspicious boy Alvin Ailey, who came to the school in 1949.

Horton worked in comparative isolation and his dancers were not crushed by agonizing pressures, other than those they placed on themselves. Horton did not ask his pupils to idolize him. Instead, he showed his candid admiration of other dance artists, like Jack Cole. Horton and his dancers aimed for the artistic heights and, at the same time, the company enjoyed great popularity when it performed, buoyed as it was by Horton's frank and perhaps flagrant theatricality. It was because of his early exposure to theatre, while a great deal of East Coast dance was still in its phase as concert dance, that Ailey so rapidly formed his choreographic principles. The structure of his works, no less than their substance, would come in large part from the impressions that had been made upon him in his formative years.

Ailey was decidedly the vogue in New York in the 1950s; he enjoyed something of the notoriety of a matinee idol. He had an arresting presence, an exotic beauty, and his sensuality was an almost perceptible aura. *House of Flowers* had only a four-month run but it precipitated a number of gifted black dancers into instant renown, Ailey and de Lavallade among them. Ailey danced in several musicals, on and off Broadway. His partners were dancers of high caliber, among them two of Graham's pupils, Mary Hinkson, and a beautiful creature named Christyne Lawson who, for a time, was paired with Ailey in much the way that de Lavallade had been.

Ailey had lost de Lavallade to Holder (and she also joined the company of John Butler) but Ailey danced in Holder's *Calypso Revue,* a show that, in 1957, went on four times daily in a Brooklyn theatre, then moved to Philadelphia and Washington. Ailey went, next, into a Jones Beach production of *Show Boat,* choreographed by Donald McKayle and, after that, was the leading dancer in Jack Cole's *Jamaica,* a Broadway musical starring Lena Horne.

Ailey danced also in concerts with Anna Sokolow, Sophie Maslow, and Donald McKayle, three distinguished modern dance choreographers. Ailey could have made his fortune in the commercial theatre but he worked there only for enough to live on, while he prepared for his own New York choreographic debut. Drawing dancers from the cast of *Jamaica,* he rehearsed three hours a day in a studio across the street from the Imperial Theatre, while *Calypso Revue* was playing in Brooklyn. He could not offer the dancers salaries but he infected them with his optimism, and something of his own gusto.

On Sunday, March 30, 1957, Alvin Ailey staged his first New York concert, a solitary performance into which had gone three months of work, "and love," for an audience at the 92nd Street YMHA, whose Kaufmann Concert Hall housed so many such presentations that it must be looked on as the cradle of American modern dance.

Ailey shared the program with another dancer, Ernest Parham, and had as guest artist Talley Beatty, who had been one of the nine dancers in Katherine Dunham's original troupe. Beatty was also a respected choreographer whose masterwork, *The Road of the Phoebe Snow,* must have been gestating just then. Ailey's program comprised three works, *Ode and Homage, Redonda,* and *Blues Suite,* and in themselves testified to Ailey's past, and to his Proustian capacity for invoking experience with universal meaning.

The *Homage,* of course, was to Ailey's mentor. It was *"respectfully dedicated to the memory of Lester Horton . . ."* now dead but not forgotten by his pupil. *Redonda* was a suite of dances to music from Latin themes, an expression of the choreographer's affinity for things Spanish, an affinity begun for a little boy who was befriended by a migrant Spanish-American family in Texas. *Blues Suite,* the most durable, and the most choreographically important of the works, had been drawn from scenes glimpsed, and scenes imagined, by little Alvin Ailey in Navasota, where, at the honky-tonk dance palace called the Dew Drop Inn, the boy had come upon his first, oblique realization of sexuality.

The program staged by Ailey was successful chiefly for its vivid theatricality, although some dancers in the audience recognized a new choreographic talent. At that time, modern dance works were most often presented in modest staging. The concert dance, to which category modern dance rightfully belonged, appealed to the discerning few rather than the audience en masse. Quite often, modern dancers performed for each other, in the way that, about the same period, writers in the "little" magazines wrote for other writers. Modern dance had its *cognoscenti,* as ballet had its *aficionados,* elite cliques that prided themselves on their informed knowledge of these two forms of dancing. The only dancing appreciated by and common to the audience en masse was that in musical theatre, the "popular" or "commercial" theatre dance. (It was not until 1978 that Martha Graham's works were danced, by her company, at the Metropolitan Opera House in New York.)

Ailey's March concert in 1958 was, undeniably, a serious presentation of dance, dance that fell into the generic term of "modern dance." Yet, by the staging alone, it broke with custom. Ailey's ideas of total theatre had come from Horton and his innate sense of drama had been further stimulated by working with Jack Cole, a choreographer whose wide range of themes and whose bold innovations were supported by the authority of authentic sources. In collaboration with Holder, whose sense of color and design were as original and adventurous as Ailey's sense of movement, Ailey managed to shock the New York modern dancers, and critics who had become the self-designated arbiters of modern dance.

The audience on March 30, 1958, may have been surprised but in its response it was thoroughly enthusiastic, so much so that some of Ailey's compeers hesitated to praise the program. There would be some who, twenty years after, would carp at Ailey's theatricality, would condemn his facility, and would try with all their might to pick holes in the argument that has centered on the contention that Ailey is the greatest of the black modern dancer-choreographers.

EIGHT

Ailey did not give another concert until December 21, 1958. Dancers, especially in modern dance, coalesced to form a transient troupe and dissolved immediately after; three months' preparation for a single performance was not an uncommon occurrence. Ailey could not hope to keep together so much as the nucleus of a troupe and he was obliged to go on dancing in musical theatre to provide enough money for him to invest in another concert presentation. He was fortunate in being able to win the trust and respect of some fine dancers, who worked with him without monetary recompense.

For the first concert in 1958 Ailey secured some skilled dancers, among them Claude Thompson, Christyne Lawson, and Liz Williamson. For the second concert Ailey had Carmen de Lavallade as his guest artist and three dancers were added to the first roster; one of these, Minnie Marshall, was to become a renowned member of the Ailey company.

Ailey called himself and his dancers "Alvin Ailey and Company," in a program that featured *Blues Suite* and that premiered *Ariette Oubliée,* to music by Debussy. The theme of the piece was Paul Verlaine's poem *"Il pleure dans mon coeur,"* and the roles of the Man and the Moon were danced by Ailey and de Lavallade. The Man traded "the flower of reality" for "the dreams of illusion," and de Lavallade seemed—to the critic P. W. Manchester, in the February 1959 issue of *Dance News*—an incarnation of Diana, chaste goddess of the moon. De Lavallade, it may be observed, was dressed in "ravishing white draperies," to contrast with "an amazing pink negligée" worn by blues singer Nancy Redi. Ailey's concert, wrote Manchester, was truly an unusual event, and it led to engagements for Ailey and his dancers, at the Jacob's Pillow Dance Festival and in a new theatre, the Delacorte in Central Park. These, in turn, brought Ailey greater recognition and the impresario Susan Pimsleur undertook to arrange tours and concerts for Ailey's troupe, billing it as the Alvin Ailey American Dance Theater, a title that Ailey formally adopted sometime later.

On January 31, 1960, Ailey gave his third concert at Kaufmann Concert Hall, with a revised *Blues Suite* on the program and, in premiere, the work *Revelations,* which was to become his masterpiece. Ailey's revisions (additions, subtractions, and outright changes) were to be a characteristic of his choreography and *Revelations* underwent a series of metamorphoses. His company, too, was subject to an inevitable flux (and Ailey was the first to urge dancers to take more lucrative engagements) but there was now a core with permanence, as company, and to it was added James Truitte, who was persuaded by Ailey to leave Los Angeles for New York. In October of that year the Ailey company found a home in the Clark Center for the Performing Arts. It was established in a YWCA building on Eighth Avenue in New York, and here Ailey premiered his *Knoxville: Summer of 1915,* on November 27, 1960. It was the most clearly autobiographical work Ailey choreographed.

The title of the work and its theme come from James Agee's prose poem in *A Death in the Family.* Ailey set the dancing to the verse with music by Samuel Barber. He used the whole, poem and dancing, to express his own feelings as a child, when, as Ailey believed, he had been well loved but seldom understood. Agee wrote: "After a while I am taken in and put to bed. Sleep, soft smiling, draws me unto her. And those receive me who quietly treat me, as one familiar and well-beloved in that home: but will not, oh, will not, not now, nor ever; but will not ever tell me who I am."[1] Ailey's incessant quest for his identity may, in some way, have been communicated to others sensitive enough to perceive it. Ailey was invited to take a part in a play, *Call Me by My Rightful Name,* which had been written by Michael Shurtleff with Ailey in mind. Ailey's performance as "a young Negro" was called brilliant.

Ailey now seemed to have, at the Clark Center, a home for his

---

[1] From *A Death in the Family* by James Agee, copyright © 1957 by James Agee Trust, Grosset & Dunlap, Inc.

Something more of Ailey's feelings and beliefs were evoked in a major solo, *Hermit Songs.* Ailey danced it in premiere at Clark Center on December 10, 1961. The work is composed as a suite, set to music arranged by Samuel Barber and sung by Leontyne Price, and was inspired by "Small poems of anonymous monks and scholars of the eighth to the thirteenth centuries speaking of the simple life these men lead—close to nature, to animals, to God."

company in which he could incorporate the spirit Horton had given his Los Angeles school and company, and Ailey admitted that he wanted to be looked upon as a father figure by his company. He continued to dance in his works, and again took on an acting role, but he was increasingly intent on building his company and on choreographing. Ailey was now in the forefront of the American dance scene and his company, billed as the Alvin Ailey Dance Theater, was chosen by the U. S. State Department to tour the Far East under a presidential Special International Program for Cultural Presentations.

The Ailey company went to Australia in February 1962, for a tour of the country's principal cities, and then to Asia, returning, via the Philippines, and Japan and Korea, in May. Ailey was engaged to teach jazz at Connecticut College, New London, a bastion of modern dance and, that same summer, was invited to choreograph a ballet for the Joffrey Ballet, on commission from the Rebekah Harkness Foundation. Ailey chose as his theme Federico García Lorca's play *The House of Bernarda Alba,* and, to music by Carlos Surinach, choreographed *Feast of Ashes.*

Here, Ailey was drawing on the years he spent in Los Angeles' Thomas Jefferson Senior High School, where he had read Spanish literature, but the employment of the classical dance, for an Ailey work, was something new and, it seemed, illogical. Nevertheless, Ailey was following the pattern so characteristic of his choreography, drawing on things he had experienced and had observed.

When he was dancing in *House of Flowers,* and at a time when he declared himself disgusted with the "whole modern dance scene" in New York, Ailey had, reluctantly, gone with Louis Johnson to a ballet school in Greenwich Village where, as Ailey discovered, almost the entire cast of *House of Flowers* studied daily, with a teacher named Karel Shook.

Shook, like Horton, was white, and Shook, like Horton, was, as Ailey has remarked, very receptive to working with black dancers. Shook, in fact, had an uncanny perception about talent in black dancers and black dancers were drawn to him. His ability to detect potential, and the quickness and authority with which he developed professional technicians, made Shook legendary. Almost every black classical dancer of the era owed something to Shook, among them Arthur Mitchell.

Alvin Ailey and Judith Jamison.

L. to r., Judith Lerner, Paul Sutherland, Cleo Quitman, Judith Jamison, Glory van Scott, and Carmen de Lavallade in THE FOUR MARYS, choreographed by Agnes de Mille. The ballet was premiered at the New York State Theater in March 1965.

Judith Jamison and Mikhail Baryshnikov in PAS DE "DUKE," choreographed by Alvin Ailey.

Kelvin Rotardier and Sylvia Waters with Judith Jamison (holding
umbrella) in Alvin Ailey's masterpiece, REVELATIONS (1973 seaso

ve Thompson, Dudley Williams, Judith Jamison, and Kelvin Rotardier
of the Alvin Ailey American Dance Theater.

Alvin Ailey

Mitchell was on scholarship at the New York High School for Performing Arts, and he had been advised to study modern dance because it was believed he had no future in ballet. Hearing of this, Shook sent for Mitchell, then in his teens, and offered to give him classical training. Shook taught at the Katherine Dunham School of Cultural Arts, to which he procured a scholarship for Mitchell. Mitchell was to become a member of the New City Ballet, a superb classical company—in which he speedily became a star. When he resigned, in premier rank, to found the Dance Theatre of Harlem, he chose Shook as his associate artistic director.

Shook, in manner mild as milk, in appearance rather like a benign Dutch elf, was not in the least perturbed by Alvin Ailey's prickly distrust of ballet, as of all strictly disciplined dance forms. Ailey emphatically stated that he did not wish to take class, whereupon Shook suggested that Ailey sit and observe the exercises. If he was going to choreograph, said Shook shrewdly, then Ailey had better know as much as he could of all dance idioms, the classical dance being of especial note. For three centuries ballet training had proved to be the best means of preparing the human body for dancing.

Ailey watched the classes and fell into discussions on dance with the erudite Shook, with whom he became friends. Not even Ailey ever knew how much he learned, how much he stored up for the future, in that bleak, uncompromising period of the early years in New York. Now, summoned to choreograph for the Joffrey Ballet, a company whose repertoire was based on modern ballets (and on the revivals and reprises of works from the Diaghilev era), Ailey could enter a hitherto alien world with confidence and authority.

Feast of Ashes is a powerful work, its strong dramatic dance episodes culminating in a brutal climax. Given a literal reference, Ailey proved adept at dance characterization. And, important for Ailey's ego, the work established him as a choreographer well able to work in various mediums. He could no longer be typed as a "jazz" or a "black" choreographer, narrowly limited as a creative artist.

Ailey worked with the Joffrey Ballet at Watch Hill, the Rhode Island estate of the company's patron, Mrs. Rebekah Harkness. This lady, who could be a lavish donor, invited Ailey to present his company at two performances in Central Park, where she sponsored the Rebekah Harkness Foundation Dance Festival, at the Delacorte Theatre, September 5–10, 1962. The Alvin Ailey Dance Theater appeared on the two last evenings, in a program that included *Roots of the Blues* and *Revelations*. And, on the last evening, Mrs. Harkness brought, as her guests, the dancers and artistic directors of the Bolshoi Ballet, which had ended a season at the Metropolitan Opera House on September 9.

Ailey and his dancers performed the first part of the September 10 program in pouring rain, through which the Russians sat, unmoving, in the open-air theatre. But the Russians applauded after each work and, following *Roots of the Blues,* leaped to their feet and shouted their delighted recognition of classic American jazz. In the intermission, Ailey made a speech, in Russian, which further pleased the guests. The rain, as though on command, stopped for *Revelations.*[2] Another storm was raging inside the Ailey company.

There was dissent within the company, on its return from the Far East tour, and some dancers left the troupe, angered because Carmen de Lavallade had been billed as co-director as well as principal dancer. The Ailey company considered her only a guest artist. As new members came into the company one, Myrna White, a black dancer out of the Broadway musical theatre, replaced de Lavallade as Ailey's partner. Ailey went into another play, a Broadway production, *Tiger, Tiger, Burning Bright,* directed by Joshua Logan, who was trying to persuade Ailey to give up dancing and become an actor. Ailey joined a cast of veteran black actors, among them Diana Sands, Roscoe Lee Brown, and Cicely Tyson, and soon found himself out of his depth. It was brought forcibly home to him that he had no training for drama and that acting was as onerous, as serious an undertaking as dancing.

At the beginning of 1963 Ailey reorganized his company, in which only three members remained from the original troupe: Ailey, Thelma Hill, and James Truitte. Among the new members was Louis Falco, who had trained with Graham and at the Humphrey-Weidman school and had danced in the José Limón Company. Ailey had begun his company with black dancers but now he felt that an integrated company would best suit his choreographic needs and the needs of other choreographers whose works were being taken into the repertoire. He was soon to say, during a London engagement,

[2] The Delacorte Theatre program was filmed and presented on "Camera Three" by the Columbia Broadcasting System (CBS), on nationwide television, September 10, 1962.

that his dream was to form a repertory modern dance company, "completely mixed" (i.e., integrated), although he intended that the major part of the troupe would be black. To emphasize his catholicity, Ailey took into the company dancers of Caucasian, Afro, and Oriental antecedents.

The Ailey Dance Theater was by now well known in the United States, from its tours, and especially through its appearances in college theatres. One U.S. tour took the company from the East Coast into the South, following a New York State tour under the auspices of the New York State Council on the Arts. The company traveled farther to take part, by invitation, in a festival at Rio de Janeiro, after which Ailey stopped off at Bahia, to observe the celebrated dancing of the Bahianians, the proud descendants of African slaves and their Portuguese masters.

The following year was even more productive and did even more to make Ailey's company famous on the international scene. He presented his dancers in performance at Clark Center, rejoined the annual festival sponsored by the Harkness Foundation at the Delacorte Theatre, and, in September, went on a three-month tour of Europe, opening at the Théâtre des Champs-Élysées in Paris. The company had grown from six to twelve dancers and among the notable additions were Kelvin Rotardier, William Louther, and Dudley Williams. The Alvin Ailey Dance Theater was, it appeared, establishing its reputation with male dancers of outstanding gifts.

Ailey had acquired some of the Beatty works, excerpts from Beatty's *Come and Get the Beauty of It Hot* (in which "Congo Tango Palace" was a show stopper), and the Ailey company premiered Beatty's *The Road of the Phoebe Snow* at the Delacorte Theatre on September 1, 1964. In that same engagement, Ailey presented *Revelations* in its completed form. The work had undergone substantial changes since its original appearance in 1960. With these two great works, *Phoebe Snow* and *Revelations,* the Alvin Ailey Dance Theater moved to the forefront of serious modern dance. Talley Beatty and Alvin Ailey drew on "black" culture—and Beatty, like Ailey, derived choreographic inspiration from his childhood.[3] They did so with vivid characterization and in colorful

---

[3] Ailey's respect for Talley Beatty (whom he met in Chicago in 1963) is an instance of Ailey's exemplary conduct toward guest choreographers. *The Road of the Phoebe Snow* was performed in the Ailey company with such passion

stage settings, and their works were danced with the fire and uninhibited freedom of a society altogether removed from that of white
America. But these works, in Beatty's and in Ailey's choreography,
could not be categorized as "Negro" dancing, as a whole body of
"black dance acts" had been, a move away from the minstrel show.
Nor did Beatty and Ailey support their works with a scholarly
crutch. Their dependence was not on archaeological research of
black Africa, it was nearer home, closer to the bone of the living
body of "black" America. Beatty and Ailey tore the flesh from that
body and distilled its blood and tears and sweat for their choreography.

The European tour was accompanied by a paean of praise for the
Alvin Ailey Dance Theater and the company won its greatest triumph in a six-week engagement at the Shaftesbury Theatre in London, commencing on October 5. Here, as it would continue to do
everywhere in the world where it was seen, *Revelations* drew the
highest praise. Ailey's *Blues Suite* and Beatty's *Phoebe Snow* were
equally admired.

No sooner was the company back in America than it prepared for
another long trip, a return engagement in Australia. Ailey found
time and energy to choreograph a ballet to an original score by
André Jolivet. It was *Ariadne,* for the Harkness Ballet. This company, wrenched more or less bodily out of the Joffrey Ballet, in
1964, made its debut in Cannes, February 1965, with the premiere
of Ailey's *Feast of Ashes*.

With the rapid development of the company, and the necessity for
enlarging the repertoire for the long foreign tours, Ailey took in the
works of several other choreographers. Some (John Butler, Joyce
Trisler, Lucas Hoving) were white. The company was especially
strong in male dancers and Ailey performed less often than before.
He began, now, to teach his roles to younger dancers, not hesitating
to alter steps and movements to better suit the men who took over
his roles. Ailey's facility—which was to be scorned by some critics
—allowed him to rapidly rechoreograph a solo, to accommodate a

---

that it came to take a place beside Ailey's own *Revelations*. *Phoebe Snow*
takes its name from a train on the Lackawanna Railroad Line that ran
through the midwestern United States. Beatty, as a child, played near the railroad tracks along which the *Phoebe Snow* ran and his ballet is composed (ab-
stractly and dramatically) on incidents "that may have happened on or near
these railroad tracks."

dancer new to the dance, or a dancer suffering from an injury, who found the original steps too difficult to perform. Ailey seemed to thrive on emergencies and to shine under stress.

During the 1965 Australian tour Mrs. Harkness called him to Paris to rehearse her company in his *Ariadne,* which received its world premiere with the ballerina Marjorie Tallchief in the title role. In the three-month European tour in 1965, Ailey took his company to the major arts festivals and on one-night stands through the cities of nine countries, plus a two-week engagement at London's Saville Theatre. His energy, and that of his dancers, seemed inexhaustible and the second London season was danced to critical raves. The usually dour English reviewers had capitulated, almost to a man.

No single dancer in the Ailey company received more praise than Ailey. When he performed in *Revelations* the audience often responded as ardently, almost, as had the members of the True Vine Baptist Church in Navasota to their own spiritual revelations—on which, of course, Ailey based his work. Appearing with his company —designated as the representative of the United States at the Paris Festival of Nations—at the Sarah Bernhardt Theatre, May 27, in *Revelations,* Ailey gave one of the greatest performances of his career. His grace, wholly masculine in style, endowed his dancing with as much beauty as his power projected force. His size, alone, distinguished him among male dancers. As remarkable was the control that he exerted over his splendid body. As Ailey matured, the old magnetic animalism had subtly altered, to nobility. He had the beauty and the dignity of a superb animal; one thought of an animalistic character because of the freedom with which he danced. The little boy who had loved the deep woods, who had made a fearless friendship with a great snake, and drawn and annotated specimens from the insect world, was closer to the charmed natural universe than to the theatre. It was in the theatre, however, that Alvin Ailey communicated his thoughts and divulged his feelings.

One of the dancers, William Louther, left the company during the 1965 European tour and Ailey returned, full time, to dancing, taking over Louther's roles at the festival at Florence (with less than two weeks to prepare himself). Two other male dancers were performing only intermittently. Ailey found himself dancing roles that he had not rehearsed for almost a year, and that he had not danced in more than six months. The incident made him determine his future: he would retire as a dancer. As soon as the company accepted this decision as a fact, he would be free to concentrate on directing the company, and on choreography.

The Ailey company returned to New York, Truitte and Ailey following later, after a holiday, during which Ailey visited Rome and Venice, Rhodes and Crete, absorbing from each place impressions to be used in future work. Ailey was back in New York by September. He had now to reorganize his company and to rehearse the repertoire in preparation for a new year. There were engagements at several colleges where, as artists in residence for a week or two, the Ailey dancers appeared in lecture-demonstrations, as well as in performance. Some dancers were delegated by Ailey to conduct classes for the college students.

Ailey engaged Clive Thompson, who had been with the Horton company and with Martha Graham. And he engaged a new girl, a Japanese with a melodious name, Takako Asakawa, who later became a principal dancer in the Graham company. Ailey went to an audition by his friend Donald McKayle and there saw a young dancer with an interesting quality. Rejected at the audition, the girl left so hurriedly that Ailey was unable to speak to her. After three days of telephoning around town, when at length he got hold of her, Ailey engaged Judith Jamison. It was, as Ailey said later, more on impulse than by judicious choice. At the time he hardly knew what use he would make of "this girl, like a long drink of water."

Ailey's most exciting acquisition that season was a teenaged boy named Miguel Godreau, who may have reminded Ailey of himself. Those who knew the young Ailey saw something of him in Godreau, who had just such a magnetic personality as Ailey, the same aura of sensuality, and twice the technical dance ability.

Judith Jamison went into the Ailey company never knowing that, simultaneously, she was to be affected powerfully by two men: Ailey, in her aspects as a dancer; Godreau, in her aspects as a woman.

NINE

When a dancer goes into a company, she gives herself in something like marriage. Her fealty is to the choreographer who will compose dances on her, and she is expected to support the principles of the group into which she has been assimiliated. When, in a company, the principal choreographer is also the artistic director, two loyalties are owed to one man.

Alvin Ailey was, as are the founder-choreographer-directors of companies, no less than God to the dancers whose fates he controlled. Ailey, at that time, also managed the affairs of his troupe. His duties were artistic and executive. The dual responsibility, and the work load in sheer man-hours, could not for long be undertaken by a creative artist; Ailey needed to hoard his time and energy if he meant to choreograph.

The Alvin Ailey Dance Theater was just then poised on the brink of a new phase of its existence. Changes were to be made and, inevitable as they were to growth, some such changes would never be to Ailey's liking. A few would shake the company to its foundations.

Jamison was unaware of the internal problems of the company when she joined it in 1965. She had heard, chiefly from de Lavallade, that Ailey was a gifted choreographer and that his company was the greatest "black" theatre dance company in the world. By 1965 it had become known on the American continent and in Europe, in the Australian metropolises, and in the East. There was left only Russia to conquer, and this the Ailey company would do in 1970. Now, five years earlier, it was the most exciting dance company in America. The Ailey company drew its audience from the huge public strata, not from the small cliques of modern dance connoisseurs and balletomanes. Ailey was bringing into the theatre people who had never before paid to attend a dance performance.

If the company was famous, it was not rich, and one of Ailey's perpetual worries lay in his finances. He had tried, without much satisfaction, placing the company under managements other than his own, and he was now faced with the necessity of deciding to whom, and to what extent, he must entrust the company's affairs. Ailey hesitated to introduce a managing element from outside the company; he feared it would affect adversely the atmosphere he was eager to develop. Ailey was still hoping to re-create the "climate" of the Lester Horton Dance Theater, though he would soon have to relinquish his intention of forming his company in that mold. Above all, Ailey was alarmed and hurt by the fractiousness of some dancers; their jockeying for favorable billing was sometimes more energetic than the dancing.

The closeness, what Ailey has called the "loving-kindness," of the dancers in Horton's company had come out of organic growth, of Horton's principles of dance and of his pupils' dedication to them. Horton attracted dancers of a certain temperament; they all shared this temperament, regardless of the diverging styles of their dancing. Perhaps the primary element in the fusion of dancers, in the Horton company, came from an individual and a collective need for something to believe in. Horton, with his apostolic fervor for dance, presented a core from which his dancers drew nourishment. Horton's capacity for belief, his marvelous optimism, led men and women into daring to dance, and some of these might never have dared otherwise. Ailey, for one.

To a conventional choreographer, a boy of Ailey's physique, which suited him well for playing football, would have seemed too burly for a performer. Predictably, conventional teachers would have discouraged Ailey from serious dance studies.

Ailey had little confidence in himself as a dancer. Although he enjoyed working with Horton, he remained hesitant about performing. As he remembers, Ailey suffered "a private hell" every time he was onstage in the beginning of his career. "If at any time in those days Lester had put too much pressure on me, I would have cut and run. I had to go at my own speed. I had to stop when I felt like it, and start again when I felt ready. Lester let me do that. I was allowed to progress, at my own rate, in the Horton company. What other company would have given me that? Who else, other than Lester, would have had the patience and the understanding to work with kids, as he did?"

Truitte would carry on Horton's work as a teacher,[1] but it was Ailey who felt an almost religious sense of obligation to preserve the "climate" that Lester Horton made for dancers to grow in, to realize their full potential.

Horton, physically a big man, like Ailey, had a matter-of-factness that may have been instrumental in keeping the "climate" of his company a fairly healthy one, emotionally. Not that the company did not have schisms and crises. There was violent dissension within the company in 1950, and it seemed that Horton's work might be destroyed. Horton reorganized the troupe, and Carmen de Lavallade and James Truitte became the definitive interpreters of Horton's choreography. The company assumed a new style, from the new principals. Bella Lewitzky, who had been Horton's assistant, left Horton's company in 1950—and left to Carmen de Lavallade not only the roles Horton had created on Lewitzky but Lewitzky's inspiration as Horton's Muse.

Belonging, as they did, to the final phase of the Horton company, the black dancers whose presence dominated it were, understandably, possessive of their traditions. Ailey, loyal to a fault, struggled to preserve the Horton legacy; failure to do so would have been not only a dereliction of duty but rank ingratitude. Ailey choreographed odes in dance, to pay homage to Horton. Audiences received these works with more apathy than enthusiasm. Ailey insisted on reviving the Horton works, even though he was obliged to admit that they—with the greater part of modern dance repertoire from the 1930s—had gone out of vogue.

In testimony to Horton, and out of his own conviction that it was an ideal way to work in a company, Ailey tried to form a troupe on a fusion of dancers. Instead of "loving-kindness," the dancers felt envy. During a European tour of his company, one of Ailey's leading dancers abruptly left because of an acrimonious quarrel over "billing." The more they were praised by critics, the more chary the

[1] James Truitte danced in musicals and after appearing in *Carmen Jones* went —on the advice of Janet Collins—to study with Horton, with whom he remained until the latter's death. Truitte had marked influence on Ailey's company in the 1960s. He served it as principal dancer and régisseur, and as associate director. A celebrated teacher, he received a John Hay Whitney fellowship to record the Horton technique, of which he is accepted as the authoritative reference source.

dancers became about casting, and about the size of the type and the placement of their names on programs. Dancers have ways of punishing management for real and fancied wrongs. The most common is to complain of an injury. Since physical injury is an occupational hazard, the dancers did not find it difficult to produce irrefutable excuses for not performing. Ailey was aghast at such ruses, played by disgruntled dancers. He was as shocked as he was angry when a dancer walked out of the company in a pique.

"Alvin," says one of his compeers, "came to New York with a Southern Baptist conscience, a prim idea of right and wrong. He was idealistic and committed, and that made him hard to work with, and for. Alvin did not spare himself. He saw no reason to spare other people." Ailey, for his part, says that "the whole New York scene" was, at first, repugnant to him. "I was put off by the drinking, the running around—and the backbiting. It was such a 'dog-eat-dog' situation, compared to the way we had worked with Horton in Los Angeles."

Time might soften Ailey's stiff prudery but it would not change his fundamental principles. He might absorb "the New York scene" but he would remain, at heart, Alvin Ailey. Nor would time change Ailey's two predominant traits: his sense of loyalty and his love of beauty. For a while, these were concentrated on Carmen de Lavallade.

De Lavallade had become a decorative if not an integral member of the Ailey company. Her appearances as guest artist were on terms dictated by her husband, Geoffrey Holder, and some of the terms aggravated the Ailey dancers. On the company's first U. S. State Department sponsored tour, in 1962, de Lavallade was billed as the star. Holder demanded and obtained for his wife equal billing with Ailey for the artistic direction of the company. Ailey's dancers were incensed that the company, as the official representative of the United States' cultural program, appeared on its thirteen-week tour as "The De Lavallade-Ailey American Dance Company," starring Carmen de Lavallade.

On the tour, de Lavallade exercised the prerogatives of an artistic director and "utterly scandalized" the dancers by changing some of Ailey's choreography. This lèse majesté was aided and abetted by Ailey, who supported de Lavallade in all she chose to do, even when he did not really agree with her.

The company's overwhelming success—it played to huge crowds and sometimes there were riots at the box office by mobs that had been turned away from the sold-out auditoriums—did not placate the anger of the Ailey dancers, fanned, it must be admitted, by the "royal treatment" that was accorded de Lavallade, with Ailey, everywhere they went. The women dancers were especially outraged by the "rank favoritism" that Ailey was said to have shown de Lavallade.

Returning home, the dissenting dancers reminded Ailey, not for the first time, that they had been engaged to work under his direction, not under de Lavallade's. Some members of the company, which, with de Lavallade, had been enlarged to ten members for the tour, left Ailey, in bitterness and with regret. There were, after all, few other opportunities for black dancers to dance "seriously" in a company in the United States, and to cut oneself off from Ailey was tantamount to giving up all chances of dancing in the "legitimate" theatre. Ailey, shaken by the experience, and aware that things "had not been quite right" on the tour, came to what he has described as "an emotional and an artistic" parting of the ways with de Lavallade. Her image would continue to haunt him. For Alvin Ailey every woman would forever dance in the shadow of that girl, in *pointe* shoes and a tutu, who had performed at a Los Angeles high school assembly to music by Mozart.

Having recovered from the traumas of 1962, Ailey philosophically endured those of 1965. He made a hard decision about then: he would stop performing.

However unhappy he may have been made by the changes taking place in his company, Ailey cannot have been less than pleased by his growing renown as a choreographer. The Harkness Ballet, on its first U.S. tour, was dancing Ailey's *Feast of Ashes* and *Ariadne,* and both ballets were receiving favorable notices. Some reviewers went so far as to say that Ailey's ballets were the chief substance of the Harkness repertoire.

The Alvin Ailey Dance Theater staged its 1965–66 season at the Harper Theatre in Chicago, November 30 through December 5. Judith Jamison made her debut in the company, not in an Ailey work but as one of the corps in Talley Beatty's *Congo Tango Palace.* Her first performances with the company in New York were in "House of the Rising Sun" in Ailey's *Blues Suite;* in his *Revelations,* in two sections, "Fix Me, Jesus" and "The Day Is Past and Gone"; and in Beatty's *The Road of the Phoebe Snow,* where she appeared as one of a quartet. On February 14, 1966, the Ailey company began its third European tour.

TEN

"Going into the Ailey company," says Judith Jamison, "was like wearing a size fifty shoe. Everything was too big for me; everybody was way out of my reach. I could have crawled into a corner but there was no time, not even time enough for me to feel nervous.

"We had two weeks of rehearsal, followed by six weeks of one-night stands. We opened in Chicago, at the Harper Theatre, then went to Washington [where the Ailey company performed in the Howard University Cultural Series] and to Hunter College. In February we were in Europe. In April we were in Africa. In May we merged with Harkness.

"I don't know what I was like, that first year. I had no criteria for myself. There were no standards I could apply, to measure up to. A lot of that time is just a blur now . . .

"What I remember best were the dancers. The girls were Lucinda Ransom, Loretta Abbott, Takako Asakawa, and me. Consuelo Atlas was with us in Europe.

"The men were James Truitte, Dudley Williams, Morton Winston, Kelvin Rotardier, Robert Powell, and Miguel Godreau. They were *magnificent*—there is no other word! Alvin had stopped dancing but the company was still very patriarchal. The concentration was on the men.

"Jimmy Truitte was Alvin's assistant but he was still performing. He was my first partner in 'Fix Me, Jesus' [in *Revelations*]. For two years we bowed to each other in the yellow section.

"I remember, that first year, dancing in *Revelations,* in *Phoebe Snow,* and in Sokolow's *Rooms*. In Rome, where we danced at the Olympic Theatre, *Rooms* had to be taken off the program. I never knew why.

"We opened the European tour in Muenster [Germany] and that night I realized the kind of status the company had in Europe. The audience applauded for *one—solid—hour!* That made the audiences at home seem pretty tepid.

"We went through Germany, Holland, and Italy and everywhere the company got tremendous response. In Berlin, they filmed *Revelations.* We got to Milan. All the while, I was thinking: *God! Girl! You are here! This is fantastic!* How many times my Mom and I had looked up the famous foreign cities, when I was doing 'papers' at school! Now I was in Milan, the city of La Scala!"

There were centuries-old libraries and theatres, art galleries and museums, cathedrals and palaces. There were famous monuments, groups of statuary, fountains and gardens. All, fabulous, with their immense age and historic associations, were interesting to observe, enlightening to the mind, and stimulating to the imagination. Jamison, however, soon discovered that the dancer most often identifies a strange city by its theatre and the hotel or pension in which he is billeted. On the tours, the company came and went with startling abruptness; the dancers seldom had layovers between towns. Soon, all the towns began to seem alike.

That year, in Milan, there was an enforced layover and Jamison experienced the first of the crises she was to share with the Ailey company.

The European tour was under an English impresario, Michael Dorfman, who, besides the Ailey company, was presenting a black troupe in a play, *The Prodigal Son.* The drama company traveled a little in advance of the dance company. A contretemps arose, over the alleged misconduct of the black actors, and the managements of several theatres canceled the play and all other Dorfman bookings. The Alvin Ailey American Dance Theater was stranded in Milan. No other engagements were available through Dorfman and it was impractical, and too risky, to try to find another European impresario at short notice.

On tours, Ailey always withheld a week's salaries from the company, as resource against such a debacle. He had the company's fares back to the United States. But Ailey and the dancers were loath to retreat, ignominiously, from the European tour. Ailey appealed for aid to Rebekah Harkness, who had sometimes subsidized dancers.

Mrs. Harkness replied with an invitation to the Ailey company to join itself to the Harkness Ballet, which, too, was in Europe. The two troupes would rendezvous in Barcelona, in May. Ailey had now, and immediately, to find means of sustaining his company for six weeks. Help came from an unexpected quarter. Ailey was asked to take his company to Senegal, to represent the United States at the Premier Festival Mondial des Arts, April 1–24, at Dakar. Ailey and Truitte managed to raise enough funds for the company's layover in Milan, after which they went to Senegal.

There, further difficulties awaited them. Clive Thompson's wife was having their first child and he returned home to be with her. On arrival at Dakar, Morton Winston became ill with an undiagnosed complaint whose symptoms were fever and vomiting. Winston performed, with numerous unscheduled exits. Weak from retching, he would make his way back onstage and continue dancing. Miguel Godreau dislocated a shoulder. When the bone popped out of its socket, he fled to the wings, laid himself flat on the floor, and waited for one of the other dancers to push it back in place. He then leaped up and again took part in the dancing.

The change in climate and unaccustomed food had adverse effects on the dancers. Ailey recalls that there were times, at the Dakar Festival, when only four or five dancers were onstage in works that had been choreographed for eight. Nevertheless, the company acquitted itself with honor. The repertoire was new to the audiences and the dancers, above all, were a startling novelty. None there had seen dancers of the style of the Ailey company, by ones and twos, or by the dozen.

Once again, the Ailey company was praised and yet again it served the United States as a cultural ambassador. Ailey, meanwhile, had alienated a number of black dancers in America who felt that, by participating at the Dakar Festival, Ailey had "sold out his own people." Ailey had taken an assignment previously given to Arthur Mitchell and then withdrawn. Adherents of Mitchell and of Ailey were sharply divided in condemnation and defense of Ailey's appearance at the Dakar Festival. It was a row of royal proportions.

The circumstances were these: Mitchell had been persuaded to serve as Dance Chairman for the committee for American representation at the Dakar Festival, and he had worked hard to form a company of thirty-one black dancers, led by himself and by Carmen de Lavallade. Many dancers were notable. The men included William Louther and Claude Thompson; the women, the formidable

Paula Kelly. There were two girls of whom more would be heard: Llanchie Stevenson and Sara Yarborough.[1]

Mitchell served the committee without financial remuneration and the other dancers also donated their services, some of them interrupting lucrative careers to do so. They were motivated by a patriotic ardor, to represent black American culture at an international arts festival.

Mitchell was, by then, an internationally known performer, the leading black danseur in twentieth-century ballet. He danced a wide range of roles at the New York City Ballet, where he had appeared in several premieres—among them, Balanchine's *Agon*. Mitchell partnered Diana Adams in the 1950s, and Suzanne Farrell in the 1960s, in *Agon*'s celebrated pas de deux, thus spanning two of the Balanchine epochs, to both of which he lent his considerable talents.

Mitchell was also well known in musical theatre, and he acted in plays, in the United States and Canada, and in Europe. Invited to bring a troupe to the Third Festival of Two Worlds at Spoleto, Mitchell formed a company of American dancers of African, Asian, and European antecedents. Their success was enough to bring them back to Spoleto the following year.

Mitchell had a prodigious energy, and an extraordinary generosity. While pursuing his own career, he devoted himself to helping young black ballet dancers. He commuted from New York to Washington, to teach at the Jones-Hayward School of Ballet, one of the principal training grounds for black dancers. Aware of the problems existent for black classical dancers, Mitchell counseled young dancers. It was on Mitchell's advice that Sylvester Campbell, a handsome and gifted student of the Jones-Hayward School, went to Europe, where Campbell became the premier danseur of the Het Nederlands Ballet.

Because of his accomplishments and his international renown, Arthur Mitchell was the logical person to head a representative troupe of American dancers, and the committee's choice was enthusiastically approved. Mitchell was determined to present his dancers as a valid company. He worked hard to rehearse the repertoire and, in an unbelievably short time, had a qualified company, one that,

[1] Stevenson became a featured dancer of the Dance Theatre of Harlem; Yarborough, of the Alvin Ailey American Dance Theater.

had it been maintained, would have been a major acquisition of American dance.

On the scheduled eve of the company's departure for Dakar, Mitchell was informed by the committee that it had not been able to raise sufficient funds to defray expenses. The committee then lamely suggested that Mitchell might go, with a partner, as the American representative to the Festival; expenses would be defrayed. Mitchell refused and the company was disbanded. Reports are that overtures were made to de Lavallade to substitute for Mitchell, and that, in loyalty to Mitchell, de Lavallade refused. At this point, the committee approached Alvin Ailey in Milan, inviting him to take his company to the Dakar Festival.

From Milan to Dakar was a much shorter distance than that from New York, and Ailey's company of ten dancers was less than half the size of Mitchell's company of thirty-odd members. Expenses for the committee, therefore, were a great deal less for the Ailey troupe than they would have been for Mitchell's. And Ailey, caught in his own dilemma in Milan, accepted much less generous terms than the committee had originally made to Mitchell. The committee was now absolved of its responsibility, and the United States was saved from diplomatic embarrassment, by the formal delegation of the Ailey company as the American representative at the Dakar Festival. As a friend of Ailey's, who was also a friend of Mitchell's, sadly remarked, it was a case of playing both ends against the middle. As is invariably the result in such instances, the ends were ill served.

Arthur Mitchell's friends felt a natural sense of outrage at the summary manner in which he had been replaced by Ailey, and they blamed Ailey for tacitly condoning the committee's shabby treatment of Mitchell and his dancers, by acting as their substitutes at the Dakar Festival. Mitchell, to his great credit, accepted another invitation from the United States government, to serve on a committee for a cultural exchange program with Brazil. It led to Mitchell's brilliant success as choreographer and director of ballet companies in Rio de Janeiro and Bahia, positions he resigned in 1968 to found the Dance Theatre of Harlem.

The bad feeling from the "Dakar incident" would rankle for a long time. Mitchell and Ailey preserved a cool and haughty silence on the affair and, in 1977, shared the Dance Magazine Awards at a function attended by dancers of both companies. These dancers, however, remained wary of each other. Though many of them were not associated with Mitchell and with Ailey in 1966, ten years later they took up the desultory vendetta over the "Dakar incident."

Ailey, stranded in Europe in 1966, was not as much concerned with the opinions of his compeers as with the urgent need to save his imperiled company. Thankfully accepting the Dakar Festival engagement, and proud of his company's rallying against the odds to make it a successful appearance, Ailey was stung, later, by the inference that he had set his ambitions above loyalty to "his own people."

Ailey took very seriously a sense of obligation to his "people" and to the culture of black America. He named his company a "Dance Theatre" to emphasize its nature. More than "just another dance troupe," it was meant by Ailey to be the storehouse of the art of blacks in America. Ailey construed "theatre" in its old Grecian meaning as "a place to view."

He wrote, for the program of the Alvin Ailey American Dance Theater, at its engagement at the Shaftesbury Theatre, London, in 1964, a statement that fairly expressed his credo: "The cultural heritage of the American Negro is one of America's richest treasures. From his roots as a slave, the American Negro—sometimes sorrowing, sometimes jubilant, but always hopeful—has created a legacy of music and dance which has touched, illuminated, and influenced the most remote preserves of world civilization. I and my dance theatre celebrate, in our programme, this trembling beauty. We bring to you the exuberance of his jazz, the ecstasy of his spirituals, and the dark rapture of his blues."

Ailey was finding it harder and harder to support the company he had dedicated to the elegiac praise of his people. He had, as he has remarked, "always to scrimp and save" and to grudgingly compromise in order to hold a few dancers together as a group. Despite the company's great success in the international theatre, it had no economic stability. The tours, if profitable for the company's management, earned barely enough for company salaries. Year after year, Ailey found himself deeper and deeper in debt for the mere appurtenances of a dance company.

These ills were compounded by the ironic conditions in which the Alvin Ailey American Dance Theater was paraded about the world, in circumstances which made it a formal representative of the United States government as well as the official delegate of black dance in the United States.

Ailey, better than his dancers, knew how close the company had come to disaster in Milan, how providentially it had been saved by being sent to Dakar, and how necessary it now became for the company to merge with the Harkness Ballet. The dancers, having survived the Dakar engagement, were inclined to look back on it as a comedy. In this spirit they set off for Barcelona—all five of the dancers who elected to go there with Ailey. Consuelo Atlas pleaded illness and returned home. Asakawa, Powell, and Williams, who did not wish to dance with the Harkness Ballet, took engagements in London—where, all of a sudden, the formerly despised modern dance was popular. The Ailey dancers were much in demand to teach technique.

Ailey and his five dancers arrived in Spain in early May and Ailey began at once to choreograph a new work for the Harkness Ballet, a ballet to de Falla's *El Amor Brujo,* in which the leading role was set on Marjorie Tallchief.

Ailey had also to choreograph a work for his own dancers, for performing in the Harkness programs. With the facility for which he was alternately praised and scorned, Ailey choreographed *Macumba,* to music composed by Rebekah Harkness. It was presented, for the first time, in Barcelona.

The Ailey dancers went with the Harkness Ballet to Paris, for a June 8–18 engagement at the Festival du Marais, after which the tour ended. The Ailey company was then disbanded.

For ten years Ailey had struggled to found a company with a representive repertoire. It was to be admitted that he had done so and had won praise on five continents. The Ailey company was world-famous; it was also too poor to continue subsisting.

In 1966 Ailey faced the realization that he no longer had the strength for the continuous and frantic search for money—not a great deal of money, only sufficient money to maintain the company of eight to ten dancers. He was temperamentally unsuited to fundraising, and he was physically and spiritually incapable of attending to the business affairs of a company of which he was also the artistic director and principal choreographer.

Ailey, even if he did not admit it, was smarting under Mrs.

Harkness' "charitable" adoption of the remnant of the Ailey company in Europe. In proximity with the opulent Harkness organization it was impossible for Ailey not to feel resentment. The Harkness company was brought into instantaneous existence by the quick-mix of dollars and dancers. The Ailey company had been torn from Alvin Ailey, like a child from the womb. Not a man or a woman who had been associated with the company could have been bought by dollars alone. All had believed in Alvin Ailey's dream and had lent themselves to making it a reality. Now, Ailey's instincts urged him to let go of the company, of the responsibility for his dancers, and to concentrate on choreography.

Ailey accepted a commission to do the choreography for Samuel Barber's *Antony and Cleopatra* and, following the Paris engagement of the Harkness Ballet, left for Rome to work with Franco Zefferelli on plans for the production of the opera at the Metropolitan Opera House in New York City. Thereafter, Ailey occupied himself with some other projects, for which he was well paid. He went to Cologne to teach master classes at the International Dance Academy. He worked again at Watch Hill, Rhode Island, with the Harkness Ballet.

The dancers of the Ailey company scattered, as do the fragments of a fragile object that has been shattered. Judith Jamison and Miguel Godreau were taken into the Harkness Ballet.

ELEVEN

While in Paris with the Harkness Ballet, Jamison worked in a French film, for which she was paid "some francs." It cannot have been a matter of consequence to her. She never saw the film, does not know what it was called, and said, later, that her recollections of what she did for the movie were "of the haziest." Jamison was in a roseate fog; she had fallen in love.

The object of Jamison's affections was Miguel Godreau, as "special" a dancer as ever appeared on the American stage.

Born in Ponce, Puerto Rico, Godreau was pleased to describe himself as a "Puerto Rican hillbilly." In truth, he was far more complex and much more of a sophisticate than any allegorical country boy.

Godreau came to the United States with his parents at an age variously given as two and as five, and grew up a street-smart boy in New York. Under the façade of that identity, Godreau remained the product of a *macho* Spanish society. Godreau's father was a musician who played for a dance band in Puerto Rico, and, as a boy, Miguel Godreau learned to play several instruments. He studied the violin for four years. Dancing was a normal aspect of his familial society. Godreau received no formal instruction but he performed traditional Spanish folk and ballroom dances, with an elder sister as his partner. There is no record of Godreau expressing an intent to become a dancer or of his having received incentives to go into the theatre until he went to high school. At the age of fourteen he took charge of his life and thereafter lived it as he chose. Intuitively he turned to dance, for which he was exceptionally gifted.

He applied for admission to the High School of Performing Arts, as a dance major, and there began instruction in modern dance and in ballet. His teachers included David Wood, a former member of the Graham company, and Nina Popova, a former member of Ballet Theatre and the Ballet Russe de Monte Carlo.

In his first year of dance studies, Godreau performed in an amateur production of *West Side Story* at Harrison, New York, and there developed a taste for the musical theatre. In 1964 he danced at the New York World's Fair in Leon Leonidoff's *Wonderworld,* for which Michael Kidd was the choreographer, and that year went on the summer theatre circuit, dancing for eleven weeks in *Flower Drum Song.* He was next hired for the musical version of *Golden Boy,* starring Sammy Davis, Jr.

The show ran into trouble during its out-of-town engagement and the choreographer Herbert Ross was brought in to ready the production for the New York premiere. Ross thought that the show was laboring under too large a cast. He fired some of the players, including Godreau, who had been the last dancer to be hired, did not sing, and spoke English with a strong Spanish accent.

Godreau tried to get into the Ailey company. When he requested an audition, he was told that no more dancers would be hired that season. He joined a troupe, the American Dance Theater, and made his official New York debut at Lincoln Center, in programs produced for the company by Roger Englander. The works were all of the modern dance genre and Godreau danced the solo role of Donald McKayle's *Workout.* He was also cast in a role in Sokolow's *The Question.*

Godreau wanted very much to work in the Broadway theatre but he had no luck in breaking into the rather closed circle of dancers that choreographers like to draw around themselves, especially when they are working under the pressures of a Broadway show. Godreau auditioned for three major Broadway choreographers, Bob Fosse, Peter Gennaro, and Morton da Costa, none of whom he impressed sufficiently with his talents. It was not until 1969 that Godreau made his mark on Broadway, in *Dear World,* the musical adaptation of Jean Giraudoux's *The Madwoman of Chaillot.*

Before then, Godreau had danced on television and in movies, as well as with the Alvin Ailey Dance Theater. He was in the NBC-TV show "Hullabaloo," "The Dean Martin Show," and half a dozen or so other weekly TV variety shows, in which song and dance were indiscriminately scattered through the regulation antic rites of comedians, sometimes as "Specials." In June 1965 Godreau was in Hollywood, working in a movie, *Billie,* starring Patty Duke, for which the dances were choreographed by David Winters. There he resumed his studies, taking classes in ballet and in jazz at Eugene Loring's American School of Dance.

Godreau preferred the "New York scene" to the California ambience and returned home, in time to audition for a Broadway show called *Sugar City,* which was to be choreographed by Alvin Ailey. The show never materialized but Godreau was taken into the Ailey company. He made his debut with the company at the Harper Theatre, Chicago, in the winter of 1965, and went with Ailey to Europe, on to the Dakar Festival, and thence to the brief engagement with the Harkness Ballet.

Godreau's rise in the company was meteoric. Ailey liked him and admired his dancing. He cast Godreau in a principal role in the new *Macumba* and in *El Amor Brujo* as the partner of Marjorie Tallchief. Godreau earned a sobriquet: "the black Nureyev."

Rudolf Nureyev, from his earliest appearances in the Western ballet, had become the paradigm for male dancers. Godreau had the same fierce exultation in dance and much of the sensual magnetism of the great Russian dancer.

In his person, Godreau was exotically beautiful. His skin was the color of cinnamon and it had the quality of seeming to change shade and texture. Sometimes he seemed a creature whose rose and gold flesh had been laid on alabaster bones; at other times, he might have been carved from old ivory. His face, with its large, dark, brooding eyes, its wide lips with their enigmatic smile, was framed in a mop of black hair and it sometimes was the face of a seraph, sometimes the face of a faun. Godreau's particular daemon was half angel, half the child of Pan.

The fascination of Godreau's dancing lay in its tensility and its abandon. His flexible body was a rapturous flame. Jamison says of Godreau: "He burned." Some reviewers were to apply the adjective *burning* to Godreau's dancing but Jamison employed the term first, as soon as she saw Godreau working in the Ailey studios. "There was nothing else to say, when Miguel danced. He was consumed." Jamison watched him from the wings when she was not onstage. When she danced with him, she was overwhelmed by his power. "Sometimes, the illusion only carries to the audience. With Miguel, the illusion lasted close up because it was no illusion; he was really burning when he danced. The nearer the proximity, the hotter the fire." Jamison was enthralled and frightened by Godreau's intensity. "I was afraid for *him*. How could any human being sustain that intensity? I was afraid that it would burn him up, burn him out." Once again, in Godreau, Jamison saw a dancer such as she had not seen before.

It was inevitable that Jamison and Godreau would be attracted to each other. If, as is said, opposites exert a unifying principle, there were sufficient contrasts to bring them together like steel and magnet.

Technically and temperamentally, there was a strong affinity between Jamison and Godreau. They were, essentially, lyrical dancers. The differences between them lay in their natures, as marked as in their physiques.

Five feet, five inches tall, and slight in frame, Godreau nevertheless possessed a virility that radiated from him like a corona; Jamison's superior height was made negligible. Born in 1946, Godreau was, in chronological age, two years younger than Jamison; in experience, he was considerably her senior. These were the piquant contrasts that lent flavor to their feelings for each other.

Deeper than these were the psychological rifts in their two characters. As a friend of theirs has remarked: "Judi is a perfect Taurus; Miguel is a Libra, born close to the cusp of Scorpio." Jamison was direct and unequivocal; Godreau, oblique and ambivalent. In their love affair and their subsequent brief marriage they were to discover that incompatibility is corrosive to passion; it cannot even be assuaged by respect. At the beginning of their relationship, Jamison yielded herself wholeheartedly to Godreau's mesmeric charm.

He was as sensitive as a chameleon and as volatile as quicksilver. "Coming in contact with Miguel was like picking up a live wire." Godreau's integral character, a Latinate masculinity, strongly appealed to Jamison, who had formed an ideal of romantic love, incorporated in her father, of male strength and tenderness. She perceived in Godreau, beneath the *macho* dominance, a fragility and vulnerability; these were the elements of his poignant charm that colored the dark passion with which he danced. Godreau was one of those fateful beings, fated to allure out of their very illusiveness.

An artistic involvement between Jamison and Godreau should have appealed to discerning choreographers. The psychological and psychical tensions between them gave off powerful vibrations. Jamison had formed a credo, that power lay in "exquisite" control. Godreau's controlling force was the raw element of intuitive power. They polarized the dance, while, at the same time, admitting to much the same kind of intelligence.

Jamison said: "I cannot bear to count [steps, in dancing]. I dance in phrases." Godreau was constitutionally unable to accept regimentation. As a child, he took some tap dancing lessons, giving up further instruction because he "hated to count, when what I wanted to do was dance." Godreau was already a long way advanced in the discovery of himself; Jamison, just on the brink of her own. They were both romantics, who made a poetic approach to dance; an almost mystical approach. In two other aspects of her Self, Jamison was touched by Godreau.

He was one of those men who, regardless of their individual sexual predilections, are incapable of being in the presence of a woman without establishing a masculine and feminine rapport. This mysterious effluvium, emanating from males in patriarchal societies, surrounds the woman like a gauzy veil, implying a passionate possessiveness. It is, above all, the blazing consciousness of the female as Woman and it is irresistible to any woman of normal responses.

Godreau was, too, a militant advocate of the so-called American minorities, categorizing himself, as a Puerto Rican, with blacks. He often stated his feelings about dance, declaring that, to him, "the idea of dance is basically black." He sometimes expanded this statement to say that his sense of dance, his freedom onstage as the dancer, was essentially "black," in that he associated "black" with "soul." Godreau was fond of saying that the Puerto Rican and the Negro were "in the same boat." In the 1960s, he was especially susceptible to the outrages of decency and loss of dignity endured by the poor and the dispossessed in contemporary American society. Godreau identified himself wholly with his compeers in the Alvin Ailey Dance Theater and gloried in the attributes of "black soul," in his feelings, and in his performances, as a dancer.

Judith Jamison was coming, gradually, to the awareness of her nature as a woman. She was forming, subtly, her recognition of her identity as a dancer who was black. Godreau accelerated the process of her growth; he was the catalyst that changed her in this phase of her development.

At the Harkness Ballet, there was the happy probability that Jamison and Godreau would attract the attention of choreographers who would compose works for them. Godreau, giving way to the pessimism that sometimes afflicted him, was doubtful that much good would come of working with the Harkness Ballet. Jamison, more optimistic, saw that the company encouraged innovative choreography and that the dancers were very good; in fact, some of them were among the best in the American theatre.

Jamison and Godreau went to Watch Hill with the company to rehearse for the new season. It was to start with a U.S. tour, and an engagement in Hawaii. Godreau abruptly quit, responding to the often unerring instinct by which he allowed himself to be guided. He had come to believe that he and Jamison, rather than having their artistic potentials explored at the Harkness Ballet, would, instead, be exploited as novelties.

And Godreau was seized, as he was so often to be, by a congenital restlessness and impatience, a need for change. All through his career he was to vacillate between the "legitimate" and the "commercial" theatre. He resisted being "typed," as he said. His only constant resolve was that he would not become a particular kind of dancer, restricted to a particular kind of dance. The Broadway theatre, he felt, offered him a wider canvas than did a ballet company.

It is characteristic of Godreau's multifaceted talent that he would become as successful in one medium as in the other. Perhaps this facility was deleterious to his radiant gift. Godreau's star was not to stay permanently ascendant.

Jamison stayed with the Harkness Ballet.

TWELVE

In a single year, Judith Jamison traveled full circle, from American Ballet Theatre to the Harkness Ballet, with the Ailey company no more than an interlude. Perhaps her future lay in the ballet; if so, the Harkness Ballet seemed a safe place to pursue it.

The New York City Ballet and American Ballet Theatre were major companies, in size as well as scope. Secondary to them, in American ballet, were two smaller companies, the Joffrey and the Harkness. They shared a common character; indeed, one had sprung out of the other.

The Joffrey Ballet was founded by Robert Joffrey, a talented dancer who gave up performing to devote himself to a school and company. He began teaching while still a student, continued to teach throughout his performing career, and formed theories for training the classical dancer which he put into effect in his Greenwich Village school, the American Ballet Center. Joffrey had a cosmopolitan training, under American and Russian ballet teachers, and also studied modern dance forms. He was a member of Roland Petit's Ballets de Paris and danced in the company of modern dancer May O'Donnell. He began choreographing in 1952; two of his works were produced by the Ballet Rambert.

With another dancer, Gerald Arpino, Joffrey organized a small company which made ever-widening tours in the United States. Joffrey stayed in New York, to teach in the school and to build the company's repertoire on works by himself and some well-known choreographers, among them Balanchine and Tudor. Joffrey's reputation as a choreographer grew simultaneously with that as a pedagogue. Some of the greatest dancers of the time studied with Joffrey, including the premier danseur noble Erik Bruhn, while, at his school, Joffrey discovered and encouraged promising dance students.

Born in 1930, in Seattle, Washington, Joffrey, by 1960, was highly respected in American ballet. A man of immense charm and considerable erudition, he was temperamentally a romanticist and by nature a conservationist. Joffrey was preeminently a classicist, with a passionate love of traditional ballet. He set himself the awesome task of maintaining a modern ballet company, which would, also, sustain an older artistic ethic. The diligence and the integrity with which Joffrey worked won him the regard of his peers. This esteem was to stand Joffrey in good stead in his hour of adversity.

Gerald Arpino, two years Joffrey's senior, was an excellent danseur, noted for the elegance of his presence. After suffering an injury to his back—received in a fall onstage—Arpino stopped performing and directed his energy to choreography. He was to become the prolific choreographer of the Joffrey Ballet, of which he became assistant director in 1965. Arpino was also the co-director and a teacher of the American Ballet Center.

These two young men, Joffrey and Arpino, succeeded in establishing a school and company of great merit. The Joffrey Ballet began in 1954 by presenting single programs, the first of these being staged May 29 at the YMHA, in the same manner and the same place as the Ailey company started, three years later. Beginning with a group of six and then eight dancers, the Robert Joffrey Ballet— passing through changes in title, meanwhile—acquired an orchestra, an expanded repertoire, and an enlarged roster, and, with these, a distinct éclat. It was invited to appear in 1962 at the Spoleto Festival.

Rebekah Harkness offered to defray the expenses of the Robert Joffrey Ballet's participation at the Spoleto Festival. Joffrey asked that instead of the grant of funds for the Festival Mrs. Harkness donate the money to finance the company for a period of concentrated rehearsal before making its annual U.S. tour.

Mrs. Harkness generously invited the Joffrey Ballet to her Rhode Island estate, Watch Hill, and financed the summer's work period, after which the company went, in the winter of 1962–63, to perform in the Mideast and in India and Pakistan. Mrs. Harkness became the patron of the Joffrey Ballet, which returned to Watch Hill for another fruitful period of work. The Joffrey Ballet triumphantly toured Russia in the winter of 1963 and, on its return, set off on a tour of the United States.

The Joffrey Ballet was in Los Angeles when Joffrey was notified, by attorneys acting for the Harkness Foundation, that it had severed its association with the company. Joffrey was suddenly deprived of Mrs. Harkness' patronage *and* of a company.

He discovered, to his and Arpino's consternation, and to the despair of the appalled dancers, that, in the relationship between the Robert Joffrey Ballet and Rebekah Harkness, the company had passed from his jurisdiction into that of his erstwhile patron. Overnight, the Robert Joffrey Ballet ceased to exist.

In the spring of 1964 a new company, the Harkness Ballet, came into being. The dancers were from the defunct Joffrey Ballet and they had discovered, meanwhile, that, under terms of the contracts they had signed while with Joffrey, they were bound to the Harkness Ballet, to which they moved, en masse.

The creation of the Harkness Ballet out of the Joffrey Ballet—a legally valid action—was viewed as piracy. It was as though the Ford Foundation had taken over the New York City Ballet as the property of Henry Ford. Or as if the Baroness de Rothschild, another patron of the dance, had changed the name of the Martha Graham company to her own. The dance world rallied to Joffrey's side and Mrs. Harkness was looked upon as a Greek bearing gifts. However, where there had been one company, now there were two.

The Ford Foundation made Joffrey a substantial grant to start another company. The Harkness Foundation had not acquired the school or the Arpino *oeuvre,* and these were precious components of the second Joffrey Ballet, which made its debut at the Jacob's Pillow Dance Festival. Its first New York appearances were at the Delacorte Theatre, in the summer of 1965. It had a very successful season, in the spring of the next year, at the New York City Center, where it became the resident company and was renamed the City Center Joffrey Ballet. Resuscitated like the Phoenix, the company, within another decade, was world-famous. Out of the American Ballet Center was drawn a second company, the Joffrey II.[1]

The Harkness Ballet was formally started in 1964 under the patronage of the Rebekah Harkness Foundation and the William Hale Harkness Foundation. In 1965, Mrs. Harkness opened the Harkness House for the Ballet Arts in New York, as a base for her

[1] Joffrey II, headed by Sally Bliss (wife of the director of the Met), has flourished in its autonomous identity and is currently much in the news, due to the inclusion of Ronald Reagan, Jr., son of the present President of the United States, as a member of the troupe.

company and for the Harkness Ballet School. All these things were accomplished with great panache, from an apparently bottomless purse. The Harkness dance organization, which grew to encompass the Harkness Theatre, was on an almost royal scale.

The formation of a company, in her own name, was the logical development of the interest Rebekah Harkness had shown in dance over a period of many years. Born in 1915 in St. Louis, Missouri, Rebekah Semple West Pierce Harkness was another of the American millionaires who was moved to patronize dance. The patronage took the form of gifts of money and, in most instances, a personal involvement in the affairs of the dance companies that benefited from the largesse—as in the case of Lucia Chase at American Ballet Theatre, and of Lincoln Kirstein at the New York City Ballet.

Mrs. Harkness was a trained musician who had studied the piano with Nadia Boulanger at Fontainebleau in France. She also studied harmonic structure and composition at the Dalcroze School and, later, took lessons in ballet technique and in Spanish dance. Some of her compositions were for dance: *Barcelona,* a piece written for José Greco; *Macumba,* the score of a ballet by Alvin Ailey; and *The Palace,* to which Gerald Arpino choreographed a ballet of the same name.

Establishing a philanthropic organization, the Rebekah Harkness Foundation, with herself as president, Mrs. Harkness promoted dance through monetary grants to performing troupes, among them one formed by Jerome Robbins as Ballets: U.S.A., for which the Harkness Foundation paid the expenses of a U. S. State Department sponsored European tour in 1961. In 1962 the Harkness Foundation defrayed the costs of an ethnological dance tour of Africa, by Pearl Primus. During 1962 and 1963, Mrs. Harkness' Rhode Island estate, Watch Hill, became the summer home of the Joffrey Ballet, which she sent on tours of the East, and the U.S.S.R., under the sponsorship of the U. S. State Department.

The Harkness Foundation in 1962 established an annual Dance Festival at the Delacorte Theatre in Central Park, where, in the summer, as part of the New York Shakespeare Festival, performances were given free to the public, in open-air concerts. A number of dancers, in groups as companies, and also in solo and pas de deux or as small ensembles, appeared at the Delacorte Theatre. Mrs. Harkness later bought and furnished a property, near Lincoln Center, as the Harkness Theatre, intending it to become the New York home of the Harkness Ballet and to provide a New York theatre for small dance companies.

Mrs. Harkness' compeer, the Baroness Bethsabee de Rothschild, was a patron of modern dance. The foundation in her name contributed handsomely to the support of the Martha Graham company and to the sustenance of the Martha Graham School of Contemporary Dance.

Baroness de Rothschild, in 1953, sponsored a two-week engagement, in a Broadway theatre, of six modern dance companies, the greatest assemblage, to that time, of modern dance choreographers and performing artists ever seen in New York.

American dance benefited, too, from industrial grants, like those given by the foundations named for the tycoons Rockefeller and Ford, but the grants of money from institutions, however large, were not made in the same spirit as those from individual donors such as the Baroness de Rothschild to modern dance, and Lincoln Kirstein, Lucia Chase, and Rebekah Harkness to ballet. All such gifts of money to dance in America came from the personal convictions of the donors; they had a personal touch, unlike the dispassionate dole from institutions, and, for better or worse, they involved the donors with the donees in a human relationship. These twentieth-century Medicis to great extent controlled the lives of the dancers who were the recipients of their gifts. The American dance theatre was not state-subsidized, its box office receipts would never wholly support it, and it was heavily reliant on charity.

In the process of distributing her fortune to American dance, Rebekah Harkness apparently formed certain conclusions about the organization and the artistic direction of a professional troupe. These opinions she put into operation in her own company. Within the legally defensible procedures on which it was formed, the Harkness Ballet, which had swallowed up the first Joffrey Ballet, might have been born out of Jerome Robbins' Ballets: U.S.A. It could as readily have absorbed the Alvin Ailey Dance Theater in 1966, but by then, the Harkness Ballet was an entity in its own right.

It began most auspiciously, with a period of training at Watch Hill under the celebrated Russian pedagogue Vera Volkova, and with the most noted premier danseur of the era, Erik Bruhn, as guest artist.

The leading dancers, the ballerina Marjorie Tallchief and the premier danseur Nicholas Polajenko, although American-born, were better known in Europe, where they had recently been with the company of the Marquis de Cuevas.[2] The company ballet master was the dancer-choreographer George Skibine, husband of Marjorie Tallchief. The company, drawn from the first Joffrey Ballet, included some dancers of distinction, none more so than Lawrence Rhodes and his wife, the Danish dancer Lone Isaksen. There were others: a young danseur of great promise named Helgi Tomasson, the fine dancer Paul Sutherland, and Brunilda Ruiz, one of the outstanding dramatic dancers of the day.

Volkova and Alexandra Danilova mounted works for the Harkness Ballet, which took into its repertoire ballets by several choreographers: Skibine, and the assistant ballet master Donald Saddler; Alvin Ailey; the youthful Michael Smuin; and the most notable Canadian choreographer, Brian Macdonald.

The Harkness Ballet was launched on a grant of $2,000,000 from the Harkness Foundation, and on the confident expectations of its becoming one of the major companies in international theatre. It was at once the cynosure of a half-admiring, half-malicious coterie.

To estimate the worth of the Harkness Ballet, it had to be seen abroad, where it made its premiere appearances in a tour beginning February 1965. After a three-week season at the Municipal Casino in Cannes and five performances at the Opéra Comique in Paris, it toured several European cities, from Scandinavia through Italy.

The company did not appear in the United States until the autumn of 1965, and then in a short tour. Its New York debut was made in 1967, by which time it had undergone considerable changes in per-

[2] This was a company first named Nouveau Ballet de Monte Carlo, which was taken over by George, Marquis de Cuevas, a Chilean-American ballet patron. He first directed Ballet International (1943), founding it (and Ballet Institute) with money from his wife, a Rockefeller heiress. Though a European company, the Grand Ballet de Marquis de Cuevas had a large contingent of American dancers, among them Rosella Hightower, now the director of the ballet at the Paris Opéra. The Cuevas company began with Nijinska as ballet mistress and may be said to have ended with the Nijinska–Robert Helpmann production of *The Sleeping Beauty* (1960), a gorgeously costumed production in which the newly defected Rudolf Nureyev appeared. De Cuevas died, at Cannes, in 1961. His company, like that of Diaghilev, perished with the death of its founder. The company was dissolved (under the direction of the Marquis' nephew, Raymundo de Larain) in 1962.

sonnel. Brian Macdonald was now, but only briefly, the artistic director.

In 1968 further changes were in effect, and Lawrence Rhodes became the artistic director. He was joined by a trusted associate, Benjamin Harkarvy. It was in this period, that of the Rhodes-Harkarvy regime, that the Harkness Ballet assumed its strongest identity, largely through a dedicated troupe of artists who were bound to the company, and to each other, in a familial devotion. Rhodes was a splendid dancer, who reached the peak of his development with the Harkness Ballet. He and several other dancers were particularly well suited to the dramatic repertoire, which included *Feast of Ashes, Time Out of Mind, The Abyss,* and *After Eden*—some of the most notable ballets of the era. The Harkness Ballet had just reached its zenith, under Rhodes, when, during a European tour, Rebekah Harkness summarily discharged the dancers and dissolved the company.

That same year she formed the Harkness Youth Ballet, a semiprofessional company, under the English choreographer Ben Stevenson. Some dancers of the old Harkness Ballet were invited to join the new troupe. In 1972, in a gala ceremony, Mrs. Harkness opened the Harkness Theatre. Soon after, it closed.

These events followed, one on the other, with bewildering rapidity. The Harkness Ballet, suspect from the start as nothing more than the whim of a rich woman, eventually became a joke. Its only constancy was its inconstancy. Incensed that no public, civic, or federal support was given to her organization, Rebekah Harkness threatened to disband it entirely. Funding agencies ignored her. Mrs. Harkness thereupon rid herself of everything excepting Harkness House, where she maintained—into the 1980s—a ballet school.

The Harkness Ballet, launched with hyperbole, vanished without a trace.[3] Only those of curmudgeonly disposition rejoiced at its fall. The disbandment of the company was a calamity for many dancers, and a loss to American dance. Much about the Harkness Ballet remains mysterious; gossip and rumor alone provide footnotes to its rise and fall. But it failed just when it should have succeeded, in the late 1960s. Its repertoire was by no means negligible and it em-

---

[3] It must be noted that a Harkness troupe remained in existence after the dismissal of director Lawrence Rhodes, and continued under Stevenson, then under Vincent Nebrada, until disbandment in 1975.

ployed some of the best young American dance artists of the day. The most acidulous critics of the Harkness Ballet could not deny the worth of its dancers. Chiefly, the company was reproved for a lack of artistic policy—what its principles were intended to be were never made clear. Rightly or wrongly, Rebekah Harkness was rumored to have imposed her will on—and sometimes against—that of each of the company directors she engaged. Perhaps the erratic changes in direction adversely affected the company's aesthetics.

The dancers, discharged during the European tour (with extra salary in lieu of notice), tried to reorganize the company (which they intended to run as a cooperative venture, under Rhodes). When they failed, they returned to the United States, saddened and disenchanted. A few of the dancers never quite recovered from the traumatic experience. Two decades later, the wounds opened afresh at every discussion of the Harkness Ballet.

But in 1966, it seemed that, with the New York premiere, the company had good reason to rejoice. Established in Harkness House, on East Seventy-fifth Street, its state was opulent, compared to that of the rest of American dance. Had opinions been polled on the Harkness Ballet's chances for survival, only the most pessimistic would have given odds against this richly appointed troupe, the pet project of Rebekah Harkness who, possessed of an apparently indomitable will and an immense fortune, was confidently expected to do for the Harkness Ballet as much as Lucia Chase had done for American Ballet Theatre.

In 1966, the Harkness Ballet dancers—Judith Jamison among them—came happily to rehearsal at Harkness House. Before climbing the handsome stairs or taking the elevator up to their big, airy, well-lighted studios, they passed through the foyer where, in a niche in the wall, reposed a pretty curio—a jeweled urn, designed for Rebekah Harkness by Salvador Dali.[4] It revolved, perpetually, on its pedestal as though symbolizing an eternal serenity.

It seemed the best of auguries for the Harkness Ballet.

---

[4] Dali's urn is intended to contain Mrs. Harkness' ashes, after her demise.

THIRTEEN

For Judith Jamison, the best part of working with the Harkness Ballet was being able to study at the school with Patricia Wilde.

Born in Ottawa in 1930, and a professional dancer at the age of fourteen, Wilde was one of the most eminent ballet dancers of her generation. Until she took over the Harkness Ballet School in 1965, Wilde was a ballerina of the New York City Ballet. She was first with the Ballet Russe de Monte Carlo, then the most prestigious dance company in America, and danced in that company with Alexandra Danilova and Alicia Markova, the reigning primas ballerinas. After appearing as guest artist in Europe, Wilde joined the New York City Ballet, where her technique and style won her an enormous fan following. In works like *Square Dance* (1957) and *Native Dancer* (1959) Balanchine celebrated Wilde's strength and brio, and her phenomenal jump. It was said of Wilde that she danced like a man, a debatable compliment also paid to Augusta Maywood, the first internationally renowned American dancer, in the nineteenth century.

Wilde had a forthright, clear, and sparkling temperament, one reflected in her person, that of a red-haired, blunt-featured woman with a generous and unprepossessing nature. Besides the brilliance of her dancing, and the engaging quality of her personality, Wilde had some other attributes, undiscovered until she took on the direction of the Harkness Ballet School.

Wilde was a gifted teacher, with a great facility for inspiring her pupils. She excelled in teaching the bravura technique in ballet; the allegro artistry of the virtuoso dancer.

Says Jamison: "I liked working with Pat Wilde. I respected her as a teacher because, when she gave combinations, *she* did them—*full out!* She had just stopped performing and she was still, in every sense, a dancer. A really fabulous dancer.

"With Pat, it was pure technique. Technique was my god in those days, so I worshiped Pat. She taught me absolute control. Her classes built strength and stamina in a way I had not known before. And she made the most difficult things look effortless. To satisfy her, you had to do the same.

"Pat appealed to my competitiveness. I wanted to do what she did, maybe better. Kids—and as a dancer I was just a kid—have this wild arrogance.

"At Harkness I took class with Skibine, whom I liked, and with Ramón Segarra, who was later to become ballet master of the Ailey company. But it was Pat Wilde who had the chief influence on me.

"I went back to studying. It was very restful; I was a pupil again. The first time 'round with the Ailey company, I learned steps. It wasn't terribly hard for me because I'm a 'quick study.' But I didn't know what I was doing, how I was dancing. I need to know what I am doing, to control it. Otherwise, it could be anybody, not Judi Jamison, dancing. So working with Pat Wilde was very good for me, in that phase. I didn't feel I got much out of performing with the Harkness Ballet but I knew, even then, that I was getting something important in the classes with Pat Wilde."

The Harkness Ballet's repertoire, predominantly dramatic, was interspersed with "tutu ballets"—the trade name for virtuoso classical dance works, mostly pas de deux, guaranteed to bring down the house. Jamison was considered unsuited to most of the repertoire. She found that she had very little to do. "The good part of the experience was dancing with Tim [Avind] Harum. Tim, who was Norwegian-born, was a very good dancer. He was tall and I was tall so we danced together. I learned partnering and Tim and I had fun. We worked hard and kept hoping a choreographer would notice us and do something for us. It didn't happen."

Jamison was cast in two Ailey ballets, *Yemanja* and *Ariadne*. *Yemanja* was *Macumba,* remounted with set and costumes by José Capuletti. It was a risky production, without copious program notes, for an American audience.

The terms *macumba* and *candomblé* are generic to rites of the Brazilian cult of Xangô, the god of wrath in the Yoruba religion. Brought to the Americas by African slaves, the Xangô (Sàngo, in Yoruba) cult, under the tolerant Portuguese, was transformed into quasi-Christianity. The greatest of the deities of the religion is not Xangô but the goddess Yemanja, whose name (*yeye* for mother and *eja* for fish) signifies that she is the mother of Creation. Ol-ódùmaré, the god of Yoruba religious belief, is head of a vast pantheon of gods and goddesses, many of whom are the replicas of other mythological pantheons. Xangô corresponds to the Scandinavian Thor, god of thunder, and he has many of the elements of the Greek Zeus, one being his concupiscence. Yemanja has multiple personalities. As the dam—a fecund female animal—she is the Diana of Ephesus. In her sea-being, she is the African Aphrodite. And Yemanja is also the Yoruba equivalent of the Assyrian Astarte, a goddess of sensual love and implacable femininity. She is sometimes worshiped through symbolic rape. Yemanja is said to be an insatiable lover, rapacious in her desires and terrible in her jealous wrath. One of her children is Orishakô, the Yoruba god of agriculture, and his cult is celebrated with sexual license, as was that of the Greek Dionysus.

The gods and goddesses are called *orìşàs* and their powers are invoked through the *macumba* and the *candomblé,* ceremonials performed with masks, regalia, sacred and symbolic props, music and dancing. The Brazilian *orìşàs* are supplicated daily by both the white and the black populace.

The *orìşàs,* when they condescend to the chosen, do so through apparitional dance—dance in which the dancer is possessed by the god and becomes the god during the term of possession. The god is said to "ride" the dancer. The succinct sexual connotation is explicit.

Worship of the *orìşàs* is commonplace in northern Brazil and visitors are often admitted to the *macumba.* For the uninitiated, the rites are a fascinating theatrical spectacle. When the dancer is possessed, he may leap higher than his own height. Capable of superhuman strength, he will jump, and twist and turn, fall and rise, and leap again, and again. In the ballet, such an exhibition of *ballon* would command awe. For the congregation of the *macumba,* it inspires rapture. The *orìşà,* not the human dancer, is adored.

The visitor may attend the *macumba* as an observer and not as a worshiper. So powerful are the *orìşàs* that they are impervious to blasphemy. But it is believed, in Brazil, that none may come into the presence of the *orìşà* and leave it as he came. Alvin Ailey, in his brief visit to Brazil, gained superficial knowledge of the rites of Xangô and Yemanja, and of the ceremonial of the *macumba.*

As the choreographer Ailey was intrigued by the elaborate and fantastic rituals of the *macumba*. As a black man, he was moved by the mysticism of a religion, transported from Africa four centuries ago, that continues to inspire devotion in the descendants of black slaves—*and* in the descendants of their white masters. Ailey tried to infuse an aspect of Brazilian black spiritism in his *Yemanja*. He did not succeed. The critical reviews dismissed it as a ballet about a mermaid.

Jamison was cast as Josephine, a priestess of Yemanja. She knew as little of the goddess as the critics and the public. Yet Jamison might have posed for an image in Yoruba sculpture. In a long flowing wig, the mane of hair that Yemanja wears (as the foam of the wave and weeds from the river) in her Aphroditean incarnation, Jamison might have been the goddess.

She was cast in another authoritarian, hieratic role, as Pasiphae in *Ariadne*. Ailey fared no better with the critics when he turned to Greek mythology. Jamison's presence—as the mother of the doomed Ariadne—was impressive but caused no stir. The ballet, with set by Ming Cho Lee, was not a success. Jamison looks back at her "Harkness period" as bringing her one small triumph, in "something Don Saddler did for me, a little thing but with exciting movement." Lawrence Rhodes rehearsed her in Brian Macdonald's *Time Out of Mind* but she did not perform in it. "That was another dead end. What Miguel had said was true: dancing in the Harkness was a dead end for me. There was nothing in sight." She struggled against a growing depression, and the nagging fear that, if she left the Harkness Ballet, she might also have to leave New York. "If I had left the Harkness, where would I have gone? I had seen what happens to dancers when a company collapses, as the Ailey company did. I saw good dancers—great dancers—reduced to taking teaching jobs. I wanted to dance. So I kept believing that once the Harkness got established in New York things would get better for me."

She was lonely as well as frustrated. "Everyone at Harkness was nice to me but I had no close friends. I found out what it means to be a black dancer in a white company." Before Jamison, Mitchell had known. "People are polite on tour but there is an uneasiness when you are around, outside the theatre. It's all right while the company is working. Once you stop working, things change. In New York you return to your own people, when you leave the white company. On tour you don't have your own world. There is one choice: the hotel room."

Jamison, when she allowed herself to face her sense of isolation at the Harkness Ballet, consoled herself with the thought that, before now, black dancers and white companies had acclimatized. Had she counted the black dancers she would not have had to use all the fingers on one hand. Arthur Mitchell at the New York City Ballet and Christian Holder at the Joffrey Ballet sprang instantly to mind. Another black danseur, John Jones (trained in three prestigious ballet schools, Balanchine's, Joffrey's, and that of the Metropolitan Opera Ballet), had appeared with the Joffrey company and with the Harkness Ballet.

On the distaff side, the numbers were fewer. Carmen de Lavallade, despite her classical training, had been relegated to modern dance. Regardless of talent and training, black dancers with potential for the ballet were not encouraged to perform in classical repertory.

Halfway through the twentieth century, opinion on aesthetics in theatre dance and on the place of the black dancer in his national theatre had hardly changed. The old stereotype of the "Negro dancer" had been aped and parodied by the minstrels, white men in bizarre "black-face" makeup and gaudy clothing, a form of entertainment so popular with the public that black men had been persuaded to lend themselves to its perpetuating. It was believed that black dancers were admirably suited to jazz and tap dancing, as these forms had emerged from black culture. Bill "Bojangles" Robinson, a genius of a tap dancer, was the paradigm. The black artist who wished to work as a serious classical or modern dancer was handicapped by prejudice.

In the late 1960s a number of black dancers—and dancers of Asiatic antecedents—were performing in modern dance troupes. With dispassionate cynicism, Arthur Mitchell commented that critics and teachers approved of black dancers in modern dance because modern dance, as "the barefoot dance," was suited to the indigent "Negro." Prejudice against black classical dancers, however, was voiced more as an aesthetic than a social slur. "The perfect classic [sic] Negro dancer is . . . a rarity due [to] the demands of European-dominated ballet technique. In ballet, there is an arbitrary and rigid code of proper style. That style happens to be white. African movement emphasizes, goes with, African structure."[1] So dogmatic a statement was clearly arguable. "African structure," taken to mean characteristic "African" physical type, was far too generalized a description to apply to the peoples of the African continent, peoples whose physiques, like their arts and societies, have a wonderful diversity.

Between the Tusi and the Pygmy, there are striking differences in "structure" or physique. What was most misleading in the statement was the reference to the "African" when the intent, clearly, was a reference to the black American dancer. After centuries of miscegenation, black Americans are "African" only by distant antecedents. Granted that some black dancers are technically and aesthetically unsuited to ballet, it is also true that some "white" dancers are also unsuited, for the same reasons. Ballet aesthetics do not apply to skin coloration but to physique, technique, and temperament. These aesthetics are formed on the "architectural" nature of classical dance, its "line" and aplomb.

In ballet there are two major classifications: the *danseur noble,* the classicist, and the *danseur demi-caractère,*[2] who is less ideally

[1] Ernestine Stodelle, "The Negro Dancer: Gift to America Beyond Value," New Haven *Register,* January 14, 1968.

[2] *Demi-caractère* is a term applied to a type of dancer (and to a type of dancing) in which character strongly flavors the academic classical technique. The Italian pedagogue Carlo Blasis (1803–1878), on whose treatise the twentieth-century academic ballet is based, described demi-caractère as "a mixture of every style . . . noble and elegant but without grand *temps* [*temps* meaning time, step, movement] of the serious kind." It is a style of dancing innovated in ballet by Jean Dauberval (1742–1806) in *La Fille Mal Gardée* (1789), for the romantic duo Lise and Colas—who are the descendants of the commedia dell'arte's Columbine and Harlequin. In the Romantic Era, the greatest demi-caractère ballerina was Fanny Elssler, who became famous for her performances of the Spanish cachucha and the Italian tarantella—soli introduced into ballets choreographed for her. In extant repertoire, a prime example of the demi-caractère ballerina is Swanilda in *Coppélia,* Acts I and II (in Act III the ballerina must assume the classical style). The demi-caractère ballerina has the nature of an opera soubrette. The classical ballerina is defined by the exceptional purity of her technique. Her masculine equivalent is the danseur noble. Cynthia Gregory is generally regarded as being the leading American classical ballerina. Peter Martins, of the New York City Ballet, and the English Anthony Dowell and American-born Fernando Bujones, at American Ballet Theatre, are exemplary danseurs nobles. Among twentieth-century dancers, Alexandra Danilova was the greatest of the demi-caractère ballerinas. She is still unrivaled for her Swanilda and for the roles she created in Massine's *Le Beau Danube* (the Street Dancer) and *Gaîté Parisienne* (the Glove Seller). Edward Villella, a principal member of the New York City Ballet, is the archtype of the danseur demi-caractère.

classical than the first, but who is usually a virtuoso dancer and one of dramatic talents (an actor-dancer). Indeed, more often for the American public, the *danseur demi-caractère* is more popular than the *danseur noble* (as is the *danseuse demi-caractère* over the classically "pure" ballerina). Between the two categories stretches a wide range, ample enough to afford dancers of many types the prerogative of becoming ballet artists.

It was an absurd convention that a valid "American" ballet should be formed only on "white" dancers and to the exclusion of dancers whose antecedents were African and Asiatic, rather than European. Caucasian Americans, themselves the products of a polyglot culture, are of various types as dancers (as they are varied in physiques, temperaments, and shades of skin). Ballet aesthetics were as applicable to "white" Americans as they were to others of "black," "red," or "yellow" pigmentation.

Arthur Mitchell's Dance Theatre of Harlem was to prove the truth of this statement and to present, through dancers who might as easily have graced a white as a black ballet company, the best argument in favor of training gifted black dancers for classical repertoire. When Judith Jamison began her professional career, the case for the black ballet dancer had not been made. Instead, the prejudices against black ballet dancers were expressed as aesthetically based opinions on the stereotype of "the Negro."

He was—in this stereotype—hideously unsuited to the classical "line" of ballet, because of his coarse features and "negroid" head. Black women were all believed to have the disfiguring contours of large, round, high, hard buttocks. As all black persons were said to have flat feet and grotesquely elongated toes, it would be impossible for a black girl to perform *coup de pied* (with arched foot) and to dance *sur les pointes,* wearing the *pointe* shoe.

Even more insulting was the opinion that black dancers, allegedly of supernormal sense of "rhythm," were by their "African" character insensitive to classical or "white" dance.

Infrequently, a black dancer succeeded in crashing the barrier into ballet, but then only grudging concessions were made by bigots. John Martin, enthusiastically praising a dancer as one of the most exciting young artists of the day, qualified the praise by asserting that although she was a black dancer she could not fairly be described as one. The dancer in question looked almost "white." She was Janet Collins.

Collins, a cousin of the de Lavallades, and born as they were in New Orleans, was also trained in Los Angeles. She was the pupil of two celebrated ballet pedagogues, Adolph Bolm and Carmelita Maracci, and worked with Horton, in whose company she danced. Beautiful and talented, Collins made an auspicious solo debut in New York in 1949 and went on to become a Broadway star, winning the Donaldson Award for her performance in the Cole Porter musical *Out of This World*. She was later the ballerina of the Metropolitan Opera Ballet and taught at the School of American Ballet. Collins successfully combined careers in ballet, modern dance, and musical theatre, among her white compeers.

Yet, as a young dancer in Los Angeles, Collins was refused by the Ballet Russe de Monte Carlo. Complimented on her excellence as a classical dancer, Collins was regretfully turned down because, it was believed, it would be necessary to paint her white for every performance in which she danced with white dancers. Ironically, when Collins danced at the Met in *Aïda,* her skin had to be darkened with cosmetics because she was too fair to make a credible Ethiopian.

If the black ballet dancer was to dance, a place would have to be made for him. In 1937 the American Negro Ballet was formed under the direction of Baron Eugene Von Grona. Von Grona trained his dancers for three years before presenting them in a debut at the Lafayette Theatre in Harlem on November 21. The company was severely criticized. In the main, it was felt that "the Negro" dancer was ill suited to ballet. John Martin pronounced the company inept, as perhaps it was. Von Grona offered free training in classical dance to black students, hoping to develop dancers for the company. Classes were conducted in the gymnasium of the Harlem YWCA but, according to informants, who were at that time in their teens, parents in Harlem were "too timid to allow their children to do white people's dances."

While the American Negro Ballet lasted, it performed a repertoire that included a version of Fokine's *The Firebird* (a production, incidentally, that pleased Martin), an ambitious undertaking for novices. But in the 1930s the very idea of a "Negro" ballet was intolerable. The company disbanded and the dancers were absorbed into a famous musical, *Blackbirds*.

There would be no revolutionary changes. Sylvester Campbell, on the advice of Arthur Mitchell, went to Europe and danced in white companies. He performed with a French troupe, Ballet de la Tour L'Eiffel, and was guest artist with the Dublin Ballet. Tall, handsome, a virtuoso technician, Campbell was popular in Europe. For several years he was the premier danseur of the Dutch National Ballet. Homesick, Campbell returned to the United States but was unable to get a job in a company. He was, for a while, premier danseur of the Royal Winnipeg Ballet, with which he toured. In 1977 Campbell was dancing with a small regional troupe, the Maryland Ballet. At the Third International Ballet Competition in Moscow, Campbell was awarded the prize for artistic excellence; he partnered a white dancer, Camille Izard, and a Japanese-American dancer, Yoko Ichino, both of whom were taken into the American Ballet Theatre. Campbell left the Maryland Ballet, when it was taken over by a new director, an ex-member of The Royal Ballet. Campbell went to teach at the Jones-Hayward School in Washington, where, years earlier, he had been trained as a ballet danseur.

Into the 1980s conditions in American ballet for the black dancer remained the same. In the 1960s, it was against all odds that a black woman would make a great career as a ballet dancer, particularly when she lacked, as Jamison lacked, the endearing "white" characteristics of Janet Collins. The black danseur was only a little less favored than the black danseuse.

In 1970 the black danseur Keith Lee joined American Ballet Theatre. He appeared in Ailey's *The River* and even choreographed a work, *Times Past* (premiered by American Ballet Theatre at the New York City Center on July 1), but Lee's tenure was brief, and he did not reappear in another major ballet company. When Arthur Mitchell left the New York City Ballet, no black danseur succeeded him, not even in the roles that had been choreographed on Mitchell.

Despite the palpable need for providing opportunities to perform for black ballet dancers, Mitchell was severely reproved for "segregating" black dancers in a "black ballet," when he formed the Dance Theatre of Harlem. Clive Barnes deplored the necessity of doing so and other critics testily complained that a company of its sort would require a "black repertoire" to maintain its identity. A "black" *Swan Lake,* for example, would be a startlingly inappropriate production.[3]

For Judith Jamison in 1967, despite the Cinderella-like aspects of her story (dancing with American Ballet Theatre, with the Alvin Ailey Dance Theater, and with the Harkness Ballet) prospects were bleak. At the Harkness Ballet her repertoire was so limited as to make her an "unwarranted luxury" in the company. The course she feared, that would lead her to a dead end, was suddenly deflected. She broke a foot.

"We were dancing in Mrs. Harkness' hometown, St. Louis, at Kiel Auditorium. The stage was slippery and I fell, doing four consecutive pirouettes. My foot felt as though it had been knifed; the pain was excruciating. The company sent me to a doctor, who told me I had sprained the foot. He thought I could go on dancing. It was my first serious injury and I didn't know how to take care of myself. I could hardly bear to put weight on the foot but I danced, and hobbled offstage with the foot swelling up to the size of a football. I lay around on the tour, resting the foot. I worried a lot, because I could feel the foot getting weaker and weaker, even after the swelling went down.

"It was not until Alvin sent me to another doctor in New York that I discovered the foot was broken. The St. Louis doctor had not bothered taking X-rays. I was lucky that the damage could be repaired. But it was six months before I could dance full out on that foot."

Unable to dance, Jamison left the tour and returned to New York, hoping to be well enough to resume performing when the Harkness Ballet's New York season began. She had been in the city for only a few days when Alvin Ailey called, to tell her he had reactivated his company.

"Judith," said Ailey, "come home."

[3] Dance Theatre of Harlem was dancing *Swan Lake* by 1981, and was about to mount *Giselle.*

FOURTEEN

The biblical adage, "A prophet is not without honour, save in his own country, and in his own house," could have been applied to Alvin Ailey, the apostle of black American dance. After ten years of work, and in spite of the incontrovertible proof of the success of that work, he had been obliged to give up his company. It had become impossible for him to support the barest expenses for a group of dancers.

The residence at Clark Center, useful when it was initiated, did not suffice the Ailey company, which had by now outgrown the facilities. Ailey's foreign tours, alone, necessitated a great deal of work; the company, at home and abroad, required a businesslike operation. Ailey realized that, in the competitive American theatre, he could no longer hope to conduct his affairs in a cosy intimacy. The company required an efficient administrative staff, as well as dancers. It needed offices, as well as studios.

Ideally, the company should have had a home in New York, a theatre in which to develop its artistic principles, and a base of operations. In harsh reality, Ailey had seldom been able to lay hand, in any season, on enough money to pay the dancers' salaries and defray current expenses. He was compelled season after season to hunt space in which to conduct class and rehearsal for the company. The Alvin Ailey American Dance Theater, in this grandiloquent title the ambassador of the U. S. State Department's cultural wing, was in reality an impoverished gypsy troupe. The federal government officially presented the company abroad as the exemplar of black American dance but in 1966, when Ailey was in desperate straits, no philanthropist came forward to save the company from extinction. When the Ailey company was again re-formed it was at the request of the managements of foreign theatres.

In the months since disbanding the company, and even before, Ailey had been invited to participate in several festivals. No company was more popular with European audiences than the Ailey. Senegal had begged for its return. It was asked to appear in Israel.

Ailey was in low spirits after completing his commission for the Metropolitan Opera. When he began choreographing for *Antony and Cleopatra,* he found that Barber was unable to give him a score. The composer, in fact, had not yet completed the music. It was an untenable position in which to place a choreographer, who had to make dances for a new work. Ailey was compelled to make do with bald rhythms, supplied him by Barber (with the assistance of the orchestra conductor, Thomas Schippers), to which Ailey choreographed the dances for *Antony and Cleopatra.* At the opera's premiere, September 16, 1966, Ailey found little to please him in the dancing.

In this mood, Ailey responded to the suggestion of an entrepreneur, Gil Shiva, to reactivate the company for tours of Europe and Africa. Shiva applied for a grant from the National Endowment for the Arts, for the African tour, and funds were allocated for this purpose—doubtlessly on the strength of Ailey's successful showing at the First Dakar Festival. From the Rebekah Harkness Foundation, Shiva obtained another grant, to take the Ailey company to Israel and to several European cities.

Ailey was now advised to incorporate his company, with a school, making the organization eligible for grants of monies in aid from government, industrial, and private agencies, as a nonprofit-making entity. A certificate of incorporation was issued in April 1967 in the name of the Dance Theater Foundation. Under this body's jurisdiction would come the operations of Ailey's school and company.

The purpose for which monetary grants are requested requires, it seems, statements of lofty motives, but Ailey was sincere in the expressions of those he made for his school and company. The declared "major aims and goals" of the Dance Theater Foundation were for a school "to train the young Negro dancer . . ." and, for a company "to provide a continuing source and outlet for talented Negro dancers . . ."

Ailey was sensible to the seriousness of his undertakings, in the application and acceptance of grants, but he was by now convinced that, in order to establish a permanent organization for his dancers, he would have to rely on grants in aid for funding. With the acceptance of such grants was entailed the accountancy for the disbursement of the monies, and Ailey would have to double as cashier and bookkeeper while carrying out his other duties as teacher and choreographer and company director. For the time being, his main concerns lay in calling back his dancers to the reactivated company and choosing a repertoire for a six-month tour. The company would be abroad from May into November, on two continents. Besides Israel, it would visit Portugal, Germany, Sweden, Holland, Yugoslavia, Switzerland, and the South of France. It would dance in Venice and then, from Athens, cross to Africa, to appear in nine countries. Over so long a period and for so diversified an audience, the choice of the repertoire and the selection of personnel for the company were of utmost importance.

It was perhaps the happiest period of Jamison's professional life. The reactivation of the Ailey company seemed the best of auguries for the future. Miguel Godreau returned to Ailey, as did most of the dancers with whom Jamison had worked before. The plans for the company's tours were grander than those it had undertaken previously. Ailey appeared happier, and more optimistic, than she had ever known him to be. It was, as Jamison recalls, "the least complicated" time of her career as a dancer and she reveled in the atmosphere of the company, in its apparent stability, under the new organization of the Dance Theater Foundation and the glowing promise that stability ensured.

She felt as though bonds had been strengthened between the dancers of the Ailey company. For her, after the period of exile at the Harkness Ballet, it was "truly a matter of coming home again" to Ailey. Secretly she hoped that he would now work with her, on dances specifically choreographed on her. Meanwhile, she rehearsed her expanded repertoire. She was given a solo in *Reflections in D,* a minor work by Ailey, choreographed in 1963 to music by Duke Ellington, and she now danced in several of the sections of *Revelations,* including the "Processional" and the famous "Wading in the Water."

Most of Jamison's appearances were in works extant in the Ailey company but she had begun to create a few roles and she was cast as the goddess Erzuli in Geoffrey Holder's *The Prodigal Prince,* with Miguel Godreau in the title role.

The Prodigal Prince was based on real and imagined events in the life of Haiti's primitive painter and mystic, Hector Hippolyte, who believed himself inspired by the *loa,* the gods of the *voudon* religion. *Prince* was entirely Holder's creation. He composed the music, designed the costumes, and choreographed the movement. The theatre piece was a sensation wherever it was presented on the tour, chiefly because of the eroticism of the dancing and the voluptuous design and color of the decor. European audiences were unaware of the connotations between the dancing and *voudon* ritual invocation of the *loa.* Holder, with his Trinidadian upbringing (and perhaps Godreau, from his familial Puerto Rican society) may have understood the implications of sorcery, and of piety, in the dancing of *The Prodigal Prince.* To others, Jamison included, the ballet was nothing more than spectacle.

Chiefly, for the Ailey company, *The Prodigal Prince* provided Miguel Godreau with a role in which he extended his repertoire. On the European tour, Godreau was the dancer who attracted most attention. He was new to European audiences and he had arrived at the exact pitch to which he attuned his ecstatic approach to the dance. The apparent abandonment with which he danced in *Revelations* gave the choreography a wondrous oracular power. Had Godreau been observed by a Brazilian or a Caribbean society, his dancing would have been taken for an act of possession. Godreau was "ridden by a god."

Yet, his control of theatrical nuances was adroit and in the Ailey company he was given opportunities for developing his dramatic talents. Ailey resolved to revise his *Knoxville: Summer of 1915* for Godreau. This, the most overtly autobiographical work by Alvin Ailey, was a project Ailey set for early completion, with Godreau in the role of the boy and Judith Jamison in the role of his mother.

Jamison found that she was no longer so "thunderstruck" by Godreau's dancing as to be bemused by it. She discovered that they danced now as equals, in harmony, but with the old, exciting tension that polarized their identities. As she expressed it, their separate "rhythms" flowed as one.

The reformed Ailey company was quickened by an exalting spirit, that memorable year. Like members of a family, the dancers rejoiced in the reunion, communicating onstage as though by sleight of hand, mesmerising their audiences by their power. Some members of the European audience, Ailey-watchers before and after the 1967 tour, believe that the company never danced better, and never again danced in quite that rapturous rapport.

Ailey's renown this year was enhanced when a work he choreographed on his company for Swedish television won the Grand Prix Italia, the most prestigious prize on Continental television. Titled *Riedaiglia,*[1] but commonly referred to as *The Seven Deadly Sins,* it was an imaginative abstraction of the biblical itinerary of sins. The Ailey company was pronounced "magnificent" in the piece, with especial mention of Godreau, Loretta Abbott, and Kelvin Rotardier. Godreau here made his initial impact on the Swedes, with whose theatre he was to associate himself in later years. At the end of the tour, he and Jamison were invited back to Stockholm, to appear on television.

The Alvin Ailey Dance Theater traveled in a blaze of glory, appearing at the festivals in Israel and Holland, at the annual Yugoslavian music festival in Dubrovnik, and for the Portuguese Gulbenkian de Musica, where *The Prodigal Prince* was premiered.

The English writer Clive Barnes, then the dance and drama critic of the New York *Times* (who had observed the Ailey company in London and in America), attended the Holland Festival and witnessed the triumph of the Alvin Ailey American Dance Theater. In a review for his paper, Barnes (after commenting on the delirious enthusiasm of the proverbially stolid Dutch audience) asked: "Why does a New York critic have to come to the Netherlands to see a New York company?" Barnes was of the opinion that the Ailey company was long overdue a New York season.

The Harkness Ballet was just then preparing for its first New York season and, once again, Mrs. Harkness summoned Ailey to work on *Ariadne.* Leaving his company in Truitte's care, Ailey flew from Israel to New York to work with the Harkness Ballet. The Skibines, meanwhile, had left the company. Ailey was distressed to discover that Marjorie Tallchief, for whom he had choreographed *Ariadne,* would no longer be dancing the title role. Ailey had felt dissatisfied with parts of the ballet and had intended reworking

[1] The title *Riedaiglia* was coined from the names of the composer, Georg Riedel, the producer-director, Lars Egler, and the choreographer, Ailey. A film documentary of the making of the ballet won the Grand Prix Italia (prize for television).

them. Now, in a sudden revulsion against *Ariadne* and against his association with the Harkness Ballet, Ailey broke off his relationship with the company. Two days after arriving in New York he flew back to Europe, chasing his company from Amsterdam to Venice and catching up with the dancers in Athens, in time to accompany them to Africa.

The Ailey company appeared in Senegal, on the Ivory Coast, in Ghana, the Republic of the Congo, Uganda, Ethiopia, Kenya, and the Malagasy Republic, in a tour that lasted from September 12 to November 6. On this tour, Judith Jamison was the star.

For the first time in her life, she understood that she was beautiful. Growing up in the belief that she was "weird-looking," because she looked like the picture of her father's mother (the picture of a woman, in the family album, who looked nothing like the pretty girls and women of Jamison's maternal relations), Jamison had perceived herself only as "a tall dancer." It was a sexless image.

She had accepted, without quibble, the opinions that others had of her, to such extent that Jamison, at twenty-three, knew very little about herself. The perspectives in which she was viewed, and the views from which she took her identity, were sometimes in conflict.

In school, because of her high degree of competence, in academics and in sports, Jamison seemed older than her years. At the same time, because of her shyness, she was the baby at home. At the Judimar School of Dance, Judith Jamison's talents, her receptivity to instruction, her quick intelligence, had put her to the fore while, to her family, she was a quiet, almost self-effacing child, content to "hole up" in her room with books and music. There were at least two Judith Jamisons.

In the Ailey company, Jamison, the tall girl, was a junior member of a coterie whose character had been formed as much through enduring hardships together as by performing together. "Judi" was easily assimilated into the company because of the ease and speed with which she learned choreography, and, too, because of her warm and generous nature. She was a "nice" girl. Very few of her colleagues, in the early years, understood the complexities of her character and the complicated processes by which she approached dancing. No one fully assessed Jamison's capacity for emotion, or the extent of her intelligence. And none, so far, had convinced Jamison that she was beautiful. The African audience did, in 1967.

That audience at once saw in Jamison the regality of a woman who could be a queen, a woman who might be a goddess. Everything about Jamison, her size, her looks, the nobility of her presence, appealed to the African audience. Even the dark patterning on her gums, revealed when she smiled. These dark patterns, Jamison discovered, were to the African aesthetic a charming feminine beauty mark, like a dimple, or a mole, in a Caucasian belle.

In Kenya the company was seen in performance by President Jomo Kenyatta, who asked for a meeting with the dancers. He told Ailey that Jamison reminded him of his favorite wife (who also had dark gums). In his frank admiration of Jamison, Kenyatta slightly alarmed her. He asked Ailey if he could keep her in Kenya. Ailey refused. This ploy, made perhaps in jest, suddenly riveted attention on Jamison. Company colleagues looked at her in a different way.

For Jamison, the adulation she received in Africa, directed at her as a person, rather than as a member of the company, did far more than flatter her. It gave her individuality and made her see that she was a desirable woman.

Dormant femininity awakens, like the sleeping beauty to the prince's kiss, but it is not dependent on the solitary masculine salutation. A less personal but even more enkindling relationship than that of erotic love will inform a woman of her sensuality, the implicit feminine mysticism of herself. For a performer, the spontaneous, fervid response of the audience is often more impassioned than a kiss.

Jamison's femininity, awakened through her love affair with Miguel Godreau, had, without conscious volition, passed from the erotic into the maternal. She was fast becoming more concerned over Godreau's welfare, as though he were her precious and tender charge, than in their relationship as lovers. Holder cast her as a goddess protective of Godreau, in *The Prodigal Prince;* Ailey, as Godreau's mother, in *Knoxville: Summer of 1915.*

Jamison's greatest need then, as it was to remain throughout her career, was for a partner as technically and as psychologically powerful as herself. Godreau came closest to meeting her on her own ground, but he was five inches shorter and the disparity in their physical sizes would have been pronounced in partnering. They could dance, within the group, as equals, but they were not dance partners, in the sense of a pas de deux. Jamison's need was for a partner of the type of dancer that Alvin Ailey had been, when he was a performer.

It was by a wicked twist of fate that Jamison was prevented from ever dancing with Ailey, who had stopped performing little more than a year before she joined his company. Ailey, alone among the men in the company, possessed all the attributes, physical and psychical, of the male dancer who would best have complemented Jamison as a woman dancer.

Six feet in height, compactly muscled but lithe as a panther, Ailey, as the dancer, had the physical bulk and the imperious masculinity that would have set off Jamison's slender height and her instinctive regality. And Ailey's sensuality, the animal magnetism for which his dancing had been so much noted, would have been the fiery element in the dance, against Jamison's cool and controlled power.

Jamison was attracted to beauty and to authority. Alvin Ailey possessed both. He had, also, a patriarchal nature, as was to be observed in the ways by which he conserved and preserved dance works, and by his attempts to form a company more like a family than a dance troupe. Ailey admitted to his "patriarchal complex," if not to its possessiveness and jealousy. His instinct was to own and to protect. Jamison's, as a woman, was to be possessed and to be cherished.

In every great collaboration between a choreographer and a dancer there exists a sensual relationship as powerful as the artistic bond. Art and sexuality are the insoluble components of all the great collaborations in dance: between two dancers in pas de deux and between choreographer and dancer. In the second relationship, the sexual element is perhaps greater. The dancers in pas de deux may romanticize their association but, in that of choreographer and dancer, authority is implicit in one part, submission in the other.

The relationship, intimate though it may be, between the painter and his subject, is never as close as that of choreographer and dancer. The dance is intrinsically physical and, by its nature, involves the whole person. A dancer who has worked with a choreographer, a man both admired and adored, for nearly twenty years, marvels that, when they are at work, the choreographer's merest touch, to indicate a movement, is often sufficient to send through her an electrifying thrill, so sharp that, like electricity, it strikes back from her to its source—startling both choreographer and dancer.

When the choreographer works with the dancer, especially for a solo, he is subconsciously seeking his alter ego, an ideal of beauty conceived in himself, Pygmalion with his Galatea. If, to this sonorous chord of self-love, there is added another, more commonplace one, Eros takes the place of the Muse. The ballet *Giselle* was born of some such passion.[2]

The dancer, especially the female dancer, longs for an exalted union with a choreographer. The intent is to submit, to yield, to offer the self for immolation on an altar, there to be transfigured, in the flesh, from dancer into goddess. American girls, of sensible upbringing in sound middle-class families, do not reveal this longing. They may be too inhibited even to frame the thought in secret. But how else to account for their suicidal dedication to dancing, except to accept the truth that they yearn to be used, as vessels, as instruments, of the thing they call dance.

Judith Jamison did not project herself as an individual who danced. She was not a typical concert dancer, content with her person and proud to exhibit it. She had no vocation as a rebel, a revolutionary who would overthrow old shibboleths and introduce new tenets, as an evangelist of the dance. She did not make dances, for herself or for others. She was in no way kin to those bold and brave young women who had pioneered in the American theatre, to make a place for themselves and for black dance. She asked only to be used as a dancer.

Jamison went to Alvin Ailey first in trust and in eager hope. She returned to him, after the "exile" in the Harkness Ballet, in something closer to love. The trust remained, implicit in the relationship of Ailey and all the dancers who stayed with him, in the rise and fall and rise of the Ailey company. The hope was transferred, for Jamison, as for all the other Ailey dancers, to a dogged tenacity, the will to endure, as it is shared among survivors in a lifeboat.

Jamison went to work with Ailey in ignorance of what that work

[2] The concept for the ballet *Giselle* was that of the critic Théophile Gautier, who adored Carlotta Grisi, the creator of Giselle. Grisi's dances in *Giselle* are believed to have been choreographed by Jules Perrot, of whom she was first the pupil and then the mistress. Grisi preferred the handsome danseur Lucien Petipa. One of the greatest dancers of the epoch, she retired in 1853, when she was thirty-four, with the daughter she bore to an elderly lover, Prince Radziwill, to live in Saint-Jean, near Geneva. A constant visitor was Gautier, though he lived with Grisi's sister Ernesta, who bore him two daughters. Gautier died in 1872, with Carlotta Grisi's name on his lips. Grisi lived to 1899.

entailed. In her innocence, she believed that, when a dancer belonged to a company, a dancer traveled tranquilly in pursuit of what Jamison called her "best." She meant her best work as a dancer; the deeper meaning lay in her best self. Jamison went to Ailey to be used, to be illuminated. It was part of the poetic coincidence and conundrum of her life that Jamison was sent to Ailey by Carmen de Lavallade, Ailey's ideal of a female dancer.

Ailey saw Jamison as a "tall dancer." He has admitted that when he took her into the company he did not know how he would use her; where, in the Ailey company's repertoire, she would fit. Jamison's charm, for Ailey, existed in her way of moving, a way that Ailey described as being "interesting" because it was arresting.

Jamison was useful to the Ailey company because she was biddable. She fit in so smoothly that her size became inconsequential when she danced in a group. Jamison completed the first phase of her career by assiduously practicing anonymity. She was so successful at this that she almost escaped distinction. Her power, and her authority, grew season by season but they existed only in her physical presence. Where Jamison dwelled, in the recesses of the Self, she remained tentative and shy.

She was aware of the torment that Ailey suffered, deciding for and against directing a company of dancers. It was as though she had been called to witness, in a lifeboat, the captain's decision to put to sea in dangerous weather, or to ground or to sink the boat and let all hands swim for their lives. Jamison believed that Ailey should have shared his worries with the dancers, and that, in the sharing, the load of Ailey's troubles might have been lightened. Subconsciously she wished to offer herself to Ailey as a friend; she wanted to be his partner in the good times, and the bad. "If I had been a man . . ." Jamison would say, looking back at the early years of her association with Ailey.

Different as were these two, Jamison and Ailey, they shared many aspects of their separate personalities. Both were proud, reserved, possessive, and tenacious in their loyalties. Both were easily wounded by real or fancied slights, made ill by discord. They both had hard heads, as they thought, but soft hearts, and they indulged those they loved, at all costs. Both could be made resentful by imagined wrongs; both yielded to periods of depression and yet were optimists.

Though their earliest backgrounds differed greatly, Jamison and Ailey had nevertheless formed much the same dependence on their environments. Both adored their mothers. Both believed that their childhoods had been spent in love but that, despite love, they had not been understood for who they truly were. Ailey used his loneliness, his sense of alienation, as the tragic motif of his choreography. Jamison did not think of herself as having been lonely but as liking to be alone; not of being alienated in her family, but of having seemed credulous, and timid, to the people who held her most dear. Ailey would nourish anger, in the resentment he could never cease to feel over his mother's second marriage. Jamison turned back, again and again, for the reaffirmation of her values, to the rock on which her mother had built a family.

But where they were most alike—Jamison and Ailey—was in their obsessive love of beauty. It seemed, in the last resort, that there was nothing they would deny, nothing they might not sacrifice to beauty's cause.

This penchant for physical beauty was as much at the root of Judith Jamison's infatuation for Miguel Godreau as it was in her admiration of his talent as a dancer.

Jamison might have understood Ailey better, and better understood his use of her, if she had known the extent of Ailey's obsessive allegiance to beauty. Jamison, and every other woman for whom Ailey choreographed, still danced in the shadow of a lovely girl in a pink tutu.

Judith Jamison remained a cipher in the Alvin Ailey Dance Theater. Her life ebbed and flowed with the erratic currents on which the company moved. She was one with its rhythms. Nevertheless, the sheer force of her personality had by now brought her to the attention of the audience and of some of the dance reviewers. Although, as Jamison would pensively recall, no attempts were made by the Ailey company to publicize her work, she was dancing in a wide range of the company's repertoire, imposing her image in the choreography.

There was about Jamison's dancing a jubilant and rapturous quality. She was not ethereal, but she commanded space with effortless ease. The fantastic nature of her technique took on the character of grandeur.

The great charm of her dancing lay in its contradictory elements:

its power and its grace. Despite her size, in spite of her authority, she was never a monolith and always a woman. Jamison's femininity was indigenous to her dancing, as was her sense of humor. She had a comedic talent, not antic or witty, neither malicious nor salacious, a sense of the ridiculous which kept her from indulging in self-pity and from being vain.

Jamison enjoyed dancing and her huge enjoyment was communicated to the audience. She still had an almost boyish insouciance, reveling in performing difficult dance movement only because she performed them easily and well. She etched her signature on certain works, in which her extensions, still more balletic in style than those of most modern dancers, made her seem to float, to soar.

She liked to dance with James Truitte. His strength, his dignity, the radiant masculinity that she admired in male dancers, were gracious complements. They went, Jamison and Truitte, to the Kansas City Spring Gala to appear in a concert of international dance, and Jamison was stirred by the hope that they would do more such guest appearances. The loss of Truitte as a partner—when he left the company a few months later—was a bitter disappointment for Jamison. She had believed that, with Truitte, she had been on the brink of something "special," something great.

FIFTEEN

The new year dawned propitiously with a tour of the United States that engaged the Alvin Ailey Dance Theater from January through April 1968. Its appearance at Hunter College Playhouse, January 19–20, was the first time the company had danced in New York since 1964. It was remarked that it was a shame the Ailey dancers were not more often seen in Manhattan. Clive Barnes again wielded his cudgel: "One of the most surprising, perhaps one of the most shocking, aspects of our senior modern-dance companies is that they can appear in extensive seasons in Europe, but at home it appears that they are not wanted on the cultural voyage."

Barnes took the plight of the Ailey company as an all too typical example of the lethargic attitude toward modern dance. He could as readily have cited the Paul Taylor company which, despite its praiseworthy achievements, was almost unknown at home, though greatly admired abroad. Barnes continued: "Without question this [the Ailey] company, which has made its way triumphantly through Europe, deserves a properly extensive New York season. Why are we so regardless of our own treasures?" Barnes's "rather sad question" remained unanswered but the Ailey company, formerly looked upon as a commercially theatrical troupe, now assumed the mantle of "educational" art. It was engaged by the Inter-campus Cultural Exchange of the University of California for appearances at eight of its campuses, where the Ailey company made its California debut, with great acclaim for the dancing and for the repertoire.

Good luck continued to attend Ailey in early 1968. He received another NEA grant, this time of $10,000, and another grant, of $5,000, from the Rockefeller Foundation, toward the creation of new works. At the same time, Ailey received a Guggenheim Fellowship, with which he proposed revising his *Knoxville: Summer of 1915*.

Ailey had never before had so much money all at once and the accretion of the sums from the grants seemed, at the time, a fortune to a man whose modest needs had, so far, always been beyond his means. Characteristically, Ailey made the first expenditure from the grants to commission a work from Beatty, and to bring into the Ailey repertoire a work by Lucas Hoving: *Icarus*. More of the funds were expended on the designing and execution of costumes for *Icarus,* and for Beatty's *Black Belt*.

The extant Ailey repertoire was badly in need of renewal and Ailey used still more money from the grants to pay for the reconstruction of some old works and for new costumes. In addition, he had to maintain the company, in rehearsal, for its coming European tour. Once more, the Ailey dancers were to participate in the annual summer festivals.

Ailey worked in the midst of happy chaos, spending money freely but on what he considered to be essential to the company's good. His management of the budget was slapdash; nothing in Ailey's career had prepared him to become an accountant. Realizing the depth of the waters in which he was swimming, Ailey felt that it was necessary for Truitte to stop dancing and take on administrative duties for the company. Truitte refused. The break between these two friends was a shock to the company. The older members, who had worked with Ailey and Truitte for several years, expressed themselves with indignation at what they felt to be an arrogant act. Ailey was accused of being faithless and overbearing, of being selfish and unfeeling. As usual, when under attack, he became stubborn. He could, when so moved, be implacable.

The company went to Europe, and on this tour it appeared at the Edinburgh Festival. There, on August 28, Ailey premiered the revised *Knoxville: Summer of 1915* and a new work: *Quintet*. Neither found great favor with British critics. *Knoxville* was dismissed as an episode about a young black boy's grief, and *Quintet,* with its Harlem milieu for five "ladies of leisure," was considered banal. Beatty's new work fared no better than Ailey's. Retitled *Black District,* it was taken as propaganda, on the alleged mistreatment of Negroes in America. Edinburgh was not a very rewarding experience for the Alvin Ailey Dance Theater, and so ended the company's fifth European tour.

The fate that had smiled on Ailey early in the year now, incomprehensibly, frowned. Godreau, the star of the company, was summoned back to New York for the role of the Deaf-Mute in the Broadway musical *Dear World*. He had auditioned for the show earlier and when he received a contract in Edinburgh he signed it immediately, and gleefully. Godreau had, from the start, set his heart on breaking into the Broadway scene and Ailey, remembering his own youth, when he too had gladly danced in the commercial theatre, did not protest Godreau's decision to leave the company. Yet, with more and more of the repertoire being invested in Godreau, Ailey could not help feeling disappointed. Godreau would return to dance with the Ailey company and he would leave it again.

Ailey had other troubles to face, besides losing Godreau. A projected London season did not materialize because a convenient theatre could not be found to house the company. Plans had been for the Ailey dancers to perform in London and then to go to Israel, for an engagement in mid-October. With the cancellation of the London season, Ailey was once more faced with a dilemma: he had no means of keeping his company occupied for the five-week interim between the Edinburgh Festival and the Israeli Festival. It was a repetition of the nightmare that he had lived through, with Truitte, when the company had been stranded in Athens in 1966.

This time, however, nothing as providential as the Dakar Festival came along to relieve Ailey's predicament. Without an impresario, he had no hope of getting bookings for an odd month or so in Europe. And it was out of the question to appeal to Rebekah Harkness for help. Believing he had no other recourse, Ailey withdrew from the engagement in Israel and dismissed his company in London.

The dancers received a week's pay and their return tickets to America but elected to remain for a while in London, where they had been invited to appear in a production for British television. Eager to make some money, the Ailey dancers flung themselves into the project, only to be disappointed when it was rejected, because the dancing had been filmed to taped music, not with a live orchestra. They straggled home while Ailey fled, for a respite of two weeks, to Tangiers and Morocco.

Nevertheless, by November the Ailey company was again in good spirits, anticipating its performance of *Revelations* at the White House on the twenty-first of that month. The dancers appeared before President and Mrs. Lyndon B. Johnson, and invited artists, in a concert to honor the National Council of the Arts. Soon after, Ailey was able to present his first Broadway season, with a grant from the Ford Foundation. The company danced at the Billy Rose Theatre, January 27 through February 1, 1969. Clive Barnes, in the New York *Times* of January 28, said: "The really surprising thing about the triumph of the Alvin Ailey American Dance Theater at the Billy Rose Theatre last night was that Mr. Ailey had to wait nearly a decade for the experience. After innumerable tours in Europe and Australia, Mr. Ailey has finally been able to bring his 11-year-old company into its hometown for a brief Broadway season."

Another respected dance critic, Frances Herridge of the New York *Post,* wrote, on the same date: "The Ailey company, founded ten years ago, has been asked (and cheered) almost everywhere in the world except here on Broadway. And that's ironic in more ways than one." Herridge commented on the theatricality of Ailey's works, saying that the company's program was "more exciting, more entertaining, than most dance concerts."

Jamison danced a great deal during the season, in the repertoire comprising *Congo Tango Palace, The Road of the Phoebe Snow, Icarus, Quintet, Reflections in D, Blues Suite, Revelations,* and Beatty's *Black Belt* (which, in the United States, resumed its original title). In New York, both Ailey's *Quintet* and Beatty's *Black Belt* received favorable reviews. The Ailey company's finances, however, were in disarray.

At the beginning of the year the company was $45,000 in debt, a bagatelle compared to the deficits of some other dance companies. One company, in the United States, was said to have a deficit of $3 million in the early 1970s but continued in operation without visible qualms. Ivy Clarke, who had been employed as the Ailey company's wardrobe mistress, took over the administration of its affairs, and she was to serve well in that office.

Two apparently sound and sensible arrangements were made: the Ailey company went under the management of Columbia Artists Management, Inc., for its American tours, and it became a resident company of the Brooklyn Academy of Music. Columbia was a well-known entrepreneur. The Academy of Music, a beautiful theatre designed along the lines of an opera house, had come under new management and was ambitiously planning on becoming a major center for concert dance.

Ailey, as he remembers, was promised a "real" residence in Brooklyn. He was to have not only a theatre for presenting dance works but also rehearsal studios, a dance school, offices, and space for the storage of the company's artifacts, including decor and costumes. The Academy of Music would become the complete physical facility required by a dance company.

No part of this planned residence materialized, except the presentation of the Ailey company on the stage of the Brooklyn Academy of Music. Ailey's "residency" was shared with the companies of Merce Cunningham and José Limón, and the administrative staffs of the three companies jostled for office space, while in the theatre's basement they were inadequately supplied with room for storage of costumes and other properties and their theatrical equipment.

Ailey took his company on a tour of college theatres in February and March 1969 and opened his first Brooklyn season on March 21, with a run through April 2. The company also participated in the Academy of Music's "Festival of Dance 68–69," April 22–26. In the Brooklyn season, when the revised *Knoxville: Summer of 1915* received its U.S. premiere, the Ailey company aroused no great interest.

Bookings, however, took the dancers on a successful U.S. tour, and in May they appeared in a film, for a program by National Educational Television, of Beatty's *Black Belt* and Ailey's *Revelations*. In summer, the company danced, for four programs, at the Saratoga Performing Arts Center in Saratoga Springs, New York, and then filled the position of "artists in residence" at Connecticut College, New London, for two weeks. Ailey found the stay at Connecticut College—where members of his company taught student courses—a welcome pause in the frenetic schedule he and the company had been following. There, Ailey choreographed a new work, and one of his greatest, *Masekela Langage,* which was premiered at that year's Dance Festival at Connecticut College. The Ailey company was the undoubted hit of the six-week festival, in which several companies vied for attention. Ostensibly a festival of dance, the New London season took on, as do all such dance festivals, some of the character of a competition. This one was won by the Alvin Ailey Dance Theater.

Masekela Langage was set to the music of Hugh Masekela, and Ailey staged it as an episode in a squalid saloon. The theme—being black in a contemptuous white society—was easily translatable from Masekela's South African milieu to an American one. The sound of Masekela's trumpet was the strident language of a people's bitter despair, a despair so bleak that only a brutal assault, in the act of sex or the act of death, could pierce the consciousness.

Something of the American South, and, more universally, of a hot, fetid, enervating atmosphere, formed the scene. Ceiling fans turned lazily and beneath them the dancers moved about in little, isolated dramatic vignettes.

The South African segregation of its black and its white societies (and, variously, the equivalent American segregation of people by a color bar) was, for some, an uncomfortable theme for a dance work. Many in the audience were repelled by what was taken to be an unnecessarily violent depiction of death and a too explicit sensuality. Ailey's *Masekela Langage* was to be called one of Ailey's most militantly "black" works. Yet, it is doubtful whether Ailey's motives were more political than artistic. More simply, he had perceived, in the South African "racial situation," conditions with which, as a black man in America, he could identify. The immediate response to the identification was the inspiration to choreograph a dance about being black, in a totally alienated black society.

For Judith Jamison, *Masekela Langage* became a landmark. Ailey choreographed a solo in it for her. Jamison, wearing a short black shift that bared her long throat and her long arms, danced, in high-heeled black pumps, with Kelvin Rotardier, George Faison, Renée Rose, John Madeiros, Sylvia Waters, and Michele Murray. In the company of these veteran performers of the Ailey company, she felt some trepidation: "I was, of course, happy that Alvin gave me the solo—it was beautiful—but I wondered if I could fit into it. I had to build a character—a kind of woman I really knew nothing about—reciprocal with the choreography. I felt like a usurper. There were other dancers in the company who could have done the role better. I needed reassurance, from Alvin, especially. He just gave me the role. Poor Alvin! That's all he probably had the time to do!"

Jamison, the obedient choreographic instrument, was still essentially the pupil, waiting to be bidden, wanting to be used. She had not, as yet, found the source of her dancer's authority, the ego that would guide and guard her.

The Ailey company made a brief U.S. tour, October 6–November 13, and in November appeared on a television program, "Hollywood Palace," in two sections from *Revelations:* "Rocka My Soul" and "Sinner Man." The dancers were seen by an audience many times larger than any for which they had danced in the theatre.

Ailey's second term of residency at the Brooklyn Academy of Music did little to convince him of the practical benefits of his tenure. He was growing restive with the irksome arrangement. To Ailey, it seemed that all the benefits had accrued for the Academy of Music and that his company had obtained little, other than a stage and the possibility of presenting programs with a live orchestra. No move had been made toward providing him with premises for a school. The company was still squashed between the companies of Cunningham and Limón, and the Ailey personnel, rightly or wrongly, believed that the least accommodation—and the least respect—was given to the Alvin Ailey Dance Theater.

In truth, Ailey's growing dislike of the arrangement he had made with the Brooklyn Academy of Music was rooted in his detestation of the stricture it had put on him—that his company could not appear anywhere else in New York. Entrepreneurs were not falling over themselves to offer Ailey a Manhattan theatre, but, had one become available to him, Ailey would, because of the terms of his agreement with the Brooklyn Academy of Music, have been obliged to refuse it. Strictures of any sort irked Alvin Ailey. These, for his company, were particularly hard to bear. He had agreed to the Academy's stipulations because of the Academy's projected plans for the company's residency, a residency that, to Ailey, had become farcical.

Ailey's dancers understood little of his difficulties. They naïvely supposed that, with the Brooklyn residency, the company had been given a base and that, with Columbia Artists Management, they were ensured of steady employment. Ailey not only knew the deadly attrition that would be felt by the company if it subsisted on nothing more artistically nourishing than one-night stands, but also foresaw that the Brooklyn residency, unless it altered soon and for the better, would be more hindrance than help to the company. Nevertheless, the Ailey company seemed in good shape, in 1969. The dancers believed that Ailey would always recoup his losses, would always have the strength and will to re-form the company, no matter how often he complained of the difficulties of holding their little world together. In a holiday mood, the company went on a tour of Latin America, with stopovers, on the way home, to perform in Puerto Rico and in the Virgin Islands.

Despite the apparent stability of the company, its problems were again becoming insupportable for Ailey. He was in hot water—for having expended monies from the grants on projects and on purchases for which they had not been specified. Disregarding what Ailey held as a legitimate and acceptable excuse for canceling the engagement in Israel, the committee for the Israeli Festival brought suit against the company for breach of contract. These mounting troubles, added to the disappointment over the Brooklyn residency, plunged Ailey again into pessimism over the company's future. And, just about this time, Ailey suffered another and more personal setback, as choreographer.

Ailey was commissioned to choreograph a Broadway musical called *La Strada*. It was the first time he had worked in the musical theatre and he was understandably eager to make a good showing there. He still smarted over the disappointing commission to choreograph for *Antony and Cleopatra* and, chiefly, he wished to prove his mettle in the commercial theatre, where he had danced in his youth and where many of his compeers had earned not inconsiderable sums as choreographers.

Ailey worked through the autumn and early winter on *La Strada,* staying in New York while the company went to the West Coast. *La Strada* opened on December 13, 1969, and closed the following day.

Nevertheless, after a week's rest in Puerto Rico, Ailey cheerfully resumed work with the company, to rehearse the repertoire for a U.S. tour, February 5–March 20, 1970. The company, in three weeks, then prepared for its spring season at the Brooklyn Academy of Music, for which Ailey choreographed two new works: *Streams* and *Gymnopedies.*

With *Streams* (to music by Miloslav Kahelac) Ailey was, perhaps unconsciously, pursuing his aquatic impulse, which was to culminate in *The River* for American Ballet Theatre. In *Gymnopedies,* Ailey, who generally choreographed for groups of dancers, departed from custom to set the dance on Dudley Williams, with a piano and pianist sharing the stage.[1] *Gymnopedies,* as a solo work for a male dancer, preceded *Cry,* which Ailey was to choreograph for Jamison.

Early in the year, Ailey was asked by the U. S. State Department to take his company to Russia in June. Ailey acquiesced, and refused all commitments following the Brooklyn season, knowing that he would need the time to select the repertoire for the Soviet tour and to rehearse the dancers. By the end of the Brooklyn season, however, the State Department changed its plans. It no longer required the services of the Alvin Ailey Dance Theater in June for a Russian tour. The cancellation of the project, coming at the close of the Brooklyn season and at the culmination of his revolt against the Academy of Music's regulations (and its, in Ailey's opinion, flagrant breaking of its promises to him), was more than Ailey could stomach. He called the dancers together and informed them that, once and for all, he had done with directing a company.

Disgusted by the humiliation, year after year, of having to disband the company and then having to cope with the exhausting task of bringing the dancers together again, Ailey believed he would be better off, and so would his dancers, if he dissolved the company.

After every forced disbanding he lost dancers, sometimes the best dancers, to other companies or to more agreeable and lucrative ways of earning a living in dance. Ailey felt that he had toiled like Sisyphus to hold his company at the high place it had made for itself in American theatre. Unlike Sisyphus, Ailey was not disposed to make the toil eternally frustrating. He sent his dancers off, with his love and blessing, to find a rosier future than any he was able to promise them.

This time the American press expressed shock at the loss of the Ailey company. A sympathetic journalist, Joseph Gale of the Newark *News,* commented that Ailey's several reasons for disbanding

---

[1] *Gymnopedies,* to music by Satie, is actually three solos. Ailey set the work in a dance studio. The pianist plays his instrument onstage, for the dancer, who, at the start of the piece, is smoking a cigarette. He puts out the cigarette, nods to his accompanist, and begins to dance, stopping and starting as though in rehearsal. The third solo requires the dancer to move half-prone. Throughout, the work is a triumph of technical command, clearly balletic in the second part. Dudley Williams was ill and his place was taken by Keith Lee for the premiere, on April 23, 1970. In *Gymnopedies,* some observers believed that Ailey was describing the choreographer at work—himself, in the fickle spell of his Muse.

the company were polarized "in the single discouraging fact of artist[ic] life: money." Or, as Gale should have said, the lack of it. He wrote: "Dance companies come and go, but the death of the Alvin Ailey American Dance Theater would be a stain on the country's artistic conscience."

Ailey, in an interview, explained that he had explored every possibility of keeping his dancers employed "for a reasonable amount of time each year" but that he could not provide them with the means of earning a living wage, despite interminable tours, most of them undertaken under "terrible conditions."

Ailey, with understandable bitterness, related how, every year, he had had to beat on doors, all over New York, merely to find a place to rehearse the company. He spoke of the dedication of his dancers and commented that, after years of hard work and ceaseless struggle to survive, the good faith and good intentions of the Ailey company had "gone for naught." "It is a sad moment for me," Ailey was quoted as saying, "for this company and the cultivation of its ideas and artists have been my very heart for the past twelve years. But, at the moment, and facing a constantly worsening situation, I see no alternative except to quit . . . I hope that dance history books will remember that we passed here, for we have been a vital and creative force in American Dance."

The press concurred. Anna Kisselgoff wrote, in the New York *Times* of April 24, 1970: "The idea that there may be only three days left to see the Alvin Ailey American Dance Theater again before its possible dissolution owing to lack of just plain money is incredible . . . The group's uniqueness, the strength of its dancers, its interracial character, its high choreographic standards served as a reminder that there will never be another company like it."

The Ailey dancers, meek as good children, went to perform at the Shakespeare Festival at Washington, D.C., June 23–27, glad of the brief respite before the company disbanded. It seemed like the end of the world. Jamison thought: "In another month or so, I will be twenty-six years old!" Ailey had turned thirty-nine. And so the decade of the 1960s ended, and that of the 1970s began.

SIXTEEN

The Ailey dancers, thrown out of work by the disbandment of their company, behaved as do all wage earners of their ilk. They sought other engagements and, failing those, secured teaching stints. Some were obliged to work at things that had no relation to dance, and in fear that the unaccustomed activities might incapacitate them as dancers. Others went home, pretending it was for a vacation, not really to live off the family. The stoical went on unemployment rolls and used part of the stipend to pay for daily class in some studio. And prayed, and waited, and, as Jamison said, swayed with the rhythm of forces they could not resist.

Ailey was busy. He accepted a commission from American Ballet Theatre to choreograph a ballet to Duke Ellington's music, to make a suite of dances for some Ellington compositions. Ailey named the work *The River,* ". . . of birth . . . of the wellspring of life . . . of reaffirmation . . . of heavenly anticipation of rebirth . . ." Working with classically trained dancers, Ailey choreographed in the classical idiom and produced a ballet of such effervescent charm and so much beauty that the dance critics expressed their surprise at the "ease and happiness" with which Ailey worked in classical dance.

Ellington was slower at delivering the music to Ailey than Ailey was at choreographing the dances, but the two men got along so well together that there was no jarring dissension in the collaboration and no recriminations from Ailey on the slowness of the composer. Ailey had revered Ellington for many years.

Ailey was again approached by the U. S. State Department, with the request that he take a company to Russia in the autumn, and, in addition, that he take his dancers on a tour of North Africa. The State Department was willing to pay the expenses of a two-week period of rehearsal for the Ailey company.

Ailey agreed to these proposals and sent out a call for his dancers. They gathered in Washington to work while Ailey stayed in New

York, with American Ballet Theatre. Jamison and the others felt "a little lost," and a great deal of jealousy, that Ailey was working with another company instead of his own. They understood the necessity for Ailey's being in New York, to fulfill his commission; they were proud and pleased that a major company would be dancing an Ailey work. But *knowing* and *feeling* were different matters.

As it was, *The River* could not be completed, as had been planned, for a premiere that summer. American Ballet Theatre, eager to present the work, at least in part, staged seven of Ailey's completed dances as "excerpts from a work in progress" at the New York State Theater on June 25, 1970. Four days later, Ailey took his company to Africa.

It appeared in eight cities in Morocco, Algeria, and Tunisia and was everywhere greeted with the enthusiasm the Ailey dancers had come to expect—and to look forward to—in their foreign tours. Ailey noted that the works in greatest favor with the African audiences were, understandably, those from "black American roots."

Heartened by the favorable reception given to the seven parts of *The River,* and, most of all, by the success of the North African tour, Ailey began to believe, again, that he could hold the company together, if he tried once more.

Cautiously he accepted an engagement in Paris and one in London, to be filled after the Russian tour. Ivy Clarke, a tower of strength, applied to foundations and to private donors for grants in aid of the Alvin Ailey American Dance Theater. She secured the company rehearsal space at 229 East Fifty-ninth Street.

Ailey engaged several new dancers, bringing his company to sixteen. They, with their stage technicians, left New York for Moscow on September 21, 1970. The repertoire had been chosen not so much to show off the choreography of Alvin Ailey as to be representative of American dance. It comprised three of Ailey's works: *Blues Suite, Streams,* and *Revelations;* three of Talley Beatty's: *The Road of the Phoebe Snow, Congo Tango Palace,* and *Toccata;* two by Joyce Trisler: *Journey* and *Dance for Six;*[1] Lucas Hoving's *Icarus;* and Geoffrey Holder's *The Prodigal Prince.* There was one

---

[1] Earlier, Trisler had appeared with the Ailey company as a dancer, in the status of guest artist. Trisler was white. More importantly, she was an alumnus of the Horton company and a dearly loved friend of Ailey.

other work, Holder's *Adagio for a Dead Soldier,* dedicated to war dead everywhere. Holder choreographed it as a solo for Judith Jamison, to whom he had promised a dance in the days when she was wearing out the couch in the Holders' living room.

If Ailey had a qualm about taking his company into the stronghold of classical dance, his fears were soon put to rest. The audiences in Moscow and Leningrad, and in Kiev, accustomed as they were to the best in ballet, adored the "plasticity" of the Ailey dancers. Throughout performances, people screamed and applauded, stamping their feet and clapping their hands so loudly that they almost drowned out the music. Never had the Ailey company met with such demonstrations of approval.

Crowds gathered outside the theatre in silence, waiting to see the dancers get into their bus to be returned to their hotels. The stillness of these crowds, especially after the vociferous applause inside the theatre, was unnerving to the American dancers, who were made edgy by the iron discipline of the Russians. The dancers began spontaneously reaching for programs, taking them from the hands of persons in the waiting crowds, to sign their autographs, to the obvious delight of the people.

Ailey, commenting later on the extraordinary success in Russia, thought that his company had not been seen there at its best, since many of the dancers were too new to the Ailey repertoire to be able to do it full justice.

Leaving Russia on November 2, Ailey took the company to Europe, with a week's holiday before each of the runs in Paris and in London.

At the International Dance Festival, held in Paris November 10–14 at the Théâtre des Champs-Élysées, Ailey was awarded the *Étoile d'Or* for the best modern dance company at the festival, and as the festival's best choreographer. Miguel Godreau was given the prize for the best modern dancer.

In London the Ailey company had its greatest success with the English critics, and with the audience of the historic Sadler's Wells Theatre, where it appeared from November 23, for a two-week run.

London was "the exact opposite" of Moscow and the other Russian cities where the company had recently appeared, in that, though the audiences were equally responsive in the theatre, they expressed themselves differently on the street. In London the Ailey dancers, when recognized, would be greeted by faces wreathed in smiles and, often, with an amiable remark.

Jamison brought away from Russia, as she was to bring away from India, later, a feeling of unease. In Russia, it was due to the sense of regimentation; in India, the abysmal poverty and wretchedness.

The restrictions in Russia were not so much on the Ailey dancers' freedom to move about as on their relationships with the Russian people. Jamison marveled that an audience so demonstrative in the theatre could be so silent, so quiet, when face to face with the dancers outside the stage door. It was, she said, as though a veritable "Iron Curtain" had come down between them.

The notion that English audiences are not as demonstrative as some in other countries could not be supported at Sadler's Wells Theatre while the Ailey company was dancing there. A London critic, Nicholas Dromgoole (in the *Sunday Telegraph,* December 6, 1970), wrote that Ailey was a choreographer of major status. Sadler's Wells Theatre would never be the same after hosting the Alvin Ailey American Dance Theater, where, on the company's best nights, the audience's applause was like that at Covent Garden for Nureyev.

It was still Ailey's *Revelations* that brought the audience, with a great roar like that of the sea, to its feet, and Judith Jamison, in "Wading in the Water," became a memorable sight. *The Prodigal Prince* again aroused favorable comment, and Miguel Godreau was again complimented for his characterization of the Prince.

In *Adagio for a Dead Soldier,* Jamison also drew attention, not all of it complimentary. A London critic, who described her as the "beautifully-ugly" Judith Jamison and as a "statuesque Negress," admired her "elongated arabesque" and the fluidity of her expressive arms but thought that she and the Holder choreography were incapable of depicting grief: "The audience applauded Miss Jamison with not a wet eye in the place."

Jamison's honesty was the greatest hindrance to her dancing in this phase of her development. She thought it wrong to "fake" a feeling she did not understand. Still the scrupulous technician, she believed that in the performance of the steps lay all the meaning of the dance. She was timid about "emoting," for fear that in so doing she would thrust herself, the choreographic instrument, beyond the identity imposed on her by the choreographer.

Given a role like that of the mother in Ailey's *Knoxville: Summer of 1915,* in which her first thought was for Godreau, not for herself, Jamison showed a sense of drama. Put center stage, in a solo, she hesitated to radiate her full power, lest it be in bad taste. Jamison's work, about this time, was being subjected to some authoritative teaching dictates.

For a dancer of Jamison's training (primarily in ballet) and of her temperament (given to the strictest obedience to the teacher, and to the choreographer) it was fortunate that her immersion in the Ailey company was first through the Horton technique, and the Horton tenets. Jamison was not asked by Ailey to forgo the years of her classical training, to eschew those aspects of her dancing that were from ballet. She was asked to invest all that she possessed, as a dancer, in the Horton ethic of dancing.

Horton advocated a freedom of expression. Any other tenet would have driven off the shy eighteen-year-old Alvin Ailey. It was the dignity of the person, as much as the conscience of the group, that had drawn Ailey to dance.

Horton's principles have been too glibly compared to those of the Denishawn school. Horton did not, however, encourage a cultist devotion to himself and his ideas, and he was boldly experimental. However much he borrowed and adapted from his peers, Horton, in the end, was more original than derivative.

Ailey, in this ethos, did not restrict his dancers but left them to find their own dynamics, their own accents. Sometimes his respect for the individual dancer was misconstrued, by the dancer, as indifference. Ailey allowed the dancer to change; *he* was open to influences, subject to changes of his own.

His preoccupation with classical dance as a means of expression was not the only new facet of the company. Ailey, who had made the company largely on his own *oeuvre,* brought more and more choreographers into it, and the choreographers made increasingly wider demands of the Ailey dancers. The naïve fervency of the first years gave way to a technically sharper, stricter kind of dancing. The Ailey dancers were honed and refined to a virtuoso genius, in an eclectic range of styles. Accordingly, Ailey made some changes in the parent school.

The curriculum included classes in ballet, modern dance, and jazz. Ailey was inspired by the work of Anna Sokolow, a modern dance choreographer of strong social convictions whose works were motivated by a passionate sense of human suffering, of loss and despair. It was not, however, Sokolow's technical ideas that were assimilated by the Ailey company but those of Martha Graham.

Ailey, as the leading apostle of "black dance" in America, moved outside "black" culture as the choreographer, and, as the company director, changed his troupe from a segregated to an integrated one. The Ailey dancers were of Caucasian and Asiatic antecedents as well as African. Was this, perhaps, the ultimate "American" dance company?

For Jamison, a quickening sense of change came through new concepts of movement and new styles of dance. The stylized and essentially idealized movements of ballet were in contrast to modern dance's use of weight. Jamison learned to change from a rational, structured form of dancing to one more graphic, less idealized, but essentially human. She learned to use her torso in a new way and she found in her upper body a strength and massiveness that served as a pivot for her expansive arms and for the powerful thrust of her legs.

Jamison in her way was as intuitive as Ailey, so she brought to her dancing a truth and a force beyond the choreographed movements. Like every great dancer, she had the capacity for understanding a choreographer's intent and for carrying his purpose beyond the letter of the law, beyond the technical aspects. Sometimes, to find himself, a dancer must break with the choreographer. Jamison was saved from that necessity. Ailey's patience, which she had thought to be indifference, allowed her to come to her own peak, in her own way.

Ailey's choreographic predilections stamped Jamison with their imprimatur: the long, gliding step; the whirling turn, in which the head was used with as much velocity as the torso; the outthrust pelvis; the spine bent like a bow.

Jamison's body punctuated the Ailey vernacular, in the delicacy of her articulate hands, the dramatic tension of her columnar throat, the amazing arc of her leg extension.

Obedient though she was to the choreographer's will, Jamison was

Sara Yarborough and Judith Jamison in CARMINA BURANA,
choreographed by John Butler.

Miguel Godreau.

Sara Yarborough in Alvin Ailey's THE LARK ASCENDING.

Judith Jamison and Miguel Godreau in THE PRODIGAL PRINCE, choreographed by Geoffrey Holder.

Judith Jamison as the Gorgon and Clive Thompson as Perseus
in Margo Sappington's MEDUSA.

Judith Jamison as the resplendent S

ICARUS, choreographed by Lucas Hoving.

Judith Jamison in Alvin Ailey's CRY.

too powerful a dancer to be subjugated by it. There came a point, in every dance, when it became Jamison's own.

Yet, Jamison hesitated to assert her persona and Ailey appeared reluctant to call it out. They waited, each on the other, for a cue.

This was, for Jamison, a period of hiatus. She seemed, as she looked back at that phase of her life, to have been poised and waiting, unsure of exactly what it was she expected, just what it was she hoped for. She was, she believes now, conscious of waiting to be "discovered" for who and what she was, "so as to be used." She had, she thought, proved herself ready and willing for this artistic use and her expectations were chiefly from Ailey. Surely he, by then, recognized her potential and would be, in a word, "inspired" by it to choreograph especially for her.

In another compartment of herself, Jamison waited for the complete realization of her relationship with Miguel Godreau. They were lovers and, in the elastic morality of the theatre (and the times), were as good as married, but Jamison could not yet consider the relationship as sealed.

Jamison's respect and admiration for Godreau's dancing were joined to an anxiety over his welfare. She knew him to be immensely talented; she had learned that he was congenitally incapable of enduring the everyday drudgery of a career. Godreau either lived, intensely, on the peaks or languished in the valleys between. He had meanwhile been scaling the heights.

His European triumph, in 1968, had been crowned by the return to Stockholm to choreograph and dance in a jazz work, to music by George Riedel, for Swedish television's "Golden Hour." The year after, Godreau had his great success on Broadway, in *Dear World*. In the Ailey company, Godreau was the star attraction, unrivaled, except by dancer Dudley Williams, in the company's repertoire.

Godreau formed his own dance group, and established himself as the managing and artistic director of the Godreau Workshop, for which he choreographed. His twelve dancers appeared in some concert engagements and on television. Godreau recruited his dancers from Broadway, because, as he said, dancers of the musical theatre were accustomed to moving in a variety of styles, according to choreographic demand. He had himself assimilated the Horton technique, through which he shone in the Ailey works. In late 1970, living in a brownstone apartment in Manhattan's Chelsea district, Godreau was working on a ballet to the *Missa Criolla,* Ariel Ramírez's composition of an Argentinian folkloric Mass.

Jamison was much in Godreau's company those days but her true artistic growth was being made with Dudley Williams, from whom she also took class.

Williams, yet another graduate of the New York High School of Performing Arts, had been trained, as a scholarship student, at the Juilliard dance school, and the ballet school of the Metropolitan Opera. Williams danced in the companies of Martha Graham, Donald McKayle, and Talley Beatty; appeared, as a dancer, on European and American television; and joined the Alvin Ailey Dance Theater in 1964. Williams, a native of New York, was a handsome man and a dancer of distinctive personality; he had the most elegant mien of any of the Ailey dancers.

Jamison was immediately attracted to Dudley Williams, because of his talent and his beauty. She soon came to respect his intelligence and to depend on his approval. "I learned," said Jamison, "to watch Dudley like a hawk. When we were dancing together, his face, his eyes, told me what I was doing, if it was right or wrong." An almost wordless communication developed between them, by which Jamison learned to estimate her own dancing. Williams' sincerity, his integrity, and his taste, were the means by which Jamison set her standards. Onstage, in the power of her dancing, the authority of her persona, Jamison seemed invincible. Offstage, she remained vulnerable, achingly dependent on a guide and mentor.

SEVENTEEN

The Ailey company opened an eight-week ANTA dance series for the New York City Center in 1971 and for their January 18–30 engagement Ailey choreographed two works: *Archipelago* and *Flowers.*

Archipelago, set to music by André Boucourchiiev, was the third of Ailey's "water ballets," and, following on *Streams* and *The River,* it was seen, by the dance reviewers, as evidence that Ailey had entered into an "aqueous" stage of choreography. Ailey described *Archipelago* as "an experiment in movement relationships." Jamison, who had danced in the "Lamentosa," at the premiere of *Streams,* appeared in the ensemble of *Archipelago.*

Flowers, set to rock music, was based on the life and death of the singer Janis Joplin, and it featured a guest artist, Lynn Seymour, of The Royal Ballet.

Seymour, a Canadian born and trained dancer, was a protégée of choreographer Kenneth MacMillan, in whose works she had attained the status of British ballet's leading dramatic ballerina. Though in physique and temperament she was utterly unlike The Royal Ballet's paragon, Margot Fonteyn, her type of dancer was by no means rare in American ballet. After the gala premiere in New York, when Seymour left Ailey, the starring role in *Flowers* was taken by members of the Ailey company, Linda Kent, Consuela Atlas, and Rosamund Lynn, and, according to some critical assessments, each of these gave the Joplin figure more pith and credibility than had Seymour. Joplin, though white, had been closer to the "black" synthesis of musical genius, and of the blackness of pain that is called "the blues."

The Ailey company took *Flowers,* and the selection of a ballerina for the leading role, as indication that Ailey was deeper than ever in his "ballet phase." The dancers were alarmed and chagrined over what they took to be Ailey's growing preoccupation with ballet, not only in his choreography but more specifically in the trends of the Ailey company and the school.

No one in the company argued over the need to attract audiences, and the employment of a celebrated "guest" was so general and so usual in American dance that it had become hackneyed. It was understandable that Ailey, all for the good of the company, would engage a guest artist whose renown would draw attention to his company's season at the New York City Center.

Nor was it incomprehensible that Ailey, in his selection of a guest artist, might wish to draw one out of ballet, rather than out of modern dance. A melding of the once rival forms of dance was symptomatic of American dance in this era. Martha Graham, the doyenne of modern dance, featured The Royal Ballet's great romantic pas de deux partners, Margot Fonteyn and Rudolf Nureyev, in a New York season.

Nevertheless, the dancers of the Ailey company were less than enthusiastic over the introduction of a ballerina into their midst, and they were jealous of the attention that Ailey lavished on her.

Judith Jamison was by now so thoroughly committed to the Ailey company that she had come to think of herself as an Ailey dancer and, by this categorization, as a modern dancer. She had begun to speak, even to think, as did modern dancers, with a veiled hostility about ballet dancers.

Jamison and her colleagues were puzzled and hurt by what they described as "Alvin's *thing* with the ballet," as though it were a disease. To the dancers, Ailey's increasing interest in ballet was a gross infatuation, a perversion of Ailey's own beliefs, rather than an extension of choreographic ideas.

If it was the worst sort of artistic prejudice to infer that, by a species of "Uncle Tomism," Ailey had become seduced by "white" dance, it must be recognized that for most of his company Ailey's dedication in forming a black dance theatre represented an ideal and a vindication for black dancers. To turn away from "black" dance culture toward "white" ballet (and to bring into the Ailey company white ballerinas) was to renege on a grand undertaking.

For Judith Jamison, at this point of her career, there was an even more personal hurt to bear: Ailey had become interested in another dancer.

She was named Sara Yarborough and she was one of two daughters of Lavinia Williams, a noted black dance teacher. Williams' older child, Sharon, became a musician; the younger, Sara, a dancer.

Born in New York in 1950, Sara Yarborough went to Haiti as an infant and grew up in that country, where Lavinia Williams directed a dance academy. Yarborough's formal training in dance began when she was six and almost at once she was cast in roles from the classical repertoire: *The Nutcracker, The Sleeping Beauty,* and *Swan Lake,* all produced by Williams in Haiti.

Yarborough's training in her mother's Haitian academy included ballet, modern dance, tap dancing, and jazz. The child was groomed for a performing career. Yarborough's intelligence and nerve were extraordinary for a little girl. Before she was technically trained to dance *en pointe,* she put on a pair of toe shoes and substituted in a performance for an ailing dancer.

In summers, Yarborough's training was expanded by classes in New York, where Williams taught at the International School of Carnegie Hall and, later, at Harkness House. At eleven, Yarborough was sent for a summer session to the School of American Ballet. She was awarded a scholarship and studied at the school for two more years.

In 1967, while Williams was teaching at Harkness House, Yarborough studied with Benjamin Harkarvy, whose protégée she became. Soon, Yarborough was invited to share the Harkness Ballet's company class; she was taken on tour, to learn the repertoire. At the end of two months, she joined the company. She danced in Macdonald's *Firebird* and *Time Out of Mind;* in Butler's *Sebastian;* in the Harkarvy works and in Jerome Robbins' *New York Export: Opus Jazz.* Alvin Ailey met Sara Yarborough while he was setting his *Feast of Ashes* on the Harkness Ballet.

After the demise of the Harkness Ballet in 1970, Yarborough returned to Haiti, where she taught, and performed with a concert troupe. It was a hiatus in her budding career and one that was perhaps necessary for her well-being. As Yarborough was to admit to colleagues later in her life, she had become conscious of the unremitting pressures to succeed—to excel—as a dancer. She was destined to become the great "black" American ballerina. The years of her adolescence were not easy for Yarborough. In New York, she lived with a Haitian family, and struggled to acclimate to a new lifestyle. A serious impediment in her academic education was her lack of fluent English. Her parents were divorced, in a row over Lavinia Williams' commitment to her career, and with the divorce came financial problems. But for the S.A.B.–Ford Foundation scholarship, Yarborough might not have been able to study dance in New York. Yarborough was homesick, for her mother and for sunny Haiti; New York was terrifying, in its hugeness and anonymity.

As soon as she began dancing in the Harkness Ballet, Yarborough found her métier. She was at once noticed, for her beauty as much as for her artistry. Yarborough had a lovely face, with large dark eyes and luscious lips; her looks were made the more arresting by the sweet melancholy that haunted her expression. She looked like a ballerina, with a beautiful body, capable of high extensions, and lyrical port de bras.

Yarborough was a musical dancer, partly through her mother's training. Lavinia Williams' methods of teaching were to involve the dancer in theatre, to make the dancer one with the other contributing artists of the ballet. An early immersion into theatre had given Yarborough stage presence; her love of dancing was fostered by Williams, in the most intimate way. Yarborough's childhood was spent with dancing and music, steeped in her mother's work. Williams thought nothing of staying up far into the night, teaching her daughter. If Yarborough tired, or momentarily wavered in her concentration, Williams would coax her daughter to dance: "Do this for me . . ."

There was another influence on Sara Yarborough, that of the Haitian sacred dance rituals, those associated with *voudon*. When Williams began teaching at the National Theatre of Haiti, she took her daughters with her and, with other children, the little girls went to "voodoo" ceremonies, where they observed, and imitated, the dancing of their elders. Sara Yarborough was playing the *voudon* drums by the time she was four and among the *voudon* dances her favorite was the dance sacred to Dambala, the serpent god, in which the dancer must move as articulately as possible, to take on the sinuosity of the snake.

Yarborough had an eclectic education, growing up with one foot in the twentieth century, as this was espoused by New York, and the other in antiquity, the world of the black Haitian, in which religion and myth (or, variously, superstition and fable) are paramount to a mystical society. Even the "real" world seemed dream-like to the little girl. It was glimpsed briefly in summers spent in New York, and through the dance films that Lavinia Williams imported to Haiti. These films, and dance books and periodicals, were Yarborough's physical links to "the outside," while she was growing up in Haiti, speaking the language, dancing the dances, one with other children in her adopted country—a country that was an island, isolated, and immune to the influences and to the artifacts of twentieth-century America. Yarborough was bred as a dancer, mind and body; and in spirit, as a devotee to a cult.

Lavinia Williams was resolutely protective of her child and she welcomed the opportunity given to Yarborough to join the Harkness Ballet. Williams liked the familial nature of the company, the warm association between the dancers, believing that these would be nurturing factors in Yarborough's development. The abrupt disbandment of the Harkness Ballet closed this phase of Yarborough's career.

She was too talented, and her mother was too ambitious for her, to remain in Haiti, dancing for a small audience. In early autumn of 1970 Yarborough came back to New York, to join the Ailey company. She went with it to Russia, to the Paris International Festival of Dance, and into the London season.

Yarborough was immediately notable in the Ailey company's repertoire, appearing in Beatty's *Toccata,* and in *Revelations* and *Blues Suite*—the last two the signature works of the Ailey company, in which a dancer's measurement was taken (in much the same way as, at that time, the ballerinas were tested in *Serenade,* and the danseurs by *Apollo,* in the New York City Ballet).

Yarborough continued studying in New York during the months following the Ailey tours, rejoining the company in 1971. Ailey made no secret of his admiration for her, he extolled her as the most beautiful and gifted young dancer of the day, and it was observed that Sara Yarborough had some of the qualities of a young Carmen de Lavallade.

Their likeness to each other, however, lay only in their attributes as beautiful women and as accomplished dancers. In Sara Yarborough, Ailey had a distinct personality, far more substantial than the image by which he was haunted, of a lovely girl in toe shoes and a pink tutu.

Yarborough was a young woman of complex and sometimes

perplexing character. Some of her colleagues thought her cold and selfish, self-seeking rather than contributing to the company. Her admirers, arguing against her detractors, maintained that Yarborough was reserved, and meticulous as an artist. Ailey's lavish public praise of her did not make her popular in the company.

Yarborough had the gentility, and the reticence, that Ailey admired in a woman. Yarborough combined in herself the dignity and the soft, sweet vulnerability that Ailey conceived as the essence of the feminine. They were qualities by which Ailey was moved, perhaps because they called up his own gallantry, and his overwhelming tenderness.

Yarborough appealed to Ailey, too, because she was a nymph, elusive and seductive. Her face was a beautiful little mask, behind which Yarborough remained a mystery. Only her body was eloquent, and impassioned.

As Ailey succumbed to Yarborough's enchantment he seemed, to the other women in his company, to be so bemused as to forget them, except for their names. Who could compete with the incarnation of Beauty, in someone as obsessed as Alvin Ailey with its form and its spirit?

But Yarborough did not fall under Ailey's spell, as Jamison was so willing to fall and to remain. Very like Miguel Godreau, Sara Yarborough exercised an almost arrogant prerogative, to come and go in the Ailey company. This factor, Yarborough's seemingly casual independence, rankled in the Ailey dancers who had given Ailey their unquestioning fidelity.

It was a difficult time for Jamison. She would not complain about what she took to be Ailey's indifference. She resisted the temptation to confide her hurt and anger to the friends who, in the belief that this might console her, berated Ailey to her for his neglect. Godreau, possessed of a caustic tongue, said—not for the first time, nor for the last—that Jamison was being wasted. With the inexorable fall of each leaf of the calendar, Jamison drew nearer to an age she dreaded: *thirty*.

Jamison's trouble, in the early 1970s, was that she had arrived at a plateau, one of those measureless and lonely spaces in the career of the artist from which the view is bleak and empty. To look back is aimless; the course already traveled appears arid. To try to foresee the future, in anxiety rather than with eagerness, is fruitless and fearful. Jamison felt obliged to take stock, to "see where I had been, and where I was going." And it appeared that, squarely in her path, stood Sara Yarborough.

Jealousy is a corrosive emotion and for the dancer it can be a crippling one. Used as a crutch, it may become the excuse, the poor explanation, for failure: I missed my chance because of so-and-so . . . Dancers experience jealousy of each other over casting in certain roles, over billings on programs, in the frequency and the infrequency by which company management promotes them through press interviews and newspaper and magazine articles. The worst jealousy, however, is over the choreographer's interest in the dancer. When, as in the Alvin Ailey American Dance Theater, the repertoire is largely represented by the works of the company's artistic director, the jealousy reaches its keenest point. The choreographer's merest whim is then capable of inflicting piercing pain or of lifting the dancer to the height of ecstasy.

In dance companies, when dancers began to pine away because of neglect by management, they look elsewhere, for companies where they believe they will be shown to better advantage. Hence comes the game of musical chairs, so assiduously played in American ballet, by which dancers change places seasonally. The dancers of the Ailey company had few other places to go, and almost no choices to make, if they wished to dance professionally. Jamison's feeling of floundering did not blind her to the realities of the situation.

Sara Yarborough, more readily than Judith Jamison, might have found other companies than the Ailey in which to dance. Arthur Mitchell had coveted Yarborough for the Dance Theatre of Harlem but Mitchell had made no offer to Jamison to join his company. There were rumors, from time to time, in the early 1970s, that Yarborough would be taken into American Ballet Theatre. Yet, privileged though she seemed, Yarborough was enduring her private grief and disappointment that, despite having been trained at the School of American Ballet, she had not been invited to join the New York City Ballet. Against this loss, there was no compensation for Sara Yarborough, not even as a principal dancer of the Alvin Ailey Dance Theater.

She cannot ever have doubted that she would be cast in ballerina roles; she was brought up believing in her right to ballet. While her daughter was a member of the Harkness Ballet, Lavinia Williams said, "I never wanted Sara to believe that a Negro would never be accepted as a ballerina, as I was made to feel in my young career." Had the Harkness Ballet survived, Williams' hopes for her child might have been realized. All her expectations would have been fulfilled, had an influential choreographer interested himself in the young Yarborough. But, though changes had come about, sufficient to ensure a black girl a place in a white ballet company, the American dancer was still subject to the erratic rise and wasteful discard of dance companies. There were no assurances of success for even the most gifted and dedicated dancers. Sara Yarborough's ballet career, begun so auspiciously at the Harkness, seemed to die with it.

She was forced, with Judith Jamison, into an invidious rivalry. Their careers were curiously parallel, in that they both danced with the Harkness Ballet and with the Alvin Ailey Dance Theater. It was by antic chance that these two women reluctantly entered into their private *agon,* the struggle to command Ailey's attention. Both dancers, at the same time, were dependent on Ailey as for their lives, in crucial phases of their careers. Jamison and Yarborough were equally proud and each pretended to ignore her own, and the other's, clamorous need of Ailey. And, just as Jamison believed herself forsaken, Ailey made her a star, in the *mater dolorosa* he called *Cry.*

EIGHTEEN

The Ailey company had so great a success at the New York City Center in January that it was asked back for a two-week engagement in the spring. After a U.S. tour, February 4 to April 5, Ailey took his company back to Broadway, setting a precedent in the American dance theatre. His company was the first of its kind to be featured in two consecutive Manhattan engagements within a year.

For the season April 27 to May 9, 1971, Ailey choreographed two more works: *Choral Dances* and *Cry*. They were premiered within a few days of each other.

Choral Dances, with Kelvin Rotardier in a leading role, was unlike most of the works of Ailey's *oeuvre*. Ailey was often accused by dance critics of being overly literal as a choreographer but in *Choral Dances* he left it to the audience to determine the meaning of the piece.

Structurally, the work was set on six themes, to the music of Benjamin Britten (from *Gloriana*) and, sometimes, to silence. *Choral Dances* had a sense of communal sharing, in act and feeling, that made it a testament to Ailey's credo of the brotherhood of mankind.

Womankind was on Ailey's mind for *Cry,* which he dedicated to "all black women everywhere—especially our mothers." To accentuate the dedication, Ailey brought his mother, Mrs. Lula E. Cooper, to New York, on her first visit to the city, for the premiere of *Cry*.

For a score, Ailey used recorded music: Alice Coltrane's "Something About John Coltrane," Laura Nyro's "Been on a Train," and the Voices of East Harlem's "Right On, Be Free." To rock and rock-bottom blues, Ailey choreographed a dance about black people in America, their endurance of poverty and pain, their yearning for freedom, and, eventually, their assumption of pride. He did this through a long solo, in which the dancer incorporated the stages in a woman's life and the phases of black life in white society.

The dancer begins the dance wearing a long white dress, her head wrapped in a cloth. She unwinds her turban and uses it to wash the floor of the white master's house. Down on her knees, she is servile but not beaten. She lifts up her arms, and her hands call to, and claw at, freedom. She is struck with anguish, and her body bends at the waist, in a contraction of pain as intense as that at childbirth. She sinks back to the ground, writhes upward again, her arms flailing the air, her legs rising and falling in great arcs, her head swinging, rhythmically, until its dizzying whirl envelops the dancer in an invisible coccon, like that mysterious and inviolate spinning space in the universe which the Dervish dancer inhabits. At length, the dancer rises up to her full height, on tiptoe, extends her arms, lifts her head high, and moves in another rhythm, one that sustains the triumphant presence of her declaration of freedom.

Cry is a dance like a shout, a dance like a paean. Choreographically, it is spare, and the steps taken, the movements made by the dancer, are basically simple. The dance depends not on its form so much as on the content—the meaning and the intensity of that meaning that the dancer conveys. Every contortion of the head and torso, each extension of the limbs, must be freighted with emotion, if Ailey's *Cry* is to be heard, and understood.

Ailey made *Cry* on, and for, and, as Ailey said, *because* of Judith Jamison. "And, also," Ailey added, "because I wanted to say something about the black woman who is my Mother."

Cry was a work of collaboration. The choreographer and the dancer worked together in such harmony, with so much perception of the meaning of the dance, that the solo spun itself out like a long, seamless thread. It would be impossible, ever after, to know where Alvin Ailey's choreography stopped in *Cry* and where Judith Jamison's interpretation began.

They worked, alone for most of the time, in a big studio on the West Side of Manhattan, a studio that adjoined a vast ballroom atop a big old wooden building grown seedy by transient use. Dust motes danced in the long, pale beams of thin sunlight that penetrated the dusk of the studio. The place smelled of wood rot, of stale sweat and damp wool. On the turntable, in endless repetition, Alice Coltrane sang, and Laura Nyro, and all the Voices of East Harlem. At the last word of "Right On, Be Free," Jamison wiped the sweat from her eyes and began again, on the first step, to the first note of the score.

Ailey stood, a man with a torso as thick as a tree, with still-powerful legs, and a face, now heavy, on which the beauty of the young Ailey still lingered, benign where once it had been fierce in its brilliance. He stood a little aside, giving Jamison all the space she needed in which to turn and turn again, to enter into the whirling spasm of her emotional immolation. He watched but he scarcely spoke, and then, more to confer with Jamison than to direct, or to correct her. Ailey, with *Cry,* had given Jamison a dance; Jamison, in *Cry,* gave a dance to Ailey, and to her audience.

In their rapt collusion, Ailey and Jamison were like lovers but they were more trusting of each other than lovers dare to be. Ailey deliberately relinquished his authority and allowed Jamison to take it upon herself, for *Cry.* Ever after, Jamison would always be more than a choreographic instrument.

Other women of the Ailey company were to perform *Cry.* They would do so well, sometimes beautifully, but none was the replica of or the substitute for Jamison. She assaulted the audience with a pitiless and glaring confrontation. At the same time, the audience became privy to a secret, the one by which black pride had been sustained, and absolved.

Ailey had, quite simply, made use of an old-fashioned device in *Cry.* He took a single, undeviating point of view, almost monotonous in its perspective, save that the intensity of the vision, the passion of its feeling, transformed one woman's Gethsemane into a universal suffering.

Cry appeared on the American stage at precisely the right time, danced by the perfect dancer, choreographed by the one man with the power and authority to create it. There is, in astronomy, a position called *syzygy,* when earth, moon, and sun occupy an almost straight line; when this is arrived at, the world is shaken. The shock of *Cry* reverberated in the American theatre and, throughout the decade of the 1970s, the shock was felt, in an emotional seismograph, around the world, wherever Judith Jamison danced Alvin Ailey's *Cry.* Time and again, when the curtain fell on *Cry,* faces were wet with tears, as audiences became caught up in the convulsive revelation. More than once, Jamison, coming offstage in the wings, wiped something else than sweat from her cheeks. Many times, she found members of her own company weeping, as they watched her.

There were, of course, critical arguments as to the merit and demerit of the work. Some reviewers thought *Cry* too long and too unremitting in its fury. Jamison danced it through, at an almost unbearable pitch, emerging, each time, from the dance as from an ordeal, her skin streaming with sweat, her body aching with tension. Jamison was sometimes too terrible, in her splendor, for those who went to the theatre intending only to be entertained, and who were affronted by being made to feel, and, perhaps, to think.

Ailey's choreography was examined by some reviewers and dismissed as a mélange of modern dance and "black" dance, with his—and Jamison's—now patented grand arabesque interpolated between the modern "contractions" and the African dance "isolations." Little was understood of the spontaneous, almost combustible nature of *Cry,* except by those who had seen it in the making.

In rehearsal, Jamison had worn a plain leotard. And, in order to get the "feel" of her movements, she had, at Ailey's suggestion, asked wardrobe for "some long skirt, anything that will move." The same skirt, with the addition of a flounce, became Jamison's costume for *Cry.* She always wrapped her head, in silk or chiffon turbans when she dressed up to go out and in light woolen turbans when she worked, to keep the sweat from running into her eyes. This headcloth, worn to rehearsal for *Cry,* became the cloth which Jamison wrapped and unwrapped, as the symbol of her servitude, and as her black woman's stately tiara. Never before and perhaps never again would Ailey and Jamison, together, or with others, work in so contained and persuasive an atmosphere, where each aspect of the dance came together in an almost miraculous cohesion to make a whole.

Ailey knew instinctively the steps and gestures that would be most effective for this dance, on Jamison's body. Her height, the breadth of the extension of her arms, the power of her long legs, the flexibility of her torso, were all explored for *Cry.* Jamison's small, neat head, erect on the swelling column of her throat, provided Ailey with another force, a style of movement, by which to punctuate and accentuate the movement in *Cry. Cry* had to have Jamison's face, as well as her body. The rictus of her lips, the roll of her eyes, were as important to the expression of this dance as was the downward writhing of her body, and the upward thrust of her spine.

And Ailey worked from memory, from the many times he had

seen his mother bent to some task, like the scrubbing of a floor. Ailey worked from his perception of a black woman's servitude, from the rage and grief he had felt at his mother's, in the houses of her employers. Loving little boys grow up and get rich enough to buy their mothers shiny automobiles and fur coats. Little Alvin Ailey grew up and made a dance for his mother when he found a dancer who could express what he wanted to say in *Cry*.

Although Ailey meant the dance to be about black women, its communication was to any man or woman who had ever been oppressed. It was a dance that could be understood by all who had ever toiled or who had been witness to the toil of others, in circumstances that demeaned and that threatened to debase the human spirit. Within the next decade, as Jamison danced *Cry* around the world (with the Alvin Ailey Dance Theater, and, frequently, as a guest artist) she never ceased to marvel at the universal responses of audiences to *Cry*. People, she remarked, behaved the same way in Bucharest and in Havana when they saw her dance *Cry*.

Jamison's intimate relationship, as a dancer, with *Cry,* obscured the work for her. "It was more than a dance; it was an experience. I have never been able to judge myself in *Cry*. I have to let the audience judge me." Walter Sorell, a distinguished American dance critic, had no doubt of the validity of *Cry*. It was, he said, writing for *Dance News,* "as perfect a work as anything can be . . . unforgettable because it is artistically irrefutable." Sorell saw *Cry* as "penetratingly human," and he commented on Jamison's femininity and the "blackness" of her persona, noting that, in one part of *Cry,* she seemed "all woman, enduring pain and giving strength and joy . . ." and that, in another part of the dance, the "specific color of her skin became clear . . . when the challenge of the environmental space around her grew."

Clive Barnes, writing for the New York *Times* on May 5, 1971, remarked: "For years it has been obvious that Judith Jamison is no ordinary dancer . . ." It was true. Jamison was no adolescent dance neophyte but a woman of twenty-seven years who, for six of those years, had been performing. She was not made an overnight star in *Cry,* in the truest Cinderella traditions of the theatre, but the woman who came offstage, after the premiere of *Cry,* was a different dancer than the one who waited, that evening, for the curtain to rise. The difference lay less in Jamison as the dancer than it did in the audience who looked at her. That audience had seen Jamison dance many times before; now, in *Cry,* they saw her as Jamison. "It was the same difference," commented a friend, "as between hearing and *listening."*

In *Cry,* Ailey gave Jamison a gift such as Michel Fokine gave Anna Pavlova in *The Dying Swan*—a dance so closely identified with the dancer that all other dancers in the role would be usurpers. And, as with *The Dying Swan, Cry's* glory reflected equally on the choreographer and the dancer. Jamison glowed in her triumph; a reviewer described her as a woman with an iridescent smile. The premiere season of *Cry* was, it seemed, a turning point for Alvin Ailey. After that, his company achieved more security than it had ever had before. And Ailey, past his fallow period, blazed again with creative fires.

The school Ailey had long wished to establish became a reality, as the American Dance Center, through a grant from the National Endowment for the Arts. The Ailey company and the company of modern dancer Pearl Lang shared facilities at 229 East Fifty-ninth Street in Manhattan, where the school was headed by Ailey and Lang. Guest instructors, from both companies, amplified the teaching of the faculty. Ailey confided his hopes to the press: he wished to make his company the nucleus for year-round subsidized modern dance in America.

Ailey dispatched his company on a U.S. tour, coast to coast, ending in a six-day engagement in Jamaica. He stayed in New York to complete *The River.* The ballet was premiered on June 25, 1971, by American Ballet Theatre at the John F. Kennedy Center for the Performing Arts, in Washington, D.C., with great acclaim. Ailey choreographed one section, "Giggling Rapids," as a pas de deux for the Russian ballerina Natalia Makarova and Erik Bruhn—a jazzy tour de force, like a vaudeville turn, for those august ballet artists.

Ailey's star was once again ascendant. He remounted his *Feast of Ashes* for the City Center Joffrey Ballet, bringing to culmination the project that he and Robert Joffrey had begun in 1961. And he choreographed for the Joffrey Ballet a new work: *Mingus Dances,* to the music of jazz composer Charles Mingus. Both ballets were presented at City Center in autumn 1971, and *Feast of Ashes* was highly praised.

For the opening of the John F. Kennedy Center in Washington,

Leonard Bernstein was commissioned—at Mrs. Jacqueline Kennedy Onassis' request—to compose a work, which he did as a Mass. Bernstein chose Ailey as choreographer for the theatre piece, and the Ailey company as the dancers. Ailey accepted the commission, though he was given less than thirty days to complete it.

The Bernstein *Mass* opened in Washington on September 8, 1971, and the Ailey company had the distinction of being the first dance company to appear in the new theatre. Ailey's pleasure was less than it might have been. He and the Ailey dancers felt that they had been "shoved about" and reduced to second-class performers in Bernstein's *Mass*. The trouble, as a member of the Ailey company reported it, came from Bernstein's preoccupation with the singers and the orchestra. The dancing was gradually reduced to minimal movement, "as far back onstage as possible, and a little in the corners." Another Ailey dancer said that part of the problem lay in the fact that the dancers sang, and the singers danced.

Nevertheless, the Ailey company toured for three months with the Bernstein *Mass,* and appeared, in two consecutive years, in the *Mass* at Kennedy Center and at the Metropolitan Opera House in New York.

Ailey's dancers felt that they "redeemed" themselves by appearing, as the Alvin Ailey American Dance Theater, in an engagement October 5–10 at Kennedy Center, after the premiere season of Bernstein's *Mass*. Ailey had learned to cut his losses and not to waste his energy in brooding over "ifs" and "what might have been." He was no sooner finished with Bernstein's *Mass* than he started on another: *Mary Lou's Mass.*

In 1971 Ailey choreographed six works for his company and began work on two more, for the coming season. The winter engagement at the New York City Center opened on December 9, 1971, and featured Ailey's new *Myth,* to music by Stravinsky, which excited little interest, and *Mary Lou's Mass,* which was hailed as the successor of *Revelations*. At the premiere of *Mary Lou's Mass* the orchestra was conducted by Mary Lou Williams, the composer with whom Ailey collaborated; Miss Williams, billed as "Queen of Jazz," also played the piano part of the score.

Composed and choreographed in thirteen sections, *Mary Lou's Mass* had the religiosity of *Revelations* and the same overt style of "black" evocation of a Divine Spirit. It was biblical in theme. Indeed, the piece included readings from Scripture, about the rich man who cannot enter Heaven and about Lazarus.

Dudley Williams appeared as Lazarus and was seen resting on the bosom of Kelvin Rotardier, as Abraham. *Mary Lou's Mass* received a great ovation at its premiere and, inevitably, was criticized as being not quite up to the masterwork, *Revelations.*

The company was now relieved of its tedious one-night stands on tour, appearing, instead, in one- or two-week residencies, mostly in the college theatre circuit. During the 1960s, while civic theatres were being built throughout the country, colleges and universities had also erected good theatrical facilities. There were now many handsome and well-equipped auditoriums and stages.

And, too, the Ailey company was now a fixture at the New York City Center, to which it returned for an engagement April 18–30, 1972. It was then that Ailey premiered *The Lark Ascending.*

Set to Vaughan Williams' *Romance for Violin and Orchestra, The Lark Ascending* was one of Ailey's most classically romantic works and one of the most meticulously structured. Ailey used two of his favorite dance forms: the arabesque and the diagonal, both common to ballet. Musically, the violin was represented by a woman—Judith Jamison—and the orchestra by the corps. Dramatically, Ailey's Woman was cast as co-principal with a Man, who seemed first the hunter and then the protector of the Woman. The Man might, just as easily, have been the eternal seeker after Beauty, and the Woman, Beauty itself.

The Lark leans upward, in flight, aspiring to space yet fearful of it. The fulfillment of her desires comes through the Man, who lifts and supports her. And the Lark is set free.

Ailey, with the inscrutability of the artist, was still writing his autobiography in dance.

At the premiere performance of *The Lark Ascending,* Judith Jamison danced with Claude Thompson. Thompson, a native of Jamaica, had danced briefly with the Ailey company in 1965 and had returned to Ailey in 1970.

Lark was not *Cry* and, for the time being, *Cry* eclipsed everything that Jamison danced. Reviewers seemed scarcely disposed to accept her in anything else. *Cry* had an insatiable audience and Jamison, now much in demand as a guest artist, was invariably asked to appear in *Cry,* as she did for the gala program on January 24, 1972, at the New York City Center, staged as a benefit for the Dance Collection of the New York Public Library–Museum at Lincoln Center. For the Ailey company, Jamison continued to dance in a wide range of the repertoire and, again and again, in *Cry,* by popular demand. Although she shared the solo with other dancers of the company, Jamison danced *Cry* so often that she injured her neck in the rapid head rolls that she had to perform in the solo. For several months she was obliged to wear a neck brace, to relieve the strain.

Her performances in *The Lark Ascending* gave Jamison great pleasure. She loved the lyricism of the dancing and the theme of the work. But, as Jamison found, she had become typecast as Ailey's protean earth mother, the "goddesslike" dancer—as Walter Sorell described her—of *Cry*.

On the cresting wave of her success in *Cry,* and on the fame it brought her, Jamison was interviewed by the press, was photographed for the covers of national magazines, and was given the Dance Magazine Award for 1972, sharing it with The Royal Ballet's premiere danseur Anthony Dowell. She was now acknowledged as the principal dancer of the Alvin Ailey Dance Theater. When the Ailey company was at the Metropolitan Opera House, with Bernstein's *Mass,* Jamison occupied the "star" dressing room, the same one reserved for Rudolf Nureyev when he danced at the Met.

The greatest change in Jamison's career came about through the agent Paul Szilard. Szilard, born in Budapest, was trained for the ballet in Paris and London, by Olga Preobrajenska, Lubov Egorova, Alexandre Volinine, and Stanilas Idzikowsky. Szilard was a successful dancer but his career was abruptly brought to a halt in 1941, when he was stranded, for four years, by the war in the Philippines. He thereupon formed a company, for which he was choreographer, premier, and entrepreneur, as well as teacher and business manager. After the war, Szilard became one of the most successful impresarios in the West. He arranged the foreign tours of several American ballet companies, among them the New York City Ballet, and brought to the United States foreign companies, among them the Dancers of Bali. During the 1950s, Szilard, with the ballerinas Nora Kaye, Colette Marchand, and Sonia Arova, toured the Orient with a company which he directed and with which he danced.

Szilard was the personal representative of Ailey the choreographer, and, in the 1970s, he represented the Alvin Ailey American

Dance Theater for overseas tours, taking the company throughout Europe and the East. About the same time that Ailey choreographed *Cry,* Szilard suggested to Judith Jamison that she engage him as her representative for appearances outside the Ailey company, as a guest artist. Jamison agreed and Paul Szilard became her agent. He and his wife Ariane became Jamison's good friends. Szilard was an energetic and purposeful manager and, at the start of their association, Jamison did not know the extent of his ambitions for her.

Her guest artist assignments began without fanfare, at the San Francisco Ballet, in a season when the star attractions were the Panovs, a pair of dancers whose defection from the Soviet Union had been highly publicized. Valery Panov was a Jew who had requested permission to emigrate to Israel. He had been denied permission until the weight of public opinion, in theatres of the Western nations, apparently persuaded the Russian government to allow him and his wife to leave Leningrad.

Jamison enjoyed the experience of "guesting" because it proved her ability "to function outside the Ailey." She was also delighted to discover that her earnings from guest appearances were more than she had ever before been paid.

Her appearance with Mikhail Baryshnikov, in Ailey's *Pas de "Duke,"* was well-timed. Baryshnikov was then the cynosure of the American press. He too had defected from the Soviet Union, while appearing in Canada with a troupe led by some of the reigning Russian ballerinas. Baryshnikov was a fine classical technician and, after a debut with American Ballet Theatre, he had the New York dance critics at his feet. They compared him to the titan of ballet, Rudolf Nureyev, and, in an effort to determine who was the greater danseur, a venomous rivalry was fomented in the press.

Nureyev, since his defection from the Leningrad Kirov Ballet in 1961, had become the most famous dancer in the world. As the star of England's national ballet, The Royal Ballet (where, as her partner, he revivified the career of prima ballerina Margot Fonteyn), Nureyev excelled not only in traditional repertoire but also in that of contemporary ballet. He was even more adventurous in appearing with the modern dance companies of Martha Graham and Paul Taylor.

Baryshnikov was anxious to take on similar challenges and he was skillfully advised at American Ballet Theatre, of which he had become the leading danseur. He appeared in a jazzy ballet, *Push Comes to Shove* by Twyla Tharp, a choreographer who gained critical praise for her works for the Joffrey Ballet. Baryshnikov eagerly accepted the invitation to dance with Jamison for a benefit gala by the Alvin Ailey City Center Dance Theater. Not only was the Ailey company unique among international dance troupes, its leading female dancer, Judith Jamison, was an authentic star, since her appearance in Ailey's great solo, *Cry.* Moreover, Ailey, in the year just past, had done another work for Jamison, *The Mooche,* to music by Duke Ellington, and in it Jamison had gained another kind of praise, this time as a glamorous and sensually exciting dancer. She offered Baryshnikov a contrast in style, technique, and personality which would not fail to emphasize his own.

Pas de "Duke" had a sensational success. While the novelty of the unorthodox partnership lasted, it was exploited by American Ballet Theatre for its gala benefit program on July 29, 1976. Shortly after, Baryshnikov and Jamison were invited as guest artists to the Vienna Staatsoper, the leading opera house in Austria and one of the most famous theatres in Europe. Here Baryshnikov and Jamison repeated their success in *Pas de "Duke."* In *Cry,* Jamison made an even greater effect on the Viennese audience.

She was already known to Continental audiences, through tours with the Ailey company. Her appearance at the Vienna Staatsoper brought her a new status, one derived from her personality as much as her dancing. At the Dance Magazine Awards in 1972 Szilard told a friend: "Give me five years to make Judi an international star." Szilard needed only four.

Baryshnikov and the Vienna Staatsoper were just then discussing a plan by which Baryshnikov would appear with the Vienna State Ballet in a new production of Richard Strauss's famous *Josephslegende,* with choreography by John Neumeier, one of the most distinguished choreographers working in Europe. The drama of the ballet lay in the events following the enslavement of Joseph, son of Jacob, in Egypt, and Joseph's meeting with Potiphar, the crux of which was the seduction of the boy Joseph by Potiphar's Wife.

Potiphar's wife, in the Bible story, was a lustful woman. Her characterization, in the proposed ballet, was to be the principal feminine role. At Baryshnikov's suggestion it was offered to Judith Jamison.

NINETEEN

Outside Vienna, not thirty minutes' drive by car from the Staatsoper, there is an old suburb, a place of precipitous, winding cobble-stoned *allées,* nestled in the vineyards for which the Grinzingerberg is famous. Close by flows the River Donau[1] and at dawn and dusk the air there is fresh and damp, as it must have been on that dew-wet day when the world began. In summer, at high noon, when it becomes as warm as the shores of the Mediterranean, the air is perfumed with the scents of fruits and flowers.

Nearly two centuries ago there was a regular visitor to the region, a man of average height, thick-set and powerful, with a massive leonine head. As he strolled the fields and forests, and paced the river walks, he would suddenly stop, appear to be listening intently, and then scribble with a pencil on a sheaf of manuscript paper. One may still walk here where Beethoven walked, as he composed his music, and dine in the cafés, with their big open kitchens, where he ate sausages and drank beer.

The studios of Wien Film are on the Sieveringstrasse and here, in August 1977, UNITEL Film and Television Production Company of Munich assembled a crew to film the Vienna Staatsoper production of *Josephslegende.* Appearing with the Vienna State Opera Ballet, in the lead roles of Joseph and Potiphar's Wife, were the American dancers Kevin Haigen and Judith Jamison.

UNITEL is an internationally known film company whose highly praised productions include 198 symphony concert programs (by conductors of the first rank, such as Herbert von Karajan, Leonard Bernstein, Karl Richter, Georg Solti, and others); nineteen operas and seventeen operettas; and twenty-four ballets. One of the ballets was the American Ballet Theatre's production of *Giselle,* with the Italian prima ballerina Carla Fracci in the title role and the Danish premier danseur Erik Bruhn as Albrecht.

[1] The Danube, river of romance and song.

UNITEL's decision to film *Josephslegende* was understandable. The ballet had caused considerable furor in Vienna both before and after its February premiere, though for different reasons.

When the production was announced, as a work by John Neumeier, there was general approval from the public and the ballet at the State Opera House. Neumeier was a celebrated choreographer, highly respected as the director of the ballet of the Hamburg State Opera. He was an American, born in Milwaukee, Wisconsin, in 1942, who had received part of his training in the United States and part of it with the Russian pedagogue Vera Volkova and as a pupil of The Royal Ballet School in London.

Neumeier danced with the American modern dancer Sybil Shearer and became a member of the Stuttgart Ballet, under director John Cranko, from 1963 into 1969. He was a danseur of exquisite exactness, with a genius for characterization, but he much preferred to choreograph, and began doing so for matinee programs of the Noverre Society in Stuttgart. An early work was done for the Harkness Ballet.

Neumeier left the Stuttgart Ballet to become director of the ballet of the Frankfurt Opera, 1969–73, where he made a name both as a company director and as a choreographer.

Through an influx of American and British choreographers, European ballet was having a lively renaissance—in the wake of John Cranko's success in turning a dull opera ballet troupe into the Stuttgart Ballet, a vibrant company autonomous of the opera. Neumeier was wooed by several companies, among them the centuries-old Royal Danish Ballet, and elected to become director of the ballet at Hamburg. There his rule became virtually absolute, a remarkable achievement for the ballet director of a European opera house, where the intendant has nominal power.

Neumeier was a prolific choreographer but he preferred to stage his works in premieres in Hamburg and only occasionally mounted them on other companies. More infrequently, he accepted commissions for new ballets. Dr. Gerhart Brunner, ballet director of the Vienna Staatsoper, scored a coup when he persuaded Neumeier to produce *Josephslegende*.

It had first been planned as an opera-ballet, with the diva Maria Callas in a starring role. Roland Petit was mentioned as the choreographer, Mikhail Baryshnikov as Joseph of the biblical legend. The plan hung fire and, with the death of Callas, the idea of an opera-ballet was abandoned. When Baryshnikov suggested that Judith Jamison should be engaged for the part of Potiphar's Wife, Dr. Brunner negotiated a contract through Paul Szilard, by which Jamison would perform with the Vienna State Opera Ballet. This announcement was met with consternation and dismay. Viennese music critics considered it nothing short of desecration for "a Negress" to appear in the Strauss work at the Staatsoper. They admired Jamison but in "her own métier," as a black dancer in the Ailey works.

Jamison, on the other hand, was cautioned against appearing with classical dancers, with whose technique hers—as a modern dancer—might be adversely compared by conservative audiences in an opera house. How would she be treated at the Vienna Staatsoper? Would there be prejudice against her, if not as a black dancer then as an American interloper? She knew nothing of the choreographer's work and received only dismal accounts of it in the United States. Neumeier was not admired in America as he was in Europe.

He was known to be a radical choreographer in his treatment of the traditional repertoire. Neumeier's *Nutcracker* dispensed not only with its Mice, Tin Soldiers, and children's party but even with the Tree. The *Don Juan* he mounted for the National Ballet of Canada —in which Nureyev was provided with one of his greatest roles— had a startling premise: the infamous libertine was not a cynical sensualist but a lover in search of a beautiful ideal, suffering "the irremediable anguish of molecular man." Invited to do a work for American Ballet Theatre, Neumeier in 1974 reset the Hamburg production of *Le Baiser de la Fée* (*The Fairy's Kiss*), but the ballet received so appallingly poor a premiere that it damned the choreographer's reputation in New York. In 1975 his *Epilogue,* a pas de deux for Makarova and Bruhn to the "Adagietto" of Gustav Mahler's Symphony No. 5, was presented by American Ballet Theatre, which the following year commissioned from Neumeier his *Hamlet Variations* for Baryshnikov as Hamlet and Gelsey Kirkland as Ophelia. These, like *Baiser,* vanished from the company's repertoire, without in any way advancing Neumeier's reputation in the esteem of American dance critics.

Possibly because of other commitments, Baryshnikov did not take the title role of *Josephslegende* and Dr. Brunner left the choice of

Judith Jamison speaking on "Art and Politics" at the symposium
on "The Arts: Years of Development, Time of Decision,"
September 29–30, 1975, at the LJB Library, Austin, Texas.

Judith Jamison with Harry Belafonte in her dressing room at the New York City Center.

Judith Jamison and Mikhail Baryshnikov in 1977.

Judith Jamison presenting the 1978 Dance Magazine Award
to Mikhail Baryshnikov.

© VAN WILLIAMS

Judith Jamison and her maternal grandmother, Mrs. Annie Brown, at the Dance Magazine Award presentation, 1972.

Judith Jamison as Potiphar's Wife in JOSEPHSLEGENDE,
choreographed by John Neumeier.
In performance at the Vienna Staatsoper.

Judith Jamison in FACETS,
choreographed for her by John Butler.

Judith Jamison with Betty Ford, wife of the current
President of the United States of America, with members
of the Alvin Ailey American Dance Theater, backstage at
the New York State Theater, August 1976.

the lead dancer to the choreographer. Neumeier chose Kevin Haigen, out of the corps of the Hamburg Ballet, a boy of about the same age as Leonide Massine had been when he danced Joseph in Fokine's version of *The Legend of Joseph*.

Jamison, expecting that she would be dancing with Baryshnikov in *Josephslegende*, was taken aback to be told that, instead, she would be cast with a young man barely out of his teens. Arriving in Hamburg for her first meeting with Neumeier and Haigen, her immediate impression was that she would be dancing with "a baby."

Haigen, born Higginbotham, began his ballet training in Florida and was taken, on scholarship, into the School of American Ballet at fourteen. He was a gifted pupil, good enough to hold the interest of the school's noted teacher, Stanley Williams; good enough to attract the notice of Balanchine, who coached the young student in a role. The School of American Ballet's workshop provided opportunities for students to choreograph. The executive director, Eugenie Ouroussow, was impressed by Higginbotham's work and showed it to Balanchine. To the boy's amazement, Balanchine invited him to choreograph a work for the Stravinsky Festival. He felt "as though God had reached down from heaven and touched me," overwhelmed with mingled terror and joy. Balanchine delegated to Higginbotham Stravinsky's *Circus Polka,* to whose music Balanchine had choreographed a ballet "for 50 young elephants and 50 beautiful girls" for the Barnum & Bailey Circus at Madison Square Garden in 1942.

The Stravinsky Festival was a mammoth undertaking by the New York City Ballet, staged as a memorial to Igor Stravinsky in 1972, and commemorating the Balanchine-Stravinsky *oeuvre,* one of the most important in contemporary classical dance. Other than ballets by Balanchine, the Stravinsky Festival featured works to the composer's music choreographed by John Taras and Jerome Robbins. Higginbotham's efforts at choreography did not satisfy the standards for this grand festival. *Circus Polka* was given to Robbins, who choreographed a "children's ballet" to the piece.

Higginbotham was not asked to join the New York City Ballet. Carrying the ineradicable wound borne by students of the parent school, who are rejected by the company, Higginbotham went into American Ballet Theatre, where Tudor promptly changed his name to Haigen. The rechristened Haigen became a soloist but he recognized that he was doomed to "ABT's short boys corps," a virtuoso

ensemble, and that he would never be cast in "serious" male roles.
He left American Ballet Theatre for the Stuttgart Ballet but found
the atmosphere "claustrophobic," in the persistence of the "Cranko
Cult." He auditioned for the Hamburg Ballet and accepted a job in
the corps, a demotion from his former position as a soloist. His
choice by Neumeier for the title role in *Josephslegende* gave Haigen
another spasm of mingled terror and joy. It was a major assignment
in a major production. Neumeier, as guest choreographer, was in-
vesting his reputation at the Vienna Staatsoper on a corps de ballet
boy from the Hamburg Ballet.

Jamison's shock was pardonable: Haigen at twenty looked not
more than sixteen. Of average height, well proportioned, talented,
and well trained, he was in all these respects indistinguishable from
many other young danseurs. But his face would have delighted
Donatello. Arresting in its beauty, it was a study in harmonious con-
tradictions, at once virile and tender, sensual and angelic.

Jamison, with her quick response to physical beauty, was cap-
tivated by Haigen's looks. "I *saw* him as Joseph and he made *me* see
myself as Potiphar's Wife. I could understand how a love-starved
woman would find it impossible to keep her eyes off him; *or* her
hands off that velvety skin."

Neumeier, as was his custom when working with dancers, talked
at great length to Jamison and Haigen about their characterizations
in the ballet, the relationships between them, and also with the other
two principals of the plot: King Potiphar and Joseph's divine guide,
the Angel of the Lord.

Jamison enjoyed Neumeier's way of working, by which she felt in-
tellectually stimulated. "John gave me the sense of working in a real
collaboration with him, with Kevin, with everyone in the ballet." She
was charmed by the deference shown her, in the European observ-
ance of protocol for a distinguished guest artist.

Work began in the studio but on the first day Jamison fell, breaking her right ankle. Haigen took her to his house, where she was
"waited on like a queen." It was as a queen that she would appear in
Josephslegende. In the biblical story Potiphar was merely the captain of Pharaoh's guard but in the ballet Potiphar was a king and his
spouse thereby became a queen. The regality of Potiphar's Wife was
an important factor in Neumeier's ballet. Jamison had to convey a
sense of this regality to emphasize the lofty height from which Pot-

iphar's Wife fell to her abasement, in the consummate folly of a proud and lonely woman driven mad for love.

As soon as she could hobble onto a plane Jamison returned to New York. She thought much on the role she would dance for Neumeier but she felt no anxiety about it, "only a thrill, that I would be making that woman come alive in the ballet." Joseph she knew well, from Sunday School Bible class.

Jacob, asleep one night in the desert, was visited by the Lord and a host of angels and when he awakened he anointed the stone where his head had lain, calling it Bethel, "the house of the Lord." It was a holy place, where Abraham had made sacrifice, and it was revered by the Israelites. The site remains, twelve miles north of Jerusalem, on the main highway.

The ballet called *La Légende de Joseph,* produced in Paris in 1914 with choreography by Michel Fokine (set designed by the Spanish painter José Sert and costumes by Léon Bakst), was to a score commissioned by Diaghilev from Richard Strauss. Diaghilev chose to mount the ballet not in its biblical locale (Egypt, c. 1600 B.C.) but in the Venice of Paolo Veronese (c. A.D. 1530), so as to evoke a scene of semi-Oriental splendor, in which the voluptuous character of Potiphar's Wife would be in strong contrast with the simplicity and purity of young Joseph's.

Strauss's *Josephslegende* had later been choreographed by Heinrich Kröller for the Berlin Staatsoper, by Balanchine for the Royal Danish Ballet, and by Tudor for Teatro Colón in Buenos Aires. In 1935 Goleizovsky choreographed a ballet, as *Joseph the Beautiful,* to music by S. Vasilenko, noteworthy for the furor it caused at the Moscow Experimental Theatre because of the unbridled eroticism of the dancing and its modernistic choreography, in purely constructivist patterns and poses. Neumeier's *Josephslegende,* with the casting of an American Negress as Potiphar's Wife, was expected to cause yet another theatrical scandal.

Neumeier treated the biblical legend as the basis for his libretto but he concerned himself mostly with the extravert and introvert aspects of the relationships between the protagonists of the plot. Neumeier's ballet opened new dimensions on the biblical legend of Joseph, in his sojourn in Egypt. Potiphar's Wife was moved to quick and intense covetousness for Joseph, but did not Potiphar himself, in his caressing kindness, betray an incipient love for that beautiful boy? The impression of an ineluctable allurement was made by Haigen in the role of Joseph. He became the incarnation of Rilke's unicorn, *"das Tier aus Licht, das reine Tier"* (the animal made of light, the innocent [or pure] animal).

Jamison's foot healed and she resumed working with Neumeier in Hamburg, going with him and Haigen to Vienna when the choreographer was ready to work with the company at the Staatsoper. Here Jamison met Franz Wilhelm, King Potiphar; and Karl Musil, the Angel of the Lord. These two men, the premiers danseurs at the Vienna Staatsoper, were entrusted with key characterizations in the ballet. They looked their parts to the life.

Wilhelm's King Potiphar was a monarch as golden and as beaming as King Arthur of Camelot. Musil—who had an international reputation—was a magnificent Angel, in a golden helmet and a pair of snowy wings.

These two represented sacrosanct authority—Potiphar, that on earth; the Angel, that of the Lord in heaven. As depicted by Wilhelm and Musil, they were distinguished by a golden beauty, and by such dignity of presence that they appeared emblematic. Potiphar's queen and the young Joseph were beings of flesh and blood.

The queen might have been a statue cast in bronze, but her being was on fire. Joseph was a pubescent boy, his heart sore with longing for his father and his homeland, his head filled by visions of the Angel, his body awakening to the discovery of its appetites and pleasures.

The court in which the scenes of the drama were played was of a rich and leisured society, in an atmosphere of weary decadence. Under the musky scent of perfumes could be faintly smelled the taint of decay. The king was surrounded by sycophants. There were priests to counsel him on the state of his soul and ministers to advise him on affairs of state. There were courtiers as vain as peacocks, worldly, venal, and cynical. In this court of a thousand treacherous intrigues only King Potiphar was devoid of guile and malice. He strolled about with benign majesty, at once naïve and gracious. The queen, silent and still, withdrawn from the court, was enthroned, veiled by curtains of saffron silk. Though she sat with bent and averted head she did not seem submissive. She looked more like a panther in a golden cage.

Dressed in a long garment, vaguely hieratic in style, no more than two panels of orange-colored silk, Jamison was simply attired. (She danced in bare feet and wore as an undergarment a bodystocking of brown nylon so that she seemed nude beneath the orange silk shift.) Potiphar's Wife was in dress and manner alien to the king's court.

Early in the drama Neumeier sketched the tension of the relationship between the king and the queen: he was tenderly solicitous; she, scornful of his attentions. Her isolation was emphasized not only by the veiled throne but also through the polite innuendo and the sly glances of the courtiers. Strauss's Shulamite dance is a dance of desire, performed to arouse the sensuality of the king. Neumeier used all of this music for Jamison's variation, a dance of unrepressed fury and yearning.

As the ballet opens, Joseph is sold into slavery by his jealous brothers, who strip from him his coat of many colors, the gift of Jacob to his beloved son. A party of Midianite merchants brings the boy to King Potiphar, as though they were selling the king a pretty, graceful young animal for a pet. Joseph, a simple boy from a poor desert tribe, is dazzled by the luxury and abundance of King Potiphar's court. The king himself seems godlike to the boy. And because this king is kind and orders that Joseph shall be given food and drink, Joseph offers the king the only gift in his power to give: a dance. Joseph dances, as young David in like circumstances would have sung and played on his harp. Joseph, in his innocence, does not know the effects of his youth and beauty, their allure to the senses, on the courtiers, and on the king and queen.

Joseph is scantily dressed and light seems to flow like oil on his bare limbs. His thick dark hair is bound by a band about his brows. As the boy dances he smiles, Haigen's sweet smile with its hint of tender melancholy. The queen looks upon him and desires him.

The court retires, Joseph lies down to sleep and to dream of his angel. It is not a golden, winged apparition by which he is visited this night but a ghostly dark one, Potiphar's Wife in her white robe, stealing from the king's bed to that of the Hebrew stranger. She kneels beside Joseph and awakens him with gestures both imploring and demanding.

As he wakens to kisses and caresses Joseph almost succumbs to temptation; almost he responds to his seductress. Then, in panic, more in fear of the wrath of his Angel than of King Potiphar, he repulses the woman. Wrenching himself from her hands Joseph leaves in them the brief garment in which he had lain down. In nothing but a loincloth, he turns to flee, as King Potiphar and the king's guard burst in, alarmed by the sounds of the struggle.

Joseph stands, half-naked, in the light of the torches. Potiphar's Wife holds out to him Joseph's garment. In the Bible she says: "And it came to pass, as I lifted up my voice and cried, that he left his garment with me, and fled . . ." And it is said that the stranger, the Hebrew servant that Potiphar brought into his house, had sought to lay with Potiphar's Wife. Whether in thought or in deed, he has dared to violate the woman. Vengeance is swift. Joseph is flogged with knouts and flailed by clubs. The guards would tear him limb from limb were it not for the mercy of King Potiphar.

Throughout Joseph's terrible punishment the queen stays mute. To confess her fault would be to stand accused of sin and to lose her place beside the king, perhaps to lose her life. As she witnesses the boy's suffering, Potiphar's Wife is smitten by remorse and love. Each blow that falls on Joseph strikes her cringing heart. In anguish, her body arches and contracts.

Joseph is thrown into prison and there the Angel of the Lord comes to him with promises of a glorious destiny, a fate already sealed in heaven.

Who is the woman that, in secret, will haunt Joseph's memory as he shall haunt hers? The Bible makes cursory mention of the seduction of Joseph and gives no name to his temptress; she has no identity except that of Potiphar's wife. Neumeier and Jamison were free to interpret her as they chose and at the Vienna Staatsoper she was tall, dark, slender, graceful, and powerful, a woman of icy hauteur warmed and melted by concupiscence.

Jamison's characterization of Potiphar's Wife was so nobly phrased that it provoked conjecture on the antecedents of this unhappy queen. Had she come, a Nubian princess, to King Potiphar to seal a diplomatic treaty between Africa and Egypt? Or was she from the line of black pharaohs who, it is said, once ruled Egypt, and in whose negroid image the Sphinx was carved? This provocative element of the characterization was organic to Jamison's interpretation and it gave a tragic aura to her queen.

At the premiere in February 1977, *Josephslegende* ended all speculation on the propriety of an American Negress appearing at the Vienna Staatsoper in Richard Strauss's ballet. When Jamison was later temporarily unable to fulfill her commitments for *Josephsle-gende* her role was danced by Donna Wood, a black dancer from the Alvin Ailey Dance Theater.

Haigen and Jamison returned several times to Vienna to perform in *Josephslegende,* which was regularly featured in the Staatsoper's ballet seasons. When UNITEL and John Neumeier agreed to make a film of the work there was no question but that Haigen and Jamison would re-create their roles.

Accordingly, Jamison arranged her schedule to allow her to join Neumeier and Haigen in Vienna in the late summer of 1977, after completing tours with the Ailey company in the Far East, Africa, and Europe.

TWENTY

Jamison was on tour with the Ailey company, performing at Avignon, in the South of France, early in the summer of 1977. She loved dancing in that city, in the open-air theatre, where, on balmy nights, she felt one with earth and sky. Audiences were always enthusiastic in Avignon and they were especially pleased by the Ailey company, sending little gifts of flowers and trinkets backstage to Jamison, with affectionate messages. She was on top of her form, having fun and looking forward to the filming of *Josephslegende,* when she slipped during rehearsal on a rain-slick stage and hurt herself. Laid up by the wrenched ankle, she groused about, sick at heart that she could not finish the season in high style. As soon as she was well enough she flew to Vienna and went, alone, to the hotel where Neumeier had reserved accommodations for her, and for himself and Haigen. Confiding her whereabouts to no one other than Paul Szilard and a few friends, Jamison settled down to a regimen of exercise and dieting, to get in shape for the grueling filming session.

As always when she was inactive and discontented, she had put on weight. This she shucked off on a spartan allowance of one salad a day, some red wine in the evening, and "too many" cigarettes, smoked in a long holder, the smoke inhaled in three or four deep gasps and the glowing end ground out so that she would not "get down to the bad stuff, that makes it into a cancer twig." She went for long walks, briskly along the tree-shaded *allées,* and loiteringly on the path along the Donaukanal. She loved having people tell her that this was where Beethoven had walked while he was composing the *Eroica.* It did not really matter what Beethoven had composed at Grinzingerberg. It might have been the *Eroica* (Symphony No. 3 in E Flat, Opus 55) or, again, it might have been the *Eroica Variations,* the theme of *The Creatures of Prometheus* (composed as a ballet for the choreographer Salvatore Viganò). Incontestably, Beethoven had frequented these streets and the cafés. People spoke of him with affection and familiarity, not with awe. He might have died five years ago, instead of one hundred and fifty. Jamison found a comforting sense of permanency here. It was not so much that things were old as that they were well used. Nothing was a museum piece for the lively people and the long-lived place. The sausages in 1977 were made with the same recipes as those Beethoven had eaten.

Jamison, tall and angular, dressed in faded blue jeans and a nondescript sweat shirt, became a celebrity in the Grinzingerberg. At first she was taken for an African tourist who, incomprehensibly, had come to spend summer on the Donau. When it was discovered that she was an American much was explained about her independence as a woman, the casual aptitude she showed in traveling alone. On finding out that she was a dancer, they understood all her idiosyncracies. Artists of the theatre have something of the prestige of aristocrats. Foibles are to be indulged.

There was hardly another spot more conducive to the mood of reverie than this pleasant suburb of Vienna. Karl Musil, the adored premier danseur of the Vienna Staatsoper, sometimes came with the Americans to eat a late supper, after looking at the day's film rushes in the studio. Often, they ate a rough meal, of sausages and cheeses, with bread and soup, wine or beer, in the working men's cafés. Sometimes they dined sumptuously at the little Hotel Grinzingerberg on Austrian delicacies prepared by a fine chef. Karl Musil knew the Grinzingerberg district well. He and his brother had grown up there and their parents still lived nearby, in a house set amid grape arbors, with rose gardens front and back.

Musil, fluent in English, confirmed the stories that the natives liked to tell about Beethoven, and the pretty superstitions: that in the Grinzingerberg hearts opened like flowers in summer, and that those who drank the summer wine together would remain friends forever. Looking into the ruby or the amber depths, smelling the fruity perfume of those wines, it was easy to believe Karli.

Jamison was alone in her hotel for two weeks before the others joined her. For days she heard her voice only when she asked for her mail, ordered a meal, or bought a trifle in a shop. When her friends arrived, she rejoiced in the sounds of English; the wines of the Grinzingerberg had perhaps opened her heart. Jamison had begun long conversations about herself in 1972 with a friend. These conversations were resumed whenever they had time to share. In the

Grinzingerberg, during the filming of *Josephslegende,* Jamison talked more fluently than she ever had about her life and her work. At first, she talked only of *Josephslegende.* "I worried more before we started the film than before we danced the premiere because I knew we were going into a new medium, and it would be hard for us to adapt. I felt that John did not want a super-video of the ballet, he wanted a film of *Josephslegende.* I didn't know if he had any experience in films, and working in film with *dancers,* not screen actors.

"So I felt that for the film to succeed, we—the dancers and the choreographer—had to keep ourselves fresh. On film, we had to produce *Josephslegende* as though we were dancing it for the first time."

She willed herself not to think of the ballet, not to think of her role in it, so that she would come, again, newborn to the experience of "John's ballet." And when Neumeier joined her, and the UNI-TEL technicians were installed at Studio Wien, Jamison found that Neumeier's intentions for the film were just as she had thought they would be. He was intent on putting *Josephslegende* on film, as a permanent record.

It was a long and laborious process. Jamison had been pleased to know that the choreographer would be producing and directing the film. There would be occasions, though, when she would be disposed to curse that arrangement. Neumeier's demands were exacting and unremitting. The UNITEL technicians were more easily satisfied with a "take" of a scene than the choreographer. Over and over, the same steps had to be performed for the camera, at various angles. In the incomprehensible jargon of the cinema, the technicians discussed their work while the dancers waited, patient as sheep. In full costume and makeup, fatigued by inaction and the oppressive heat of the arc lamps, the dancers worked through the long hours of a day, and returned, again and again, to repeat the same scene in which they had performed the day before. Every evening, after the "shooting" had ended, Neumeier, with Haigen and Jamison, joined the UNITEL technical crew in the little cinema attached to Studio Wien to look at the rushes from the day before. The film was processed as rapidly as possible, so that, scene by scene, it could be examined and judged. The primary question at every screening was: Is it good enough to keep?

There were some unexpected interruptions in the shooting of

Josephslegende and afterward it became necessary to accelerate the schedule. Gone were the jaunts to the Flea Market over the weekend holiday. Haigen and Jamison worked on Saturday and Sunday as well as during the week. Under pressure Neumeier did not relax his vigilance, he merely turned the screw tighter.

A young man close in height and coloring to Haigen's was employed as a stand-in. Jamison had none, for where in Vienna, she asked, would UNITEL find a woman the height and color of Judith Jamison? Occasionally she became laconic and looked impassive but these were the only signs by which she betrayed stress—and always she would recover her good humor when the day's work was done. Otherwise, she commented, she would not be able to do a good day's work the next. Haigen, of volatile temperament, showed strain in the loss of appetite. He was warned that Joseph would look cadaverous instead of lithe. Jamison insisted that they have their meals together so that she could make sure he ate.

Protective and supportive, Haigen and Jamison helped each other work toward their characterizations in *Josephslegende,* in the purest desire "to give John what he wants." From their first meeting in Hamburg, Jamison had refused to permit Haigen to give her "star treatment." They were, she told him, "in this thing together." Haigen loved Jamison for her generous nature; he admired her exceedingly as an artist, and for her professional integrity. He said she was the strongest woman he knew. Their rooms in the hotel adjoined and Jamison left the door open, so that Haigen could come in to talk to her when he wished. She was a good listener.

Unlike the majority of performers, Jamison liked talking about others more than about herself. Other people interested her. She liked to know "life stories" as much as some women like to read romantic novels.

Jamison has a small vanity. She believes her personal seismograph signals her to "like" or "dislike" those she meets. Now and then she has had cause to rue it, but that is because she is so quick to place utter trust in the one she loves. Her friends marvel that someone as sensible as Jamison (who, in matters of money, is as pragmatic as an accountant) will so entirely give herself over to an impulse to like and sometimes to love. Once her affections are placed, they are sustained by a fierce loyalty.

Kevin Haigen she liked at first sight. She saw more in him than a facile gift for dance and the good looks which impressed others. "I knew that Kevin was much more than a pretty ballet boy." Haigen had been a "battered" child; the faint scar on his face was a souvenir of a wretched childhood. Miraculously, instead of becoming brutalized by violence, he had become loving and gentle, possessed of a degree of compassion surely rare in someone of his age. Experiences that might have warped or deadened emotions seemed to have given Haigen an extraordinary sensitivity. The particular radiance of his Joseph, the look of sublime innocence, had been born out of a dark wisdom. The knowledge of pain was the reason for the tender melancholy of his smile.

Her relationship with Haigen, Jamison said, was different from any other she had had with a man, in or outside her professional life. She spoke of Haigen as an "exquisite" dancer and a "rare" person, and said he was so beautiful that it was a pleasure just to look at him. "Kevin and I are not 'in love' but we truly love each other. It's not any motherly instinct on my part, it's a new sort of feeling that I am just starting to analyze."

Haigen has a mysterious attraction for people. His friends are possessive of him and, at the same time, dependent on him. Out-of-work American dancers frequently turned up on his Hamburg doorstep, expecting aid and comfort, and assistance in getting jobs in European ballet. During the filming of *Josephslegende* a young woman came to visit Haigen. Every evening at dinner she monopolized the conversation, with a recital of her dismissal from a ballet company in New York and discussions of her and Haigen's friends. Others were necessarily excluded from these talks. Jamison resented the intrusion of "a stranger," and she detested the young woman, a classical dancer, who, Jamison believed, was patronizing to modern dancers.

"I'm jealous," she said frankly. "Not only of that girl spoiling our evenings but of her taking up Kevin's time. He should be resting and relaxing, so he can rev himself up to get back to the studio at eight o'clock in the morning." The evening hours in the Grinzingerberg were cherished by Jamison. After working before the cameras she would shower and change into clean jeans, adding a patterned silk chiffon blouse, a scarf in a turban on her head, and some gems from the pouch in which she carried her jewels. She touched perfume to her ears, throat, and wrists. These things were part of a ritual with which she preserved the identity of the woman within the dancer. They were the stern measures by which Jamison divided herself between *dancing* and *living*. After they had seen the day's rushes, Jamison and her friends went to dine, at their leisure.

After a few evenings of enduring the company of Haigen's friend, Jamison vowed she would not expose herself to the irritation. She stayed in her room, but without the harmony of friendly conversation the food was tasteless, the wine not so red. "I'm miserable and I'm jealous," she told a friend. "I can't stand that stupid, rude girl because something is broken, something is spoiled, since she came. Working as hard as we are, we need the concentration, just being by ourselves. Kevin is being distracted. If I said these things to him I'd sound evil. But he should be getting ready to dance the Joseph variation, *thinking about nothing except being Joseph*."

She knew something of Haigen's past. "He is someone who needs love, he wants everybody to love him to make up for when he was not loved enough. So he gives all he has and that's as bad as taking too much.

"Kevin wants too much to please other people. Since the premiere at the Staatsoper, he has been a star. God knows, he earned the right to think of himself as special. That was a terrible ordeal for him. I saw him that night turn green with fear—a corps de ballet boy in the title role of a big, new, important production in an opera house! Kevin knew how much was riding on him: John's reputation. It was John who put him in the Staatsoper production. Kevin proved himself that night and he has proved himself every time he's done Joseph. He ought to realize that. But he's not yet begun dancing Joseph for Kevin Haigen; he's still dancing Joseph for John Neumeier."

Of course, the dancer had to try to satisfy the choreographer and it went without saying that "the dancer's aim is to communicate the sense of the dancing to the audience, to work at making a rapport" but, Jamison believed, it was perilous to dance to please others. "If you dance only to get other people's approval, sooner or later you find yourself dancing in a state of constant anxiety, scared that they won't like you, won't admire what you're doing." Dependency of this sort was as dangerous as self-indulgence; the dancer had to find in dancing "a personal reason."

Haigen's friend departed and a day or two later filming began on Joseph's long solo.

The cameras were kind to Haigen. Under stage lighting, his flesh seemed to be anointed with fragrant oils; on film, he had a luminosity. Jamison was difficult to film in the same light that was used for Haigen. Because of the dark shade of her complexion her image appeared grayish. She disliked the lighting for her dancing in the film but she stoically accepted it.

Haigen's was the most taxing dance role in *Josephslegende*. From his first entrance he was continuously onstage and the focus of much of the drama. Neumeier had the reputation for choreographing fiendishly difficult variations. For Joseph, Neumeier composed a long, beautiful, and technically difficult solo.

Neumeier stipulated that the variation was to be filmed in a single camera take. Toward this purpose, three consecutive days were devoted to dancing the Joseph variation. It was rehearsed for the lights and for camera angles. When Haigen began to dance it for filming, there were numerous interruptions, some by Haigen, others by Neumeier, as choreographer-director and dancer struggled to extract the most perfect possible performance of the solo for the film of *Josephslegende*.

Earlier, Jamison's solo, as Potiphar's Wife, had been filmed, after several performances for the cameras. She was still limping from having lost skin, where the friction of her body stocking had burned into her flesh. Rubbed raw, Jamison had Nobecuton, a plastic film, sprayed on for "temporary skin," so she could continue dancing. Pain was part of the business, she said, as was boring repetition. When they were not on call the dancers of the Vienna Staatsoper stayed away from Studio Wien. Jamison might have done the same for Haigen's solo, but she went every day to watch him dance, to lend him a comforting presence. Between camera takes, he sought her out, for her opinion and her encouragement.

Late on the third day, Haigen gave a performance of the Joseph variation that Jamison described as "flawless." The words *exquisite* and *flawless* were those she used as superlatives, to describe the best in dancing.

Haigen's performance evoked bravos from the UNITEL technicians. The dressers, ladies of imperturbable mien and phlegmatic temperament, burst into spontaneous applause. Neumeier was observed to be smiling. Singing merrily, Haigen ran off to shower and then went down to the anteroom of Studio Wien to order wine. While Haigen was on his cheery errand, Jamison returned to her dressing room, walking with an odd flat-footed gait, a wooden expression on her face. She lighted a cigarette, as she did in moments of stress, inhaled the smoke and then let the cigarette burn to ash. She had heard the bad news. Haigen would have to dance the Joseph variation again. There had been some fault or error in the camera take.

It fell to Neumeier's assistant, Ray Barra, to tell Haigen that he must report for work at Studio Wien next day to repeat the variation. The predictable explosion occurred. The usually gentle and sweet-tempered Haigen became almost hysterical, declaring that he would not resume dancing the variation for the film. Neumeier and UNITEL could go through the discards of three days of shooting and edit them for a full-length version of the solo. This would require patching film. Neumeier was adamantly opposed to the procedure and demanded that Haigen again dance the solo. "Wait until tomorrow, after you have a night's sleep," soothed Barra, a model of tact and good sense. "Then just do it like a performance." Barra wisely put as much space as possible between Neumeier and Haigen. Jamison took Haigen to dine with a friend who was staying at Hotel Grinzingerberg.

The little hotel overlooks vineyards and a very old church. Jamison's friend lived in a large room, with dormer windows, on the top floor.

Rage and despair had fought for dominance over Haigen. He could not swallow his food at dinner. In Jamison's friend's room he drank some brandy and fell across the bed, on the downy quilts in their covers of starched linen that smelled of hay and sunshine. Sleeping in the moonlight that shone in at the tall windows, Haigen looked as exhausted as a drowning man. Sipping her brandy, Jamison talked about him.

"I am torn between John and Kevin as I used to be between Alvin and Miguel. It's terrible to have to take sides. I understand John's position but I know how Kevin feels. I've been through similar experiences and it makes you hateful. You have no control over things like this [the rumor at Studio Wien was that someone had forgotten to load a camera with film]. All that machinery, all the manpower—

two men to a camera, one just to wipe the lens, and still . . . John says it's human error, and people *do* make mistakes. The cameramen can be human, but not Kevin. Dancers are supposed to be able to make others feel, but *we* are not allowed to have feelings. You rage, because of the waste—of yourself, your time, your *best*. You kill yourself trying, because you care so much about what you're doing, and then it's spoiled, because no one else cares the way you do. It's just a job to other people.

"Other people don't really understand us. They may enjoy looking at dancing, they may get very intellectual about it, but they don't truly know anything *about dancers.*

"Psychoanalysts say we are masochistic, that we enjoy the punishment, the rejection. That we are narcissistic, and we get our kicks from exhibiting ourselves onstage. Maybe we do what we do for another reason: because we want to accomplish something that is perfect, flawless.

"It's not easy to do what Kevin has done, to keep on and on, and then dance as he did today, after the eighth attempt. It was not the same as giving a performance in the theatre. It was for the film. It didn't take, and that means that he wasted the dancing. It's the waste that is so frustrating.

"All through dinner I gave Kevin a sales talk about John Neumeier's ballet. It's not called *Potiphar's Wife,* I told him, it's called *Josephslegende,* and Kevin Haigen is Joseph. I told him to behave like a star if he was a star. I told him to quit being sorry for himself. I was very rough on that child.

"But I hate to be the one to moralize. I hate to be the one to have to psych that boy up to go back and start in again. Nobody made me do it; *I* elected Judi.

"I know what will happen: Kevin will sleep like the dead and wake up looking like an angel. You can do that after the worst trauma when you are his age. I'll drag myself out of bed in time to get him to Studio Wien by eight o'clock and I'll stay with him as long as it takes for him to dance the variation, until he and John are satisfied it's good enough for the film.

"Kevin is not going to be able to dance the way he danced that one time today but he'll do that some other place, some other time. And Hohfeld [the chief UNITEL executive] will have this story about Kevin, like the one he tells about Erik Bruhn: how, when they were making the ABT *Giselle,* Erik danced *his* variation straight through, six times."

The following day, after only a few false starts, Haigen danced Joseph's variation well enough to satisfy himself and Neumeier that it should be kept in the film. Shortly thereafter, filming having been completed on *Josephslegende,* the company was dispersed.

Jamison returned at once to New York to resume her voice and dance studies in preparation for beginning rehearsals of a musical. She had signed to appear in a Broadway revue, *The Only World in Town.* For this, she was taking a leave of absence from the Ailey company.

"The first long leave I asked for," she said, the night before leaving Vienna, "was when I married Miguel. Alvin gave me a year off because I was going to dance with Miguel in Europe. That didn't work out, we separated—and I had to humiliate myself and beg Alvin to let me go back to work." It seemed, she said, a long, long time ago. The years of the decade of the 1970s seemed to be flying past at a faster rate than those of the 1960s. Time had "telescoped" so that when she looked back at just a few years ago pictures of incidents blurred in her mind. She had been working so industriously that there had been no time to recount, to remember. She was grateful for that time in the Grinzingerberg. It had given her a respite and a chance to "analyze" herself. Jamison, who tried hard to keep a balance between *dancing* and *living,* now divided her career into two phases: *before* and *after Cry.*

TWENTY-ONE

As *Cry* changed the public view of Jamison, so its success altered some aspects of her life. Despite having worked since 1965 in professional theatre, she was still naïve enough to be surprised and hurt by enmity. She was shocked by the implication of disloyalty to Ailey when she received the Dance Magazine Award in 1972, before the award had been given to Alvin Ailey. His friends were angry at what they took as a deliberate slight. One of them protested to an editor of *Dance Magazine* against giving the award to Jamison, on the theory that it would be humiliating to Ailey and the Ailey company.

Jamison stoutly resisted the imputation that she was made recipient of the award solely for *Cry*. She believed that any distinction she may have earned had come to her for her six years of work as the dancer. She feared that she would be haltered to *Cry* for the rest of her career, typecast as Ailey's great earth mother. Yet she failed, for the first time, to satisfy Ailey, in the next work he choreographed for her: *The Lark Ascending*. Set to the famous composition by Ralph Vaughan Williams, this was an important departure from "black" dance for Ailey. Jamison danced the lead at the premiere, in the Ailey's third consecutive season for that year, at the New York City Center, April 18–30, 1972, when the company had just reached a new peak of popularity. Sara Yarborough, following Jamison into the lead of *Lark,* eclipsed her. (Yarborough was soon to leave Ailey, to join the Joffrey Ballet in 1975.)

There was no rift in the relationship between Jamison and Ailey, only a widening gulf, but this gulf existed now between Ailey and all the dancers, within the enlarged Ailey organization. Ailey was launched on a quixotic mission: the preservation of all the major works from the beginning of American modern dance. Ailey revived Ted Shawn's *Kinetic Molpai* and other defunct works, and he again announced, but now with more authority, that he intended to make his company a repertory ensemble that would be the headquarters for contemporary dance in the United States, the year round. At the same time, he continued to encourage young choreographers by commissioning new works from them for the Ailey, not always with chief regard for the merit of the works but always with the intent to develop talented artists.

No other company director, black or white, had done, or showed any inclination of desiring to do, as much as Ailey did, in these conjoined efforts, to preserve and develop American dance. His friends worried that he was expending too much time and energy on these projects and too little on his own work. The business administrators of the Ailey organization were dubious about making money from the revival of old works. They would have preferred Ailey to choreograph new works, of the kind that would be big draws at the box office. Ailey, since the institution of a board of trustees for the company, was under increasing pressures. The administrators of the company would have liked it to become self-supporting. The critics, meanwhile, carped that the company had begun to sacrifice aesthetics to commercialism. (The preponderance of dances set to "pop" music was cited as the Ailey company's failure to maintain its artistic standards, which were thought to be deteriorating because of the company's popularity with the audience en masse, as opposed to the "dance audience"). Jamison perceived that Ailey was under a great many pressures and that one was the nagging inquiry as to whether or when he would do another work for her of the substance of *Cry*. She believed that when she went into a studio where Ailey was working with other dancers, he made excuses to stop what he was doing. She was careful not to embarrass him with a loitering presence and she felt lonelier than she had been since leaving Philadelphia. She requested and was granted a year's leave of absence.

Jamison and Miguel Godreau lived together in New York. Their relationship was broken off when Godreau left the Ailey and went to Europe, where he became a member of the Swedish Birgit Cullberg company. He also danced in revues and on television and gained an estimable reputation in England and Europe. When he and Jamison resumed their relationship he told her that he was buying a London flat and forming a company. To the consternation of their friends, they were married in 1972, in a civil ceremony in Stockholm.

Marriage made no perceptible change in Jamison's life, not as much, she was to remark, as buying a dog. She acquired a Great

Dane, Emma, to whom she became devoted. For Emma, she scrupu-
lously adhered to a schedule when she was in New York, putting
Emma's needs and Emma's pleasures ahead of everything except rehearsal and performing. When she went abroad, she eagerly awaited
the reunion with Emma. She went on tour with the Ailey company,
leaving Emma and all her household goods in the care of her husband. On her return, her year's leave would commence, allowing her
to work with Godreau in Europe, to assist him in launching a
troupe.

Jamison recalls that on tour she had difficulty reaching Godreau
by telephone and that, at times, she did not know whether he had
returned to London or had stayed in New York—a matter of concern to her, as it affected Emma's welfare. When the Ailey returned
to New York, Jamison was relieved to be met at the airport by
Godreau. He airily informed her that he was living on a friend's
boat, moored on the Hudson. Jamison was surprised and upset. Her
first queries were about Emma. Godreau assured her that Emma was
safe and sound at the apartment of a friend. As Jamison recollects
the episode, Godreau took her to the boat, where a party that had
been in process for several days continued that night, after which the
Godreaus left for Jacob's Pillow, in Lee, Massachusetts. Godreau
had accepted an engagement for them to perform at the annual
Jacob's Pillow Dance Festival.

Tired from the tour and, above all, angry over Godreau's haphaz-
ard domestic arrangements, Jamison was in a bad mood—the worst
of moods for her, one of simmering fury and frustration. She felt as
though she were walking on quicksand. Godreau told her that the
flat in London—toward the purchase of which Jamison had sent her
husband money—did not belong to him but to a friend. The
Godreau company, with which Jamison was to dance, had not materialized.

Jamison thought that Godreau was evasive in answering her questions, that he was less than truthful about the state of his affairs.
Later, she would admit that part of the clash between them came
from what Godreau may have perceived as an affront to his masculine authority. Jamison, by then, had grown accustomed to handling
her own money, to making decisions as they concerned her life. She
was not the adoring novice in love, as she had been in the early
stages of their relationship. Meanwhile, she had had love affairs, one

a torrid romance with a Swede whose passion for Jamison had been so intense that, ten years later, he blanched at the mention of her name.

At an earlier time, during her "fixation" with Godreau, he had been incapable of doing wrong in Jamison's eyes. She mourned his leaving the Ailey company, torn, as she described herself, between loyalty to Ailey and to Godreau. Knowing how greatly Ailey valued Godreau, she had thought that no effort should be spared to keep him in the company, however "difficult" he might be.

Now, in the unhappy reunion at Jacob's Pillow, Jamison looked at Godreau with new eyes. They were dancing together in *Prodigal Son*. Godreau appeared in his *Paz,* Jamison in a work called *Nubian Lady,* choreographed by John Parks, and with Parks in Lucas Hoving's *Icarus*. There was no pleasure for Jamison in the engagement. She brooded over her plight. Godreau seemed threatening to her peace of mind, inimical to her well-being. It frightened her to think of sharing the kind of life he seemed to wish to live, one that lacked the stability she needed.

One evening during a performance she felt ill. Later, she collapsed, regaining consciousness many hours after in her room, to which a friend had taken her. She was always to believe that she had been drugged, perhaps with LSD. Someone may have dosed her food or drink, as a bad joke, or even in mistaken charity, to "loosen up" the "uptight" person she was considered to be. Humiliated, and angrier than she had ever felt, she welcomed a quarrel with Godreau when he appeared. The row was shattering. Each of them uttered such wounding things as could never be forgiven and forgotten. Jamison left the Pillow and left Godreau. It was the end of the relationship, so much so that the annulment of their marriage—granted in Sweden in 1974—passed almost unremarked for Jamison.

Returning to New York, Jamison set about trying to retrieve her "nest," the physical things in which she set store—her tape recorders, phonograph, and television—and Emma. The stroke of good luck that came of this debacle was meeting the man with whom Emma had been lodged and boarded. He was Tom Yust, who was to become her close friend—the person most responsible for what Jamison thinks of as her "stability."

Yust had a big apartment on Riverside Drive and Jamison stayed there while she looked for a place of her own. "There were two

Toms at the apartment then—Tom Yust, who worked in the Bursar's Office at Columbia University, and Tom Hudspeth, who worked at the Whitney Museum. There was also a girl, Eileen, a college student, who had a dog too, a big Newfoundland named Panda. Emma and I were 'crashing,' but as time went by I stopped thinking about leaving. Emma and I just stayed. When Eileen and her dog left—as did Tom Hudspeth—there was just Tom, Emma, and me." It was an arrangement well suited to Jamison. She and Tom Yust liked and respected each other, each prized privacy and so never intruded on the other. And Jamison could be sure that, in her absence, Emma would be well cared for and well loved.

She had to work at repairing her career. It infuriated her to discover that someone had notified the press that she had left the Ailey company. The arrangement with Ailey had been that she would take a year off.

Jamison asked Ailey to put her back to work and she appeared with the company that season, dancing, among other roles, a leading one in *Carmina Burana*.

The work by John Butler, choreographed for a New York City Opera production in 1959, was well known in America, and in Europe, where Butler had since mounted it. It had been made as a film, within the setting of a ruined castle in Holland. On Butler's return from Europe he set *Carmina Burana* on the Pennsylvania Ballet (a classical company that was referred to as the "other" New York City Ballet) and on Alvin Ailey's company.

Carmina Burana was danced to a choir. The music was by Carl Orff, who based it on a sheaf of worldly Latin poems he had discovered in Bavaria, in a Benedictine monastery. Butler's ballet, in three parts as "Springtime," "In the Tavern," and "Court of Love," followed Orff's composition. *Carmina Burana* was more in a priapic than a conventionally churchly mode. The poems that inspired Orff were about monks and nuns who forswear their order to resume the naturalistic rounds of life, with its joys and sorrows. Butler's *Carmina Burana* is a faithful depiction of the exuberant musical theme and ranks among the great dance works of twentieth-century American theatre.

At the premiere the four principal roles were performed by Carmen de Lavallade and Veronika Mlakar, a Yugoslavian ballerina, and Scott Douglas and Glen Tetley. It was one work, said Jamison, in which she wished she could have danced in premiere.

Jamison believed that in *Carmina Burana* she danced one of her greatest roles and that, had it been created on her, it would have been of enormous significance to her career. She admired Butler's choreography so much that she hoped he would work with her.

Ailey was preoccupied by the music of Duke Ellington, the theme for his adolescence and his maturity. Working together on *The River,* the men became close friends and on the composer's death in 1974 Ailey seemed to become intent on immortalizing his friend as much through dance as he had been through music. Ailey was preparing a memorial program for Ellington, to be danced during the American Bicentennial year, and in autumn, 1975, he premiered *The Mooche,* with Jamison.

The Mooche was a spectacular jazz work, for which Jamison wore a brilliant scarlet gown glittering with sequins, and a headdress of fluffy red plumes. The dance had an electrifying effect. Instead of the matriarch of *Cry,* Jamison became the epitome of à glamorous entertainer, the sexiest black female dancer of the day. *The Mooche* altered the public conception of Jamison. She was asked to model couturier fashions. She was asked to do a Broadway show. It was suggested that she headline a Parisian revue, *à la* Josephine Baker.

The Alvin Ailey City Center Dance Theater opened a season at the New York State Theater on August 10, 1976, offering a week-long tribute to Duke Ellington, and on that evening Jamison appeared again in *The Mooche.* Before the performance, she was visited in her dressing room by Betty Ford, wife of the incumbent President of the United States, and after the evening's performance Mrs. Ford (wearing a "Chinese-style" pink dress) was photographed "dancing" with Judith Jamison in her red gown from *The Mooche.*

A month before, Jamison had been the guest star of American Ballet Theatre, partnered by Mikhail Baryshnikov in Ailey's *Pas de "Duke."* Featured in American Ballet Theatre's gala benefit program, it was the most sensational offering of the evening.

The dizzy progression that started with *The Mooche*—which led to *Pas de "Duke,"* which led to appearances in *Pas de "Duke"* and *Cry* at the Vienna Staatsoper—carried Jamison into *Josephslegende.*

She considered *Cry* and *Josephslegende* to be milestones in her career. Oddly, *Cry,* her first great success, closed a phase in that career, while it was from *The Mooche* that a new phase flowed, one she hurried home to start, after the filming of *Josephslegende.*

After considering several offers Jamison, through Szilard, accepted one, the lead in a Broadway musical to be called *The Only World in Town.* It was for this that Jamison obtained a leave of absence from Ailey in 1977. The leave was of indefinite duration, since it would not be until the Broadway opening that Jamison would know approximately how long she would stay with the show. At least a year was needed, for rehearsals, out-of-town openings, and the Broadway premiere—scheduled for early fall, 1978.

The choreographer of *The Only World in Town* was Billy Wilson, well respected on Broadway. He had choreographed and staged the musical numbers for *Bubbling Brown Sugar,* a nostalgic revival of dance and music from the era of Harlem night life made famous by Duke Ellington, Cab Calloway, Fats Waller, Eubie Blake, and their compeers. Calloway's music was the theme for *The Only World in Town* and, in the vogue for "black" musicals (*Sugar, The Wiz, etc.*), *The Only World in Town* was likely to have a success on Broadway.

Jamison's friends were thrilled at the thought of seeing her on Broadway, none more than her steady beau, Tom Ellis. Ellis, a singer and painter, had met Jamison when he was singing and she dancing in the Bernstein *Mass.* Their friendship had become a romantic attachment, one in which neither made demands on the other. Jamison enjoyed having the handsome, intelligent Ellis as her escort. They dined together at the White House and were seen at some other social functions, Jamison invariably wearing a black silk crepe dress with long sleeves, a high round neck, and a low scooped back. It had been made for her by a costumier in the Graham company and served her, for several years, as her social uniform.

She was wearing the black dress when she attended the sumptuous reception given for the Ailey company at the presidential palace in Manila, with as much pomp and circumstance as Buckingham Palace. She wore it on the evening of the reception given by the American Ambassador to Austria, when the Ailey company danced in Vienna—the memorable occasion on which the Ailey dancers, arriving at the American Embassy, were astounded to be each given a hot dog and a bun. (Szilard, not waiting to find out what brand of

American cola was being served as liquid refreshment, speedily took Jamison to dine at Vienna's celebrated Hotel Sacher.)

The black dress eventually wore out and Jamison discovered, when she was asked to present the Dance Magazine Award (in 1978) to Baryshnikov, that she had nothing suitable to wear. "I begged Mari [Kajiwara, Jamison's closest woman friend in the Ailey] to find me something. At three o'clock in the afternoon, Mari rushed to Hanae Mori [the Manhattan shop of the celebrated Japanese couturier designer] and bought me a dress . . ." Two hours later, Jamison appeared in the Hanae Mori creation, a printed silk chiffon in her favorite shade of orange, to face a battery of television cameras, news photographers, and journalists clamoring for interviews.

The pace of her life, throughout the second half of the decade, left Jamison little time to think about herself. Her time was spent more in the aspect of dancing than in the aspect of living. *Josephslegende* was an epochal event, and she so frequently appeared in it that she almost had "permanent guest artist" status at the Vienna Staatsoper. Other guest engagements were filled. Jamison danced for the annual Chicago dance festivals organized by Ruth Page. She went to Havana, to dance *Cry* at the Cuban dance festival organized by Alicia Alonso. And, to her great joy, Ailey commissioned a work for her from John Butler: *Facets*.

Facets, in which Jamison portrayed several different characters, was one of the rarest of theatrical creations: a one-woman show. Its demands of Jamison were different and in certain ways harder than any that had been made of her before. *Facets* is concerned with love, with women in love, and the manner in which women, according to their natures, respond to loving.

In *Facets,* Jamison, wearing only a slip, sits on the edge of a black steamer trunk, out of which she extricates items of clothing. With every costume change she assumes the character of the woman she is portraying, to the accompaniment of appropriate songs by Bessie Smith, Ethel Waters, Dinah Washington, Lena Horne, and La Belle, five famous black female entertainers.

The range is from pathos to bathos. Jamison is melancholy as the woman who has loved and lost her man; she is a raunchy, hard-boiled dame, who having loved and lost is going to live for sure, and *maybe* love again. Her capacity as a tragic dancer had already been proved in *Cry,* but in *Facets* Jamison revealed unexpected gifts as a comedienne. Dance critics praised *Facets* as a tour de force by Jamison but disparaged the choreography. Butler's work was considered little more than a vehicle for a great performer. The adverse criticism of Butler distressed and irritated Jamison.

"That's much the same sort of criticism that was given to Alvin and *Mooche.* I feel that *Mooche* and *Facets* are works of a special kind and that each is perfect of its kind. Critics would like only to see masterpieces. Dancers love dancing in masterpieces but, realistically, we know that all works are not masterpieces.

"I passionately respect a man's craft. I passionately respect the work the choreographer does. Dancers are starved for new works. We need them to challenge us, we need them like other people need food to grow on. I would hate to see choreographers—especially young choreographers—get too scared to produce anything except masterpieces. In America we have the freedom to dance in every way we choose. That is what gives American dance its excitement for audiences in Europe, Asia, and Africa. You need to go around the world to know the effects of American dancers on audiences.

"I love *The Mooche* because Alvin made it for me and because it gave me the chance to show another side of me than the side in *Cry.* I love *Facets* because John made it for me and because it has given me a truly great opportunity to show that I have qualities as a dramatic dancer.

"I feel that it is wrong to call *Facets* a 'slight' work. *Facets* is one of the most difficult things I dance. I cannot relax my concentration for one moment in the solo. In *Facets* you don't rely on muscle memory as you sometimes can in other kinds of dancing. In *Caravan* [a work choreographed by Louis Falco for the Ailey and performed by a group of dancers] I often find myself just listening to the music and letting myself go; it's a dance orgy. Critics may not like *Facets* but I notice that audiences love *Facets* when I dance it— maybe because in every audience there will always be women who know something about the facets of loving. Of being a woman, and loving a man."

Jamison danced *Facets* in its premiere during the spring 1977 season at New York City Center. The ballet was again in the programming for the fall season of the Alvin Ailey American Dance Theater. Thereafter, the even tenor of Jamison's career altered.

She suffered two keen disappointments. After only two rehearsals, *The Only World in Town* was aborted. Its backers were unable to obtain sufficient funds to get the show onstage. And though UNI-TEL's film of American Ballet Theatre's *Giselle* had been seen in America, no representative was found for the release of *Josephs-legende* in the United States and Canada.

The film was widely circulated in Europe, where it was televised, bringing to Jamison and Haigen further accolades for their performances as Potiphar's Wife and Joseph. Jamison assumed an incomparably romantic image, as the black Venus of twentieth-century ballet. Suggestions were made for other works for her, one as a ballet about Dido, queen of Carthage, who died for love of Aeneas of Troy. Nureyev, no less, was thought to be the perfect Aeneas to Jamison's Dido. Nothing came of that idea, but Maurice Béjart invited Jamison to dance as guest artist with his company, the Brussels-based Ballet of the 20th Century, the most popular ballet company on the Continent.

There were persistent rumors that Neumeier would be invited to bring his Hamburg Ballet to the Metropolitan Opera House in New York and the Kennedy Center in Washington, and, perhaps, take it on a tour of the United States. In that event, as Jamison thought, *Josephslegende* would be included in the repertoire and she would be seen by her American public in the ballet. The Hamburg Ballet did not come to America. Jamison felt she was blighted by bad luck.

She was still heartsore over the theft of her beloved dog, the Great Dane Emma. In New York they had been inseparable. Emma was a beast of immense sagacity, with an almost human nature. Jamison declared that Emma did not know she was a dog but believed she was a girl. Jamison had owned her from a pup, had nursed her through an illness so grave that a veterinarian had advised she be put to sleep, and had watched her grow into maturity, weighing one hundred and fifty pounds, standing as tall as Jamison's thigh.

Jamison and Emma played together in the park and went on long walks. Emma lay quietly in the studio during rehearsals and stayed in the dressing rooms of the theatres where Jamison performed. She had a remarkable aplomb in public, though she was clownish when she played with Jamison. Jamison swore that Emma had a sense of humor. People gazed at them in wonder, that a woman and a dog could look so absurdly like human and canine manifestations of each other, the woman and the dog each tall, slender, and elegant.

One morning, coming home after a walk, Jamison stopped at the neighborhood grocery store and, as usual, tied Emma's leash to a parking meter outside the shop. Less than ten minutes later, when she came out, Emma had gone, her leash untied by someone who had presumably stolen her. Jamison was distraught, blaming herself for having trained Emma to be too friendly and biddable, too fond of people. New York newspapers sympathetically printed news of Jamison's loss. She appealed on radio and television for the return of Emma, but she never saw Emma again. She could only hope that the dog was well cared for and loved but she feared that, from their close attachment, Emma might pine and sicken. Jamison would not buy another dog and she refused to accept a pet from friends. To try to replace Emma would be fickle. "I grieved for Emma as I knew Emma, if she was still alive, was grieving for me."

Emma had not been merely a pet. Jamison had made her a companion, as close and dear as a mute human friend.

"Emma was my child," said Jamison. "Other people fed her and cared for her when I was away, but Emma knew that she had a one-to-one relationship with me, that I was her mother. I loved Emma because she loved me. And I loved her because, in all New York, Emma was the one creature who needed me. I learned from Emma that *for me* "love" is not only needing someone, it's being needed. I learned from an animal, not from a man, one of the most important things I know about myself."

Jamison found a new interest and activity, in an off-Broadway project. She was curious about the innovative and unconventional theories of "experimental theatre." Jamison's friends were at first cool to the idea of her working in an amateur project and they later bitterly resented the claims it made on her, and her willingness to be treated as a novice. Jamison insisted that it was good for her to be "starting over" at something strange and new. She was cast as Juliet II to Juliet I in a version of *Romeo and Juliet* and, while her friends suffered because she was in a minor role, Jamison announced that she was thrilled to be Juliet's psyche because she "got to know what Juliet was thinking" (while Juliet I performed the acting part). She recalled that she had intended majoring in psychology at Fisk University before she gave up thoughts of a college education. She declared she loved being involved in what she was doing. While she pursued her interest in experimental theatre, Jamison frequently described herself as "involved" and "committed." She was absorbed to an almost fanatical degree in the off-Broadway project, while waiting to begin work in *The Only World in Town*. For the better part of twelve months, Jamison was contracturally bound to the projected Broadway musical that never materialized. She and Szilard were assured that the show was only temporarily postponed and accordingly Jamison took no engagements, and continued working hard, on voice lessons with a teacher named Paul Gavett and on dance routines with another teacher, Chip Garrette. It was only when Szilard lost patience and forced an admission from the show's organizers that they were unable to raise the necessary funds that Jamison freed herself from the ill-fated *The Only Show in Town*.

The financial loss was not small, but even worse was the drain on Jamison's spirits. She was so unused to inactivity, so accustomed to a strict and cramped schedule of work, that she felt lost, almost disoriented. This time she could not go back and ask the Ailey company to cancel her leave of absence. The company, although still headed by Alvin Ailey, had become a large organization, under an administration. It was no longer a cosy and warm group of dancers with easy access to their director but a businesslike organization that budgeted and programmed its work a year and more in advance of performing and touring schedules. At loose ends, for the first time in almost ten years, Judith Jamison turned to the off-Broadway project in the belief that its techniques would enlarge and educate her for a different kind of theatre. *Facets* had encouraged her in a long-held desire to act. Despite the fiasco of *The Only World in Town,* she still hoped to do a Broadway show, but she was deflected from this —and her voice and dance routine studies—by a more "serious" involvement in experimental theatre.

The involvement for Jamison was more than professional. She affiliated herself with a group of amateur actors who worked in a studio, converted from an old radio station, on West Forty-fifth Street and fell in love with the group's director, a personable young American Jew. Jamison's love was mingled with hero worship, in an impulsive, headlong emotion that, however seemingly paradoxical to her public image, was actually characteristic of her nature.

She behaved like a newly initiated novice toward a new religion, prepared to sacrifice herself, and all her worldly goods, to her commitment. Szilard was instructed to accept only the guest engagements contingent on her commitment to the Forty-fifth Street theatre group. She kept her contractural obligations with the Ailey company and for *Josephslegende,* but she temporarily ceased to desire the new challenges she so much loved to set herself. While her passion lasted, for experimental theatre and for the off-Broadway project's director, Jamison was impervious to all except her rite of passage. Like the characters of Butler's *Facets* she was learning what it was to be a woman, and a woman in love.

TWENTY-TWO

Sara Yarborough returned to the Ailey and, at once, again imprinted her delicate personality on the company. She was to Alvin Ailey a perpetual and poetic source of inspiration, like that of Suzanne Farrell for George Balanchine.[1] Yarborough's image all but eclipsed that of Carmen de Lavallade for Ailey. Yarborough was cast in the title role of *Portrait of Billie*—which de Lavallade had created—Butler's poignant ballet about the vulnerability of the female performer, equally to love and to success. The rise and fall of Billie Holiday in Butler's ballet could be taken as a warning for the black woman in theatre.

But Yarborough's great role in the Ailey company's repertoire was in *The Lark Ascending,* a work of particular significance to the choreographer. Inspired by the music he heard, during the company's 1968 engagement at the Edinburgh Festival, Ailey had choreographed a work to Ralph Vaughan Williams' violin romanza. *Lark* took Ailey outside the "black experience" as choreographer and it symbolized his feelings about growth and the revelations of the development of the Self, phase by phase. Williams' elegiac music and

[1] Suzanne Farrell, born a year after Jamison, came to New York from Cincinnati to the School of American Ballet on a Ford Foundation scholarship. She joined the New York City Ballet in 1961 and was made a soloist in 1965. By 1969, when she left the company, she was its reigning ballerina—a fact made more remarkable because it occurred in a company that had eschewed the star system. In 1968–69, of the forty-one ballets in seasonal repertoire for N.Y.C.B., Farrell was cast in principal roles of more than half. Balanchine choreographed a number of roles for Farrell, and in an amazing range, from his grand passion play, *Don Quixote* (in which he sometimes took the title role) into *Slaughter on Tenth Avenue,* a reprise of a Broadway show piece, composed for Farrell and Arthur Mitchell in 1968. In the first half of the seventies, Farrell danced with the Ballet of the 20th Century, in Europe and America, and Maurice Béjart choreographed several roles for her, some in large works like his *Nijinsky, Clown of God.* Farrell returned to the New York City Ballet in 1975, where she has since created roles in works choreographed by Balanchine and Robbins.

Yarborough's lyricism perfectly complemented the choreography of Ailey's *Lark*. Of Yarborough in the work, Ailey said it was dancing as close as humanly possible to flight. Complimented on the loveliness of the dancing, Ailey replied: *"Lark* is not Alvin Ailey. It is Sara Yarborough."

Other young dancers were coming to the fore in the company. Two were Sarita Allen and Donna Wood. Wood alternated with Yarborough in *Cry* and in *Lark* and though she was overshadowed there by Jamison and by Yarborough, Wood's own image was secure.

Gifted with the mulatta's lovely coloring, Donna Wood had, besides, exquisitely modeled features and enormous, doelike eyes. She was exceptionally accomplished, trained in classical dance from early childhood in Dayton, Ohio. At the age of twelve she started performing with the Dayton Ballet so that, despite her youth, she already had stage presence, and considerable panache, when she came to New York in 1972. Greatly impressed, Ailey took her into the company where, like the gazelle to whom she was poetically likened, Wood blithely leaped into leading roles.

Wood, though unlike Jamison in physique and temperament, was highly praised by her. It was Wood who substituted for Jamison as Potiphar's Wife in *Josephslegende,* at the Vienna Staatsoper and in the Hamburg Ballet, when Jamison, because of an injury, could not dance her role.

Jamison also took an interest in Sarita Allen, a former scholarship student of the Dance Theatre of Harlem's school and of Ailey's American Dance Center, who, after serving an apprenticeship in the Ailey's Repertory Ensemble, entered the senior company in 1975. Yet another dancer favored by Jamison was Ulysses Dove, who had joined the Ailey in 1973. Dove came late and abruptly to dancing. He was a premed student at Howard University in South Carolina when, on impulse, he auditioned at the dance department of the University of Washington and was taken on scholarship. He completed his studies at Bennington College, graduating from that school in 1970.

Coming to New York the same year, Dove joined the Merce Cunningham company and also danced in companies led by Pearl Lang and Mary Anthony. After joining the Ailey company he made his choreographic debut with a work for the Repertory Ensemble, one of two junior companies drawn out of the Ailey school.

Jamison marveled that Dove had been able to combine a university education with a dance career. It had been untenable for her. Her ambitions were now focused on her nephew, her brother's son John Charles. She insisted that the boy be sent to a first-rate college preparatory school, for which she paid the fees. She and Johnnie had disappointed their parents in failing to pursue their own university educations. John Charles would be educated for one of the professions.

Jamison left off wearing turbans. Her hair was cropped short and, later, worn in a "corn row" coiffure. In her pierced ears twinkled diamond studs. She was eager for new challenges. She wanted more than anything else to develop her instincts for drama.

Ailey, for long obsessed by the music of Duke Ellington, and more so than ever after the composer's death, turned to another composer, Hale Smith, for the score of a new work for Jamison. Ailey used Smith's *Rituals and Incantations* for *Passage,* a work inspired by the legend of Marie Laveau, high priestess of the *voudon* religion in New Orleans in the nineteenth century.

Passage was a long solo, performed on a series of platforms. Jamison appeared to be dancing on a steeply raked stage but she in fact maintained a perilous equilibrium by the tilt of her body. The solo explored her grand extensions and superb line, though not in the conventions of lyricism. Jamison in *Passage* radiated primal force. It was paramountly a feminine force, that of the mythical sorceress, of whom Marie Laveau—described as "the most powerful voodoo queen in the history of the United States"—was a prototype. Laveau had not been a secluded *réligieuse* of the old African rites. "Beyond her role as a priestess," read the program note of *Passage,* "her influences extended deeply into the social and political fabric of 19th-century New Orleans."

Ailey, the Southern Baptist, was, it seemed, bent on exploring the black American piety whose roots had been transplanted to Protestant America. Ailey's "voodoo" *oeuvre,* begun in *Macumba-Yemanja,* although not fully shaped, was a significant aspect of his work, but it was unremarked by American dance critics—on whom *Passage* failed to make much of an impression. Ailey, for his part, classed *Passage* with his other works that were "about transitions."

"Passage," he said, "depicts a woman passing through stages. It's a ballet about transition just as *Lark* is . . . I made *Lark* for Judi but she did not give me what I wanted. Judi was too ethereal, too obedient to the choreography. She was not vulnerable enough. I got what I wanted for *Lark* from Sara, the essence of girl turning into woman. When Judi saw Sara dance *Lark* she told me she would never do it again. *Lark* became Sara's ballet, as *Cry* and *Passage* are Judi's.

"Judith Jamison is a terribly powerful dancer, a terribly powerful personality. She challenges and in a way she intimidates the choreographer. Judith is in size, in type, in technique an *extra*-ordinary dancer. There can be no choreographic clichés in a work for Judith. She becomes the woman in *Cry,* she becomes the woman in *Passage,* by absorbing the choreography, and then she gives her own substance to the dancing.

"I made *Passage* for Judith because she is a dancer of mythical nature. Onstage, it does not take much imagination to picture her dancing in a sacred place. Part of the effect comes from Judith as the person, part from the intensity, the dynamism of her approach to dancing. Judith is a modern woman but she understands ritual, she understands the piety of incantations. In religious societies, all rites of passage are performed to incantation, and with dance."

Ailey's idea of "transitions" was not only of palpable physical development but as those transfigurations that come about through revelatory experiences. Drawn to the mystical and the oracular, Ailey returned time and again to those founts. Sometimes, he sought them in the feminine. Before *Cry*, before *Passage,* Ailey, in 1971, choreographed *Myth,* a work about a woman's exploration of love with three male lovers. Set to Stravinsky's *Symphonies of Wind Instruments* (dedicated, by the composer, as an "austere ritual," to the memory of Debussy), *Myth* was disparaged by New York dance reviewers as a paltry imitation of Graham.

Ailey thought the accusation unjustified, despite the fact that Graham had choreographed an *oeuvre* based on mythology. Myth and allegory, said Ailey, were broad, deep, and universal sources of inspiration for artistic imagery. African religion and folklore were of a greater complexity, he believed, than those of Graeco-Roman legends. Yemanja, the black Aphrodite, was by nature a composite of several goddesses, among them the mother-goddess of the Sumerians, Astarte. Ailey, deeply conscious of his own mythology as a black American, was interested in probing myth for its contemporary validity, its psychological truths. In 1978 he commissioned a work, *Medusa,* that was set on ten dancers, with Jamison in the title role.

The choreographer, Margo Sappington, proposed to use the myth of the Gorgon in a contemporary sense: "The Medusa legend also represents man's paralysis at looking into the face of horrifying realities."

Jamison was elated at having a new work and she was intrigued by the subject of Sappington's ballet. Medusa is one of the most fearfully fascinating females in history.

She was, it is said, a beautiful woman, so beautiful that, in her contumacious vanity, she dared to compare her beauty with that of the goddess Pallas Athene. For committing *hubris,* the cardinal sin of the Greeks, a dreadful punishment was meted out to Medusa. Although she retained her female form, she was changed into a monster, with a countenance so terrible that all who looked upon it were turned to stone. Her long golden hair was transformed into writhing serpents. In this terrifying guise, the Gorgon ravaged the countryside. All about her lair lay stone effigies of brave men who had lost their lives in attempts to slay the Gorgon.

Perseus, the son of Zeus and Danäe, was chosen to perform the heroic deed. Wearing the winged sandals of Hermes, messenger of the gods, and protected by the great shield of Pallas Athene, he flew to the cavern where the Gorgon lurked. Pallas Athene warned the hero to look not on the Gorgon's living face but at its reflection in the polished shield, where the Gorgon's image appeared as in a mirror. Thus Perseus slew the Gorgon, presenting her head to Pallas Athene, who fixed the fearsome visage in the center of her shield.

Medusa was scheduled for the autumn season at the New York City Center.

In the summer of that year Ailey took the company—for the first time in fifteen years—on a tour of Latin America. It was a triumphal progress, through the major South American metropolitan theatres. The company was "ecstatically" received in Rio de Janeiro, a reception the more notable for being given in a municipal theatre of conservative tastes. The Ailey opened the music festival of São Paulo, Brazil's major industrial city, to audiences "delirious with joy." A troupe from Moscow's mighty Bolshoi Ballet, led by the prima ballerina Maya Plisetskaya, also appeared in São Paulo, but to far less acclaim than the Ailey company. Brazilian balleto-manes—who paid scalpers the equivalent of $200 U.S. for a theatre ticket in São Paulo—declared that Alvin Ailey alone had shown them creativity in dance.

On the company's return from South America it was recipient of a matching grant of $175,000 from the National Endowment for the Arts. The board of directors of the Alvin Ailey American Dance Theater had been negotiating for the lease of New York University's Town Hall and it was hoped that the company would soon be housed in its own building. Ailey's chief interest, at the moment, was in organizing a gala program with which to mark the company's twentieth anniversary.

He gathered into the "new" Ailey company many members from the "old" Ailey, for a four-hour-long program staged at the New York City Center on November 26. Among the distinguished guests were Carmen de Lavallade and James Truitte. Others included Hope Clarke and Altovise Gore (Mrs. Sammy Davis, Jr.), George Faison, William Louther, Hector Mercado, John Parks, and Kelvin Rotardier. Miguel Godreau danced a portion of his *Paz,* to tumultu-ous applause. The sensation of the evening was the appearance of Alvin Ailey, dancing with Hope Clarke in the "Backwater Blues" of *Blues Suite.* He had subjected himself to a rigorous regimen in order to reduce his weight, and it was as "a lean and chiseled" Ailey that he appeared onstage, for the first time in thirteen years, to perform again as a dancer.

To those who had known him in his beauty and pristine force, it was an uncanny sensation to see Ailey dancing again. But Ailey did not organize the gala program out of sentiment, or to satisfy a narcissistic urge. His purpose was to reaffirm the truest nature of the Ailey company, to restate the principles on which it had been founded.

Ailey's philosophy was obscure to a new generation of dancers and critics. When Ailey spoke, as he often did, of the "spirit" of his work, of the content and meaning of the Ailey repertoire, he was thought of as a poseur by reviewers who had not seen the older rep-ertoire danced in premieres. Some of the critics who had observed the Ailey company for two decades liked to comment on the changes a new generation of dancers had brought about in the company, through superior technique. The 20th Anniversary Gala program, for which the "old" and the "new" Ailey dancers performed, should have enlightened a great many people, on both sides of the proscenium, on the natures, past and present, of the Ailey company.

For it was not as stately veterans that the "old" Ailey dancers returned, in the gala program, but as artists of vibrant and articulate communication, many of them possessed of awesome presence. The program was "gala" in the truest sense, as a festive and celebratory occasion. Thematically, the program spanned the company's repertoire, yet Ailey dedicated it not to his company but to three pioneers of black dance, all women: Katherine Dunham, Pearl Primus, and Beryl McBurnie.

Ailey was persisting in his intent to preserve what he considered to be the heritage of black dancers and of modern dancers in America. He had before this taken works into the repertoire by Primus, and by other choreographers from the beginning phases of black and modern dance. Sometimes he dedicated whole seasons, as well as individual programs, as tributes to these older artists. At the 20th Anniversary Gala a friend of Ailey's remarked: "Alvin is still paying his dues."

The evening ended with *Revelations,* the opening portion of which was performed by the "old" Ailey, the closing section by the "new." Jamison, who appeared in a part of *Cry,* said of the anniversary program: "I only hope that the young dancers realized what they were seeing. I only hope they took in everything that was there for them to learn . . . that dancing is more than steps and jumps and turns, that it is this sort of human communication. I hope that the audience, and the critics, understood what this company has done, what it stands for, what the Ailey is all about. It was there, in the beauty, the truth, and the exquisite dancing of Jimmy [Truitte] in the role he created in 'Fix Me, Jesus.' I stood in awe, to watch Dudley [Williams] in 'I Want to Be Ready.' And to see Carmen in *Billie* is to know *the* definitive interpretation of that role, of what it means to be a woman like Billie Holiday.

"It was a wonderful experience for me. Looking at Miguel [Godreau also danced in *Blues Suite* that evening] brought back the old days and the feeling I had about him as a burning dancer. There is no personal involvement anymore so I can look at him with a pure sense of his dancing, and see that it is unique.

"When I saw Carmen, it was a thrill for me to remember, away back in *The Four Marys,* that I had realized *then* she was a great dancer—long before I knew enough to tell what greatness is . . .

"All the dancers were real in those days; there were no plastic dancers then. They did not come off the studio assembly line. You will notice that every one of these dancers is an individual, no two of them alike—no duplicates of de Lavallade or of Godreau.

"Someone asked me what I preferred to be, an 'artist' or a 'personality.' But it's the *personality* in the performer that makes the artist, the unique artist."

Jamison was in rehearsal for Sappington's *Medusa,* in which Clive Thompson was cast as Perseus, Dudley Williams as Hermes, Mari Kajiwara as Athena. Other dancers were Sarita Allen, Ronni Favors, Marilyn Banks, Ulysses Dove, and Michiko Oka, with Alistair Butler in a minor role. Butler, a tall, handsome young dancer, had been taken into the company a year earlier, from the Ailey Repertory Ensemble. He was a native of the Bahamas who had begun dancing in Nassau. In New York he had performed with the company of Eleo Pomare. Jamison was watchful of Butler's progress; she thought they might develop a good partnership.

One of the pleasures in working in *Medusa* was that she was working within a group. Preeminently a soloist, she had been established in an isolated sphere in her career. Yet she had always enjoyed dancing with a partner and in the early days had hoped that she and Truitte would develop a valid partnership, in and out of the Ailey company.

Her height had seemed a handicap. There were few tall male dancers, in her technical class, by whom she could be partnered. She believed that her reputation as a "powerful" dancer precluded choreographers from working with her in other than solo forms, and that her soloist status had gradually but surely deprived her of a romantic repertoire. *Medusa,* she thought, would provide a new intimacy for her with partners. She danced first with Butler and then with Thompson as mortal and supernormal manifestations of the Gorgon. Jamison joked about the nature of Medusa in Sappington's ballet. It was that of a nymphomaniac. This Medusa would seduce her lovers before she destroyed them.

Jamison worked with Sappington as she worked with every chore-ographer: "I never think analytically: is the work going to be good or bad? I just give myself up to trying to bring the choreographer's ideas to reality. My contribution is myself, how I dance, how I feel when I am dancing."

Margo Sappington had danced with the Joffrey Ballet and in mu-sicals. Her earliest choreography had been for a nude pas de deux in the notorious *Oh! Calcutta!,* the show whose success advanced the genre of pornographic art in American theatre. Sappington had later made ballets for the Joffrey and Harkness companies, in more tradi-tional style, and, most recently, had choreographed a well-received work—a tribute to Alexander Calder—for the Pennsylvania Ballet. Ailey treated his guest choreographers with deference; indeed, he showed them the tenderest concern. Sappington was allowed a free hand for *Medusa.* A score was commissioned from Michael Kamen; costumes from Willa Kim, one of the foremost theatrical designers in New York.

Medusa was scheduled for its premiere in advance of another work by another "young" choreographer, Gene Hill Sagan. Sagan produced *Sunrise . . . Sunset* in Jerusalem in 1977 and now re-mounted it on the Ailey. Sagan, from Philadelphia, had danced with a black company, Ballet Americana. For the past ten years, he had lived in Israel.

Sarita Allen, Donna Wood, and Ulysses Dove were cast in princi-pal roles in Sagan's ballet which, like Sappington's *Medusa,* consti-tuted a large work for the Ailey. The two works were in dramatic contrast. Sagan's was almost ritualistically patterned and heavily symbolic, making use of a glowing chalice and lighted candle. Allen, Wood, and Dove, in turn, assumed the figure of the transmogrified Christ.

Medusa was contemporary. Other than the identifications of the leading characters, and the reference to the myth of the Gorgon and Perseus, there was no attempt to relate the work to a literary source. Kamen's composition could have served for disco dancing. Kim's costumes were minimal, and characterless, though somewhat pseudo-Grecian.

Sunrise . . . Sunset, to the austerity of *Cantus planus* (plainsong) and in the solemnity of its movement, as compared to *Medusa* with its pop music score—and Jamison in the title role—would attract widely dissimilar coteries of dance fans. The odds were that Sappington's ballet would be a big box office draw for the New York audience.

This audience, the "regular" attendants on the Ailey seasons, keenly anticipated *Medusa* as a new Jamison work. While New York critics remarked that Jamison's appearances were becoming fewer, public demand of the Ailey box office for Jamison increased. Despite the several rising stars of the "new" Ailey, Jamison remained the superstar. Reviewers who had previously disparaged her dancing, and had fretted at the enthusiasm of audiences for whatever Jamison danced, had now fallen into the habit of referring to Jamison as "Ailey's enduring star." Jamison had received reviews that excessively praised her and reviews that attempted to belittle her. There was hardly a word left in the language by which a reviewer could advance or diminish her reputation.

Jamison still found it gratifying to read perceptive reviews, "good or bad," as they applied to her work, "because you can often learn something from an intelligent piece of criticism." But her responsibility, as she felt it, was not to please the press when she danced. She was responsible first to the choreographer and then to the audience with whom she had to communicate. If she moved the audience to responses, if she was able to "touch a nerve, to establish rapport between the audience and my dancing" then that constituted, for Jamison, "a sort of success." "I don't need a reviewer to tell me how I dance at a performance. When I dance badly *I* know it, before anyone else does. And criticism of the performer is made performance by performance while, for the performer, it is the total of many performances in a work that gives you a basis for analyzing and evaluating yourself."

The audience, Jamison's prime arbiter, was in a state of pleasurable expectancy at the New York City Center on the evening of December 1, 1978. It became witness to an artistic disaster.

It was Sappington's intent to use the Gorgon as the symbolic seductress, whose allurement of men is ultimately destructive. Perseus, and another nameless young lover, would fall prey to Medusa, symbolizing contemporary man's incapability to face horrifying reality.

Sappington might have achieved her purpose in this work without dependence on a literary source but, having identified her work with one, and one so universally known as the legend of the Gorgon, her crucial error was to tamper with it.

The nature of the legend is essentially heroic, but it was Sappington's whim to make it paltry. In Sappington's ballet Athena, Zeus's noble "gray-eyed" warrior daughter—the most austere of the goddesses—became a petulant woman, jealous of Medusa, whom she feared to be more beautiful. To eliminate her rival, Sappington's Athena enlisted the aid of a doltish Perseus, who was sent to slay the Gorgon, but with the intention that *he,* after being seduced by Medusa, would also be killed.

Dramatically as well as choreographically Sappington's *Medusa* was a debacle. In the theatre Kamen's music sounded banal. Kim's skimpy costumes were absurd and one worn by Clive Thompson was an affront to the dancer's dignity. The focus of the ballet was on Medusa's seductive powers, corruption by allurement, destruction through orgasm. Jamison, as Medusa, would become the fascinating and repellent Gorgon, whose embrace meant death.

Jamison's Medusa, in her "mortal" phase, summarily dispatched the first suitor (Butler) but spent a longer time (dancing a solo) in the seduction of Perseus (Thompson). Sappington's sources for these two seductions may have been Jerome Robbins' *The Cage* and Robert Joffrey's *Astarte,* two ballets on the theme of the omnivorous nature of feminine love.

In the first "mortal" phase Jamison wore a wig and a "Grecian" headband but when she reappeared in her "Gorgon" identity the audience quailed, not in terror of Jamison's Medusa but in embarrassment for the dancer. Kim gave her a headdress of streamers, to simulate Medusa's writhing serpents. Sappington required Jamison to imitate a snake, by thrusting her tongue out as far as it could go, then withdrawing it, and repeating these motions rapidly, like those made by the flickering tongue of a cobra.

The sigh breathed at the finale, when the simulated beheading brought the ballet to its close, must have been one of relief.

With commendable fortitude, the Ailey company performed *Medusa* as scheduled throughout the season. Jamison waited until it ended before she spoke of the debacle. "Everyone connected with *Medusa* worked hard to make it a success. No one works to make a failure. If we knew what would fail, we would know what would succeed and then we would only have successful ballets. What you think is happening in the studio does not always happen onstage. *Medusa* is not a success and I'm sad about that. But Margo is tough, she'll survive. And so will the Ailey."

Athena was not lightly mocked. Lèse majesté had been committed against the gray-eyed goddess, though the ballet was referred to as "Medusa's curse." Jamison, for all the calm with which she accepted failure, would have preferred to have appeared in a successful work.

The Ailey company did not have to end the season (November 29–December 16, 1978) with a fiasco. Sagan's *Sunrise . . . Sunset* had an unexpected success. Critics may have praised it the more after having endured poor *Medusa*.

All told, it had been a good year for the Ailey, considering its wavering fortunes earlier in the decade and Alvin Ailey's despondency of just a year before. As the new decade approached, prospects had never seemed brighter. Ailey, since the Anniversary Gala, had been almost euphoric. On November 12 he had again been asked to bring his company to the White House, this time to perform at the reception given by President and Mrs. Jimmy Carter in honor of the King of Morocco, Hassan II. The king had warmly commended the dancers and had begged Ailey to bring them to Rabat, to dance at a private party in the palace on New Year's Eve. When the New York season was done, Ailey and twenty-five of his dancers flew to Rabat, to dance for the King of Morocco.

Portents were not propitious for Judith Jamison that New Year's Eve. She had by then realized how wearisome it was for her to work with amateurs, in mediocre plays. She had tired, too, of the self-indulgence of experimental theatre. Freedom, carried to license, became pretentious. She turned back, gratefully, to the discipline of the dance studio.

There was yet another severance for head and heart. The love affair in which Jamison had invested so much faith and hope, so much hero worship, had gone sour. It would not last out the new year.

TWENTY-THREE

Into the end of 1978 Szilard was patiently and persistently trying to persuade Jamison to dance more often, in and outside the Ailey. She insisted that engagements could only be arranged with consideration of her work in the off-Broadway theatre. To Szilard, the scruple was ridiculous; he could not bring himself to treat the experimental project seriously. But Jamison was adamant about what she considered "an obligation," to a schedule of dates for which she was "committed" to the off-Broadway project.

For Szilard it was far more than a matter of agent's fees. He worried that Jamison, by a too prolonged absence from the legitimate theatre, would lose her popularity with the public. Shrewd impresario that he was, Szilard knew that the Ailey company, in New York and elsewhere, capitalized on Jamison as a box office draw. His ruse was to appeal to Jamison that she was needed by the company, "needed by Alvin"; the ruse never failed to work. Jamison pledged herself to a schedule of performances with the company for 1979, including the tours. Szilard reminded her of Ailey's solicitude, shown in the care he gave to her repertoire. Ailey was forever on the lookout for choreographers who might be engaged to do works for the company, featuring Jamison. Well, there had been *Medusa*. On the plus of the balance sheet was *Facets*. And, of course, Ailey's own *Passage*. Jamison knew how difficult it was to find new works to dance. On her own, she canvased likely and sometimes unlikely sources in attempts to stimulate choreographic inspiration.

She held to the belief that, whereas critics approved only of masterpieces, dancers needed new works, in continuing supply, even if the works were not always first-rate.

Jamison relished going into a new work, though it turned out to be a failure like *Medusa*. Without constant subjugation of the self to effort and trial, the dancer would cease to have a viable character. "I don't dance because it's an easy way of earning a living. Being a successful professional dancer does not mean that you are comfort-able and secure. It just means that you are required to test yourself more and more, to find out whether you have the capacity, the tech-nical skill, to meet all the challenges." Deprived of the discipline and the stimulus, Jamison thought that dancing would become something as simple "as basket-weaving."

Her irritation, her feeling of aimlessness, was caused by a growing apprehension concerning her private life. She would not yet admit to disenchantment in the off-Broadway project because to do so would wound her vanity. She had been too vehement in her defense of her work and her love affair to easily and quickly discard her "commit-ment." And how would she explain a change of heart to friends who had so strongly disapproved of her entanglement in experimental theatre, without herself appearing temperamental and fickle?

She acquired another dog, an Akita, a Japanese breed (the first of which was brought to the United States by Helen Keller). Keetah, as Jamison called her pet, was a beautiful animal, weighing eighty pounds, with a fluffy coat of silver-gray color—altogether unlike the Great Dane, Emma, who, as much as a dog could be said to resem-ble a woman, had been the canine replica of Judith Jamison.

Keetah did not replace Emma, said Jamison; no dog would ever do that. Keetah was an object of affection, a creature demanding at-tention and care, but Jamison did not belong to Keetah, as she had belonged to Emma.

Keetah and two cats lived in the New York apartment and now when Jamison answered a ring at her door, she was escorted there by her small menagerie. When she and a guest sat in the living room, the three beasts took up heraldic positions, couchant, with their eyes fixed on their mistress.

Szilard persuaded Jamison, in autumn 1978, to accept the invita-tion of Maurice Béjart to appear as guest artist with the Ballet of the 20th Century. Béjart proposed choreographing a new version of *Le Spectre de la Rose,* in which Jamison would dance.

Michel Fokine's ballet *Le Spectre de la Rose,* set to Weber's *Invi-tation to the Dance,* had been produced by Diaghilev chiefly as a ve-hicle for Nijinsky, who, as the Rose, made a celebrated leap through a window. The slight, episodic ballet concerns a young lady who re-turns from a ball carrying a red rose, which she touches to her lips before falling asleep in a chair. She dreams that the spirit, the spectre of the Rose, manifested as a young man, enters the room and dances with her. When she wakes, the man has gone but the rose remains.

The Ballet of the 20th Century, based in Brussels, toured widely and Béjart's *Rose* aroused great interest in the European press. Although intended as a novelty, the work was treated seriously by critics. André-Philippe Hersin, the editor-publisher of the Paris magazine *Les Saisons de la Danse,* described *Rose* as reflecting Béjart's feelings on the solitariness of the successful artist.

Jamison was both the lady who returns from the ball carrying a red rose, and the rose itself. She was partnered by Patrice Touron, a tall and spectacular danseur of the Béjart company. An Algerian, he had a virtuoso technique which he used effortlessly but without the conventional suavity of ballet. Jamison first appeared in a long white evening gown, arms and neck bare, dancing with a long-stemmed red rose. Touron, as the incarnate Rose, wore a splendid scarlet costume, a great hood over his head and an enormous, swirling cloak. When the cloak parted, it revealed the dancer in leotard and tights, seemingly nude, his legs and torso bound with ribbands in an abstract design.

Jamison danced, with one leg unfolding the wide skirt of her gown, in the sweeping extensions that characterized her style. In the second part of the ballet, divested of the white dress, she wore a brown leotard, banded, to match Touron's, in the abstract design, and the two became the Rose, twin images of one being, in an enigmatic choreographic duet.

The Ballet of the 20th Century had a New York season at the Minskoff Theatre on Broadway at Forty-fifth Street, in spring 1979. Appearing as guest artists with Béjart's company were Jean Babilée, the great French dramatic danseur, and the American dancer Judith Jamison, in Béjart's *Le Spectre de la Rose*. It was a ballet season of significance. At the Mark Hellinger Theatre, Nureyev was dancing with the Joffrey Ballet, in revivals of ballets from the Diaghilev era, in a program that honored the fiftieth anniversary of Serge Diaghilev's death.

The Alvin Ailey American Dance Theater opened its annual spring season at the New York City Center, including in the repertoire a work by George Faison called *Tilt,* and another, by Donald McKayle, titled *District Storyville*. Ailey—still "paying his dues"—

choreographed *Solo for Mingus,* a tribute to the late composer whose music Ailey had used for an earlier ballet choreographed for the Joffrey Ballet. Ailey's *Myth* was revived, with Kajiwara in the principal role.

Jamison's popularity with the New York audience had been enhanced by her guest appearances with the Béjart company. The press (several members of which, in the United States, had long been inimical to Béjart, and almost maniacally disapproving of the public acclaim given him) were not well impressed by *Le Spectre de la Rose,* but Jamison's fans enjoyed seeing her in a European company and in something as novel as Béjart's pas de deux.

As Szilard had foreseen it would, Jamison's appearance in Europe with the Ballet of the 20th Century had heightened interest in her and European audiences were anticipating the arrival of the Ailey company, on its 1979 tour. Jamison was in good health and high spirits. Almost painlessly she had ended her love affair and, quite easily, extricated herself from the experimental theatre project. She had no regrets about her involvements in love and in off-Broadway theatre, and from the latter, at least, she had derived some profit. "If nothing else," she said, "I moved into another dimension [in theatre]."

Freed of extracurricular obligations, she returned to a routine of rehearsals. When she was not working with the Ailey company she was doing so with her voice teacher and drama coach. Szilard was again conferring on offers to star Jamison in a Broadway show. The 20th Anniversary Gala program of the Ailey in November had given Jamison "such a lift" that it buoyed her into the spring season. She was having more "fun" dancing, she said, than she had had "in ages."

Tensions that she had felt—some created by defending her rights to her private life—had relaxed and she had a sense of freedom, of being again "in charge" of herself, that gave her a new peace of mind. She was reunited with old friends, among them Faison, with whom she had danced a decade before in the Ailey. She enjoyed dancing, as part of the company, in something as "mindless" as Louis Falco's *Caravan,* "where you don't think, you just give yourself up to moving and to the music." She had often, in the past, felt that her work should have artistic progression. Now she had come to recognize that there was nothing so orderly, so tidily instituted, as progress in her work. It was charted by pendulum sweeps, from good to bad, and, at best, in cycles.

Nevertheless, there was a sense of continuity perceptible after fourteen years. Erzuli, in Holder's *The Prodigal Son,* and Marie Laveau, in Ailey's *Passage,* were two sides of the same coin. The roles she had danced had been, as it were, by random choice, and yet chance had defined for her a sort of convoluted progression.

On June 25, 1979, dancing for purest pleasure with George Faison in the studio, Jamison fell. X-rays showed that she had smashed the ball of her left femur. "It was such a terrible injury to get when I was just fooling around, having fun." X-rays also showed that the ball of her left thigh had, sometime in the past, been broken but had meanwhile healed.

Jamison, comparatively, had escaped serious injury in her career. She discounted the minor hurts, the sprained ankle at Avignon (even the bad falls she had taken rehearsing *Caravan*) and counted chiefly the broken ankle from the Harkness, and the other break, in her left ankle, when she had started work in Hamburg on *Josephs-legende.* Of the femur that had healed, without her ever knowing that it had been broken, she could only assume that the damage had been done at a time when she was working under so much concentration that she had not realized the extent of the damage or the degree of her pain. "It's the sort of damage that you do when you are young and you don't understand your body. American dancers have to learn to work with their bodies on their own. No one teaches us how to take care of ourselves. We learn when the body lets us know it's been ill-treated. While the body is young, it can absorb shocks and stress. Later on, you suffer from all the damage you've done to yourself."

She was forced to give up the European tour, to the distress of her fans, especially those from the eastern Socialist countries who, when they attended performances of the Ailey company, felt cheated to be deprived of seeing Judith Jamison. For a while, she yielded Potiphar's Wife to another dancer, Donna Wood. Jamison, when she returned to performing, did so with four steel pins holding together the shattered ball of her left femur. She was to be called upon for other duties than those of the dancer. For a while, Jamison would hold together the almost shattered company that was "the Ailey."

TWENTY-FOUR

On a bleak, gray day in late December, 1978, Jamison dined with a friend in New York. She arrived at the apartment on Central Park West straight from rehearsal, wearing her uniform of tight faded jeans and a sweat shirt. But the coat in which she had wrapped herself against the chill and bitter wind was of skins she had selected and had sewn to order, in a shop in Vienna, and the tall boots on her feet were of leather as soft as doeskin.

Jamison, who thought she made a virtue of simplicity, was sensitive to atmosphere. Entering the big living room, almost as spacious as her own, she exclaimed appreciatively: "Ah, high ceilings, I can breathe here!" She took keen pleasure in her senses. Her friend had bought her a gift of Jamison's favorite perfume, from Halston, in two vials, one a miniature flagon on a cord. Jamison rubbed some of the perfume on the inside of her wrists and hung the cord like a chain around her neck. As she lounged after dinner, nestled into a corner of a couch, she fondled the little flagon as tenderly as though it were alive. Textures, she remembered—satin, velvet, brocade, serge—had pleased her as a child, as much as colors and shapes.

Jamison had not yet adopted the "corn row" coiffure and her hair was cropped close to the skull. Her throat, rising from the high round neck of the sweat shirt, was a column for her head. She looked like a bronze sculpture. The lamps in the big room were low but from time to time, as Jamison turned her head, their light caught the facets of the diamonds in her ears and in those moments she blazed with points of fire. On one hand she wore an Art Deco ring, shaped as two roses, that Patrice Touron had given her to mark the premiere of *Le Spectre de la Rose*.

Deeper than the patina of love is the bloom of success. Jamison had this high gloss, the emanation of the authority that is born of power. Here, in repose, was the *monstre sacré*, the sacred monster of

American dance, as Jamison had been called in Europe—a term applied to a person who, through the idolatrous admiration of a multitude, becomes an object both of adoration and of sacrifice.

Two hours earlier Jamison and Szilard had conferred on her schedule for the coming year. It had been a skirmish, with Jamison defending her right to dates which she wished apportioned to her off-Broadway play, and Szilard pressing for the fulfillment of engagements to which she was obligated, in and out of the Ailey. Jamison was committed to the experimental theatre project only on her word; Szilard reminded her that she had other, legal obligations. Jamison yielded reluctantly to Szilard's patient, careful pressure, retaining some of the "free" dates for which she bargained. Now, in meditative mood, she referred to the matter of her "personal involvement."

"People think I am crazy. So I'm not doing leading roles, and there's no money or fame in it, and it's very, very off-Broadway . . . It's something *I* want to do.

"For the past thirteen years people have said: Judi, do this, at such-and-such a time, in such-and-such a place, and I've done it. I've worked hard and I feel I've earned the success I have—that I am supposed to have. Well, if I am 'successful,' what does that mean?

"To me, being successful is reaching some sort of goal. Success is a reward for working hard and well. You get paid, people praise you for what you are doing. So you owe yourself and other people a responsibility, to go on working as hard and as well as you can.

"But success is not slavery, not to me.

"This thing I'm doing, the off-Broadway project I'm into, is more than a personal involvement, although there's that too. What I'm doing at the Forty-fifth Street studio is something that satisfies a need I have, to open myself to a new experience. I had reached a phase where I felt it was important for me to start fresh again. To be used, like raw material. So what I'm doing is proving that I can still control my life, that 'success' is not controlling me."

Ailey and Jamison often expressed similar feelings, sometimes in almost the same terms, independently of each other. They were frightened not of success but of the enslavement of the person by success, and of the person's dehumanization. Jamison's mutinous determination to divide her private and her professional life into separate parts was an attempt to "stay in control of Judith Jamison." Ailey had even more desperate fears than Jamison but he was far more restricted in freedom. Jamison was able to make decisions for herself and to disregard the discomfort they gave to others; Ailey could not. He was very like a man with a hand on the throttle of a speeding train who knows that if he dares relax his grip, dares to turn away, the train he is driving will jump the track.

Ailey had a more fanciful simile. He called the Ailey organization a monster and declared that it was devouring him.

By comparison with other dance organizations in the United States, the Ailey's was monstrous in size, comprising as it did three companies and a school. The school, the American Dance Center, was the parent organization of two performing groups, the Dance Workshop (in which students served an apprenticeship) and the Repertory Ensemble, the vaulting ground into the senior company. All were under the Ailey aegis, and established in his name.

The Alvin Ailey Dance Theater (in which the word "American" appeared first in 1962, at the urging of impresarios booking foreign tours, and was thereafter sometimes discarded, sometimes retrieved) remained the main part of the organization. Here Ailey and guest choreographers worked with experienced dancers of versatile qualifications and, in many instances, virtuoso technique.

The Alvin Ailey Repertory Ensemble, into which were taken young dancers from several companies and schools, had a repertoire and toured under its own management, often extending activities to the West Coast.

In maintaining a senior and a junior company, Ailey was not alone. Robert Joffrey also had two companies, each autonomous, the Joffrey Ballet and the Joffrey II. American Ballet Theatre had a subsidiary group, directed by Richard Englund, called Ballet Repertory Company, brought into being in 1972.

Not only did the Ailey comprise a third company, in the Dance Workshop, but its school was the largest of its kind in New York. By 1979 the enrollment had risen to five thousand. The Ailey, in toto, represented a mammoth undertaking in American dance.

The administration of the Ailey was under a board of trustees, with Alvin Ailey the artistic director of the senior company and the nominal head of the other two companies and the school. The management of the Ailey was of such diversity and, in some respects, such obliquity, that it was difficult for an observer to thoroughly comprehend its precise definitions and dimensions. Ailey, in conversations with his friends, maintained that, since the reestablishment of the company early in the 1970s, he had lost control, that he no longer was "responsible" for the affairs of the organization and that, sometimes, he felt himself "a stranger in my own house."

Alvin Ailey had a poetic eloquence, a masterful command of words, and an intense romanticism. His dramatic sense invariably magnified crises, so that his friends were in the habit of discounting the extent of "Alvin's problems." In a conversation with one friend, soon after the triumphant 20th Anniversary Gala program in 1978, Ailey expressed his continuing worries over the Ailey—its economy, its future development, and, above all, its abiding nature. He said: "I've always realized that, after I'm gone, things will change— maybe for the better, maybe for the worse. But I've always hoped that, before I went [he was speaking of his departure not as retirement but as death] I would have the satisfaction of knowing that I was leaving something behind, something that had come out of a vision. It's not that I want to raise a monument to Alvin Ailey. I have other ways of getting my kicks. It's nothing so pompous as getting a plaque put up in your name.

"But I'm different from Mr. B. [George Balanchine], who likes to say—I don't believe him!—that he doesn't care what happens to the New York City Ballet when he leaves it. *I* care, about the Ailey. I care too much. I want too much for the Ailey—or so people tell me. But I have come this far, on the strength of the vision I had way back in the fifties, when I started with five or six and sometimes eight dancers, to try to make a company. In those days I had to beg dancers to work for me. They had to work in faith, and out of love . . . not for money.

"Now we have some kind of budget that, in the fifties, would have been a fortune. And we have a deficit, they tell me, almost as big as the national debt. What else do we have in the Ailey?

"We have twenty-five dancers in the [senior] company. I would like to have thirty or thirty-five. Our guest choreographers could sometimes use forty. But we are limited to a maximum because our company falls into a certain [union] category. There are always restrictions.

"Restrictions you live with and, perhaps, they stimulate you to a resourcefulness, an inventiveness, you might not otherwise develop. But first you have to have a vision.

"You can't build without a vision and you can't restrict the dimensions of visions. The dream I have, the dream I have talked about for many, many years, is as clear to me as if it existed already in reality. I feel sometimes that I am killing myself and, if I am, it's for this dream."

The dream had two aspects, a spiritual and a physical.

Ailey had elected himself the curator of American modern dance. One aspect of his dream was to preserve "living, in our repertory, not as museum pieces," the classic works of modern dance. He meant the company to be the repository of this collection of works, while at the same time it stayed contemporary, producing new works. But the company was only part of the entire vision.

Of the second aspect of his vision Ailey spoke like an architect, of a building that would house all the elements of the Ailey organization, school and companies, and extend into other services through dance.

Ailey's vision of such a home for the Ailey organization was treated as a pipe dream, even by his friends. But it was something to which Ailey clung for nearly twenty years, ever since he found, in Clark Center, the germinal Ailey home.

In 1960 the Ailey company's stage manager, Charles Blackwell, brought Ailey together with Edele Holtz, the director of the Westside Young Women's Christian Association, which owned a building in mid-Manhattan, not far from the New York City Center. Holtz converted the second floor of the building into premises for the Ailey company, which became resident at the Clark Center for the Performing Arts.

The company had studios for rehearsal and classes, and a storage area for costumes and, besides, a small auditorium in which performances were given. Although the company soon outgrew the premises, Ailey retained fond memories of Clark Center. "That little theatre helped us to survive, and it helped build our audience," he said. "Tickets were cheap, compared to what they are now, and we gave audiences their money's worth."

Clark Center formally opened in October 1960 and the Ailey Dance Theater presented its first program there on November 27, with Carmen de Lavallade as guest artist, dancing with Truitte in

Horton's *The Beloved* and with Glen Tetley in Butler's *Portrait of Billie.*

In premiere was Ailey's *Knoxville: Summer of 1915* and to a friend, commenting on the autobiographical significance of the work, de Lavallade said: "Alvin does not know how to work except from the truth, everything he makes is based on experience—on feeling, or on fact. Alvin could just as well have become a writer as a choreographer." And, laughing, but in earnest, de Lavallade added: "I take the responsibility for Alvin becoming a choreographer"—referring to her mesmerizing influence on Ailey in high school in Los Angeles, when he had seen her dance. Ailey now said, in 1979: "I believe that there was a reason for my becoming a dancer and a choreographer and the reason is more than making a successful career in theatre. I feel that I was given a mission in dance. It comes to other men in science, and in the church. It came to me in theatre. Dance is a way for me to serve my people, for me to serve my country. I know that I sound crazy to people who don't understand what I mean. They think: Oh, Alvin is sounding off again. People, some people, think I have illusions of grandeur. They couldn't be more wrong. My dream is not to aggrandize Alvin Ailey. It's to use the Ailey company in the service of dance, and to make dance—the humanism of dance—a sociological as well as an artistic involvement."

The "building," the corporeal aspect of the Ailey dream, would contain studios for the company and the school, with all the necessary adjuncts as premises for administration and staff to tend to the affairs of the Ailey organization. There would be, in addition, "a proper small theatre, nothing extravagant but something adequate, for experimental work. Choreographers are pressured by commissions to do works, and by time and money. I want to provide a place where there are no pressures excepting artistic pressures. I want to provide a place and an environment where the creative process can begin—and where it does not always have to 'produce' a salable product."

The architecture of the dream building included classrooms in which the students of the school could get their "normal" education, where dance training and education would be within the same environment, as it is in the European and Russian academies of dance.

Further, Ailey wanted "lecture halls, and a small cinema" for lectures on history and aesthetics of theatre, and for the showing of dance films, "not only for the Ailey dancers and students but for the community, because we must bring the public into dance, if we are really honest and sincere about making a great American dance tradition." The tradition, as Ailey saw it, could not be narrowly enclosed in the dance studio and on the theatre stage, as an elite occupation of dance artists. It had to "reach into society" through every possible means, integrating the audience en masse within the humanism of dance arts.

"Who am I to take a mission like this on myself?" Ailey asked rhetorically. But he had rights enough.

The earliest shape and substance of Ailey's dream had been for the black dance artist. While fulfilling his own ambitions, he set himself to advancing those of his contemporary "black brothers," Talley Beatty, Donald McKayle, and others. Next, he became determined to gain permanent recognition and respect for the work of the pioneer black artists, Katherine Dunham, Pearl Primus, and their compeers. But soon Ailey had passed beyond the "black" boundary into a universal sense of dance in which there was no segregation.

One of his dearest friends was Joyce Trisler, who was white. Trisler left the Horton company in 1953 for New York, where she became a member of the Juilliard Dance Theatre and formed a close and affectionate association with Doris Humphrey. She was a respected teacher, with a troupe of her own, called the Joyce Trisler Danscompany.

In 1964 (it is said, on the instigation of Truitte) Trisler joined the Ailey company on a European tour. Later, Trisler's *Journey* and *Dance for Six,* two of her most noted works, were taken into the Ailey repertoire. In the ensuing years, Ailey had become greatly attached to Trisler, in part because she was one of the "old ones from Horton," and chiefly because Trisler was one of the foremost authorities on the Horton technique, which Ailey prized.

Ailey had thus thoroughly integrated his company, in the dancers and choreographers, and in the nice balance between the old and the new phases of modern dance. And as Ailey had himself extended his work outside the modern and the Afro-American dance forms, so did his company enlarge its scope, until its character could no longer be defined as that of a "modern dance" company or a "black" company. The Ailey's unique character had to be considered: it was the most successful nonclassical dance company in North America. And the grandeur of Ailey's vision had to be recognized, not as it related particularly to the work of black dance artists but as it related generally to American contemporary dance.

The function of Ailey's "mission," as he described it, was to maintain a school and a company as headquarters for American dance. For this he had formed an ensemble, as a repertory company, capable of performing in any style and in all technical forms. The school was a means of providing the company with skilled dancers, and, besides, of supplying an inexhaustible source of talented dancers to other companies.

An important function of the school would be the discovery of gifted children, from a strata of society as yet untapped, the socially and economically impoverished.

The American Dance Center was formally opened in May 1971, at 229 East Fifty-ninth Street, with the aid of funding from the National Endowment for the Arts. Ailey and Pearl Lang were joint tenants of the building and they collaborated as directors of the school. Besides the faculty, dancers from both companies taught classes—in ballet, jazz, and modern dance (Lang was a pupil of Graham, as Ailey was the disciple of Horton).

Dance schools are more lucrative than dance companies. Students pay tuition fees; dancers have to be paid salaries. But Ailey had no intention of making the school into "a paying proposition." He would have liked to admit all the pupils on scholarships and to have fully supported those who were needy.[1]

The Ailey company, during one of its major financial crises, had received substantial funds for its reactivation, and acquired an administrative or governing branch. Good management, it was assumed, would rectify past errors and keep the shaky Ailey on an even keel. "Management" became the bane of Ailey's existence, as he saw it.

However benign the rule and efficacious the judgments, Ailey would never cease to resent a controlling branch. It might, as it assuredly did, prop and sustain the Ailey, but it seemed to cast a

[1] It was on this precept that Arthur Mitchell began the school of the Dance Theatre of Harlem. Mitchell was forced to abandon the noble principle, for lack of money, although the school continues to grant a large number of scholarships to pupils who cannot afford to pay fees.

shadow on Ailey himself. It was his instinct to lead, and when he was not, as he felt, in charge, then he believed that he had been usurped. Placed in a position of leadership, Ailey could rise superbly to all challenges and overcome all difficulties, as he had done in the past.

Ailey had survived and flourished, as he knew, not on his sole efforts but on those of devoted friends who were dedicated to him and to his work. He had come to depend on these friends for moral support and for help in caring for the Ailey. These friends, he said in 1979, had one by one been lost to him.

Truitte was the first to leave Ailey, leaving, it is believed, a space that no one else ever filled, not only in Ailey's esteem but also in the management of the company. Further changes came about, following the institution of a board of trustees, which changed chairmen, twice, between 1972 and 1979. An executive director was engaged in 1975 to administrate all the affairs of the Ailey organization, and Ivy Clarke, who since 1967 had taken care of the company, resigned or was dismissed. By 1977, Ailey was complaining that he was a stranger in his own house. Wade Williams, who had run the school (now headed by a member of the board), and William Hammond, the company's production stage manager, had also left Ailey.

The conflicts that arose between the new management and the old were chiefly over the manner in which the company's affairs should be administered. Ailey's custom was to keep everything "on the human level," and in many of his dealings with his associates "people ran roughshod over Alvin," some of them dancers in the company. It was ostensibly to bring a more businesslike style to the company's administration and to protect Ailey from unnecessary worry that the new management took over the company's affairs.

The board was meanwhile accomplishing herculean tasks, chief of which was to wipe out the large deficit and to provide funding for continuing operations. These things were done through a well-organized fund-raising campaign. A greater task was containing the company's annual budget within the spiraling national inflation. The Ailey budget, set at $700,000 in 1973, rose to $3,000,000 by 1977.

Ailey had always loathed the need to beg for money; he had never been able to overcome the feeling that it was demeaning to him as an artist. He grumbled that the board pressed him into "political appearances" at social functions, so that he would induce prospective patrons to make grants to the Ailey. If the board had been established to protect him from administrative worries, why, then, was he called on to campaign for funds? Relations were so strained that Ailey and his board communicated their feelings through the press rather than tête-à-tête.

Jamison noted, on her return from the Grinzingerberg, that Ailey looked tired and seemed "withdrawn." His poor health, mental and physical, was attributed to excessive weight. Ailey had grown heavier of late and referred to himself as "fat." He spoke disgustedly of his ungainliness, blaming it for his inability to choreograph because he could not work properly with the dancers. At other times he complained that he was prevented from working because of the time and energy that were sapped by having to try to raise funds for the company.

Ailey admitted that he was exhausted. He felt, he said, that he needed to take time off, to look at the company objectively. "I have let too much control of the company go to other people. I don't like the way in which the company is changing." He would take a year off, go on a reducing diet, rest, get his head together. But Ailey could not bring himself to stay away from the company, and he would not forgive himself for his sins: for growing old, for getting fat, for not choreographing. "We have six premieres," he said to a friend soon before the opening of the New York City Center season, May 4, 1977, "none by Ailey." He was reminded of the fecund years, thirty works choreographed since 1970, several to the music of Duke Ellington.

It was a mistake to mention Ellington. The memory of the composer plunged Ailey into a gloomier mood. If he found it hard to endure the loss of the living, it was even harder to lose someone to death. The death of Ellington in 1974 still grieved Ailey. "The Duke was my idol because of his genius, I loved him as a friend, because he was such a beautiful man, and in the end I made him the father I never had."

Ailey spoke prayerfully of Ellington, making a loving litany of their relationship. "We went back a long way, he and I, to when I was a kid listening to his music at the Lincoln [in Los Angeles]. I never got over the thrill of knowing him in the flesh. Working on *The River* was one of the best times in my life. I remember taking the company in 1963 to Chicago, to work with him and Talley in

My People [a musical created for the Black Centennial Exposition]."

When he was not animated by memories of Ellington, Ailey sank into a strange apathy. His self-esteem was low, his will slack. The old flaring optimism, expressed even in anger, was missing. Despite his corpulence he seemed oddly depleted. His face wore a haggard expression, particularly doleful on plump cheeks. His eyes, set in shadows the color of pansies, betrayed a deep, secret fatigue. When a friend kissed him, he smelled faintly of a sweetish perfume. On the advice of well-meaning friends Ailey was smoking marijuana to soothe his nerves.

Believing himself a lonely man, he isolated himself, spending his time with phantoms. In that bedeviled spring of 1977 Ailey would sit for hours at a time in a darkened room, looking at the company's repertoire on video tapes and most often the cassette on the VTR machine was of *The Lark Ascending* with Sara Yarborough. But Yarborough had once again left the Ailey company.

TWENTY-FIVE

Jamison, shuttling on her transatlantic engagements, was aware of the tensions in the Ailey company but she tried to stay aloof from them. She spoke of herself, as Ailey did, as a "stranger." There were so many newcomers, so many familiar faces were missing. She and Dudley Williams were "among the last survivors."

Ailey was obviously unhappy and worried by what he felt to be diversions from his objectives, and too many administrative edicts, but Jamison never doubted that he would hold on to the company.

"I couldn't picture Alvin ever giving up. In a way, I built my own strengths from watching Alvin, how he would react to problems. When they got too big, when they came too close, he pretended they were not there. We'd be dancing on a precipice—with Alvin not knowing how he was going to get us over that week, *that day*.

"In the early days, before I had a place of my own in New York, I slept on the couch in Alvin's living room. He and Jimmy would be working at night on the company's books. I'd turn over, pull the blanket over my head, and go to sleep. I'd wake when they switched the light off. Sometimes dawn would be coming in round the drapes in the window.

"The miraculous thing was: *Alvin at that time was choreographing.* Just up to a little while before that, he had been choreographing, running the company, *and* dancing. He and Jimmy did everything. I don't know how they managed, especially for the big tours.

"We danced literally all over the world and everywhere audiences loved us, but we never knew if the company would last out a season. It was this constant hassle. People ask me if I would like to have my own company. I want to say: 'God, you've got to be kidding!'

"After I had been to Hamburg, and Vienna, I realized that Alvin had had to work miracles to keep a company going in the States. So in 1977, when I could see that Alvin was worn out, I still believed he was infallible. No matter how many blows he was hit, he'd get up and keep going."

True, Ailey seemed to recover from the depression into which he had sunk that spring, and in summer, under auspices of the U. S. State Department, the company went on a tour of the Orient. Returning to Japan after a fifteen-year absence, it was welcomed with a rapture uncommon to Japanese audiences. Ending the tour in the Philippines, it was given a reception in the presidential palace at Manila as sumptuous as any ever presented for a visiting head of state.

The company then embarked on tours of Africa and Europe, with equal acclaim. Not for the first time Ailey was urged to establish a Continental residency.[1] Ailey refused, as he had previously refused invitations from some American cities. For Ailey, "Broadway is the company's home town." Yet, on his return to the United States, Ailey was told that a two-week season scheduled for the company at the New York State Theater had to be canceled because of escalated costs. Jamison's well-paid guest engagements provided her with a financial security that she would have been denied in the Ailey company, subject as it still was to seasonal crises and a precarious economy.

It was puzzling that, despite an enlarged administration, which had taken considerable power to itself, the Ailey company still teetered on a precipice. Much of the Ailey's troubles had been blamed on its allegedly slap-dash management. Businesslike methods were supposed to have changed procedures for the better, though they made for a chillier climate and a more distant association in the company.

Jamison never thought of severing her ties with the company, to which she had a profound attachment. "You do not spend thirteen years of your life in a company," she commented, after the 20th Anniversary Gala program, "without getting involved." Jamison seemed more moved even than Ailey by the significance of the twentieth anniversary. Ailey was beatific, in having reinstituted, as he felt he had, the true and lasting nature of his company, through the unit-

[1] With increasing interest in modern dance, the Europeans were eager to foster their own traditions. Ailey's company was the most coveted, for a Continental residency. Ailey refused it but one was accepted, by the modern dance choreographer Alwin Nikolais, in Angers, France.

ing of the "old" Ailey dancers with the "new." Jamison was almost somber when she spoke of the Gala program, as though the solemnity of the event outweighed the joyousness.

The anniversary year, as it was referred to in the company, was not without trials. Despite exuberantly welcoming audiences, Ailey had serious difficulties during the South American tour, at one point threatening to cancel the opening night performance in Rio de Janeiro because of altercations with the administration of the municipal theatre. Nevertheless, he remained in good spirits and after the Anniversary Gala, with his newly "streamlined" figure, he looked much as he had ten years earlier. To maintain his form, Ailey went, with Szilard, to a spa, for a course of exercise and massage and a rigorous diet. His mood remained sanguine even during the debacle of *Medusa*.

Ailey was working again. He choreographed *Passage* for Jamison in 1978 and that was taken as a sign that he had freed himself of his "monster's" oppression. But, complimented by a friend on *Solo for Mingus* (premiered at the New York City Center in May 1979, in tribute to the composer) Ailey sadly replied: "Man, I am tired of requiems."

One subject was guaranteed to divert him from his cares and that was a home for the Ailey. Considerable impetus was lent to his plan when the Ailey company ceased to be a constituent of the New York City Center.

Invited to become resident at the City Center in 1972, Ailey changed the title of his company to the Alvin Ailey City Center Dance Theater, taking up formal occupancy on August 4 at West Fifty-fifth Street. The company now had a permanent base in New York and a home theatre where it presented two seasons annually, spring and fall.

In February 1973 the administration of the New York City Center for Music and Drama announced stringent reductions in budgeting for its seven constituents, among which were the New York City Opera, the New York City Ballet at the New York State Theater, the City Center Joffrey Ballet, and the Alvin Ailey City Center Dance Theater. City Center had a $1.3 million deficit, caused in part by a too ambitious expansion in programming. The budget cuts went into effect immediately. The Joffrey was hardest hit, with an 80 percent reduction—$380,000 abruptly reduced to $75,000. Ironically, the Joffrey had that season broken the City Center's box office record and was more financially solvent than it had ever been in its seventeen-year-old history.

The Joffrey and the Ailey—both of whom dropped the "City Center" designation from their titles—remained at the City Center but as tenants rather than constituents. Ailey's company had the use of studios on one floor but Ailey was obliged to rent extra studio space for his guest choreographers. The Ailey continued, also, to present seasonal performances at the City Center but the Joffrey Ballet was compelled first to curtail its New York seasons and then to abandon them altogether. The Joffrey Ballet disbanded for a time. It was resuscitated in 1980.

Following the cataclysmic events of 1973, there were persisting rumors that the city would tear down the old and almost decrepit Center, freeing the valuable site for a lucrative real estate project. Now, at length, serious efforts were made toward finding a new residence for the Ailey. In 1977 and 1978 two locations were surveyed, both belonging to New York universities.

The first, the Columbia School of Pharmacy, was a vacant building attached to Columbia University, on which Ailey's board tried to obtain a long lease. Negotiations lasted for some time, while the university debated the Ailey offer and one from the A&P, who wished to expand an adjacent grocery store. The university also pondered demolishing the building and leaving the site vacant, to avoid paying income taxes on the facility. Ailey was outraged that, with the paucity of available buildings in New York, it was possible to "cynically" consider pulling down a sound edifice merely to gain a reduction in taxes. He was shocked that a *university,* above all other organizations, would be guilty of what he thought of as vandalism.

The next year, an equally abortive attempt was made to secure a lease on Town Hall, which New York University was contemplating closing for financial reasons.

Ailey resumed his pleas for a building constructed to specifications, a plan irrational in view of the Ailey's shaky financial status and the high price of New York real estate. The board offered little hope that such a goal would be realized, and positively not in the company's twenty-first year. Then, by one of the turns of fortune that Ailey and his friends called miraculous, a building materialized

—as the Minskoff Building on Broadway, at Forty-fourth and Forty-fifth streets, adjacent to the Minskoff Theater.

With a gift of $75,000 from the Kresge Foundation, which had to be augmented by $40,000 raised by the Ailey parent organization, Dance Theater Foundation Incorporated, construction was completed in time for the newly named Alvin Ailey Dance Center to be formally installed in residence on October 18, 1979.

The three companies and their administrative offices, with four large studios, were housed in a three-storied complex, in which was also contained the American Dance Center—the school Ailey had founded ten years earlier with 125 students, now grown to an enrollment of 5,000.

In December the school inaugurated a model program, the Arts Connection, whereby children from disadvantaged communities were auditioned at the Center, in the hope of discovering potentially gifted dancers. The program was funded under the sponsorship of the United States Office of Education, the National Endowment for the Arts, and the New York State Education Department and Division for Youth. Within this program Ailey meant to develop his plan to integrate into the American theatre a segment of the population for which the chances of an artistic education were remote. The program in its initial phase would enrich the lives of hundreds of children and from them, Ailey believed, would come artists whose contributions would enrich American society.

Jamison, her broken thigh nicely on the mend, officiated with Ailey at the opening ceremonies of the Ailey Center on October 18. Jubilantly, she noted that she and Dudley Williams, with Ailey, were "the oldest inhabitants" of the mansion. Of the 1979–80 roster, ten dancers were making their debut in the company. Of the twelve dancers taken into the company since 1975, seven had joined in 1978. Already, the dancers who had entered the Ailey earlier in the decade had assumed the status of veterans: Mari Kajiwara, who had been in the company from 1970; Mazumi Chaya, Michiko Oka, and Donna Wood, from 1972; and Ulysses Dove, from 1973.

Only Jamison and Dudley Williams fully realized the significance in Ailey's life of the new Center. It represented the fulfillment of a dream. Ailey was unable to bring himself to rejoice in the triumph. Joyce Trisler had died on October 6.

Once again Ailey had to make a requiem, his *Memoria* "to the joy, the beauty, the creativity of my old friend Joyce Trisler." He choreographed a large work and set it on the three Ailey companies. The work was choreographed, rehearsed, and set within a few weeks, for a premiere at the New York City Center on December 13, 1979. The Ailey company was granted a sum of money by the New York State Council on the Arts in partial defrayment of the cost of the production.

Memoria was a skillful blending of Trisler's and Horton's principles for dance. Ailey lovingly diffused throughout the work the essence of Trisler and he cleverly traced in it the evolutions of her career as a choreographer and teacher.

Donna Wood had the leading role, shown first as a hieratic figure (in a white dress, evocative of the *ballet blanc* of Trisler's *Dance for Six*); as an American gamine (a "jazzy babe"); and, in the closing movement, an ennobled almost transmogrified creature in a glittering red dress, who was lifted and carried high above the heads of the massed dancers. *Memoria* subtly conveyed Trisler's own precepts for dancing; her teaching had been characterized by a quality she described as "controlled freedom."

Joyce Trisler and Alvin Ailey had been friends for almost thirty years. At the Horton Studio, he had known her as "that floppy, crazy girl from down the street." A woman of effervescent and irreverent humor, Trisler could always jolly Ailey out of the blues. Despite her renown as a teacher, and the substantial nature of her choreographic work, Trisler had a refreshing pragmatism. She scorned self-pity and was derisive of pretension. Of the theatre she loved, Trisler remarked that "behind the scenes it's pure Woody Allen." Explaining how she had come to form her company, the Joyce Trisler Danscompany, she said that she had been working with some dancers who just wouldn't go home. She began her work in drama and changed to dance when, she said, she discovered that actors were at least ten times more boring than dancers.

Trisler's loss struck Ailey a stunning blow. He had mourned the death of Ellington and been saddened by that of Charlie Mingus, but that of Trisler brought him more than grief. Trisler had been three years younger than Ailey and her dying touched him with an atavistic fear, the chilling presentiment of his own mortality.

Horton, too, had died as Trisler died, of a heart attack, but Ailey was horrified by the manner of Trisler's death, alone in her apartment, where her corpse had lain for several days before being discovered. He pictured a scene of desolation that wrung his heart: the lonely death of this woman, whose name meant *joy,* without a hand to hold; without a hand to even perform the last act of charity and close the lids over her glazed eyes.

Trisler, in December 1977, had rephrased *Journey* for the Ailey company (on Kajiwara). Even when they did not meet regularly, Ailey was always conscious that Trisler was near. Her death, announced nine days before the opening of the Alvin Ailey Dance Center, was like a cruel warning, that for every favor granted a loss must be endured.

He choreographed *Memoria* as a paean, not as an epitaph, declaring it a "celebration" of Trisler's life. And *Memoria* was also Ailey's desperate attempt to expunge the shabby loneliness of her dying. None had attended her body as it grew cold and stiffened, but in *Memoria,* through a surrogate, Trisler would be surrounded not merely by one but by all three of the Ailey companies. The work, in its original form, was too large to tour, and Ailey revised *Memoria* for the dancers of his senior company. Wherever the Alvin Ailey American Dance Theater appeared in 1979–80 the performances it danced were dedicated in Ailey's name "to the memory of his friend, Joyce Trisler, who died October 6, 1979."

Ailey's associates were relieved and pleased that his friend's death, instead of prostrating him, had agitated Ailey to an extraordinary activity. *Memoria* seemed to burst from a fount of inexhaustible energy and invention. Less pleasing to Ailey's associates was the morbidity of his thoughts in the weeks following the premiere of *Memoria,* when Ailey spoke of the likelihood that he would come to his end as Trisler to hers: suddenly and in solitude.

There was a degree of impatience in Ailey's friends' concern over him at this period. Granted, he felt grief over the loss of Joyce Trisler. It was believed that of all the friends of his youth, Carmen de Lavallade and James Truitte among them, Ailey's relationship had been most amicable and tranquil with Trisler. But his obsession with the past, especially when he was unhappy, irritated Ailey's friends. They did not realize that for Ailey nostalgia was therapeutic. As Jamison flung herself into new experiences, to refresh her soul, so did Ailey return to old and familiar passages of his life.

His friends, few of whom had ever believed that "Alvin's pipe-dream" of a home for his company would be realized, thought that he should rejoice in the Center more than he did. Ailey was said to be moody, but no one observed the moods as the fluctuating fever chart of a tormented psyche.

As befitted the head of a conglomerate enterprise, a $3 million investment, Ailey was established in "corporation executive" state in a corner office of the Ailey Dance Center. The office was furnished with an Art Deco desk that had belonged to the cosmetic tycoon, Helena Rubinstein. Of this office, Ailey commented that it was bigger than the studio in which he had choreographed *Revelations* in 1959. He said to a friend: "Man, I'm too old for all this nonsense. I only need a place to work with the dancers—it's the dancers I love, not the show."

"Alvin was in a terrible rage," said a friend, "not so much over Joyce Trisler dying *as the way she died*. Alvin has always prized the dignity of the human being—he has always loved beauty. It offended him that death came to Joyce Trisler in the way it did.

"I believe Alvin blamed himself for not knowing that Joyce had died. He couldn't have stopped her dying but, if he had known, he would have saved her the indignity, what *he* thinks was the indignity, of lying alone after death. This is the sort of crazy sense of responsibility Alvin has, the load of guilt he drags around, as if his back is broad enough for the obligation of everybody he loves."

Ivy Clarke had said that Ailey wanted everyone to love him but, to this discerning friend, Ailey's problems "have nothing to do with *being* loved—*it's with him loving too much, caring about other people too much.*" Ailey tormented himself with caring, as he did about the inequities suffered by black people, secretly reproaching himself for his personal success. He felt, his friend said, that he "owed" his people more than he had been able to give them. He often said that, as much as founding a company, his life had been spent in trying to change the conditions for black dancers in the American theatre. Now, in his long season of depression, Ailey was telling his friends that, despite the success of the Ailey company, he had not been able to alter the conditions that had existed when he began working in New York in the 1950s. It was in Ailey's character that he should take on himself some blame for this, that he should reproach himself for having succeeded as much as he had, while other black dancers had not.

Ailey was goaded into making statements on the American "race issue," at times and on occasions that certain persons considered to be inappropriate. He earned the reputation of being "a militant black." People chose to forget that Ailey began working with the declared purpose of choreographing a repertoire for a company that was to present to the world "the cultural heritage of the American Negro."

By 1964, however, Ailey had abandoned the goal of a segregated company, and a repertoire restricted to the black experience, for a company of integrated dancers, of African, Asiatic, and European antecedents, and a repertoire concerned with the "humanism" of dance. In the early months of 1980, gripped by savage despondency, Ailey wondered if he had done the right thing.

Any claim he might have made to being the black messiah of American dance had by now been yielded to Arthur Mitchell, who, although his school was fully integrated in faculty and students, persisted in the aim of keeping the Dance Theatre of Harlem a black classical company. Ailey did not have cause to repine—his contributions to his national theatre were prodigious, far more so than they would have been through a company restricted to dancers of one color, and to a repertoire based on only one aspect of society. The contributions Ailey made to the American theatre were also to be counted in the humanism with which he had presented the black American to the world—a humanism unequaled and without precedent save in the work of Pearl Primus, the first dance artist to alter the stereotype of the black man as savage.

Any doubts that Ailey had now about the value of his work as a choreographer and a company director could only come from the deep despondency, the lingering malaise that plagued him for many years and that was observed only when his moods were drastically altered: in the spring of 1977, when he fell into a despairing resignation and, as it would happen, in the spring of 1980, when the malaise took the form of rage.

The puzzling thing, for Ailey's friends, was that the man took so little pride and pleasure in his accomplishments. His company was the most successful of its kind, unique in the international theatre by reason of its repertoire and the caliber of its artists. Ailey had drawn into theatre audiences who had never before seen a live dancer on-stage, perhaps because people discerned in the dancing a strangely evocative quality. Dance in the theatre, Ailey said, "should be a reflection of life, the dark side as well as the good and happy side . . . [it should] show man's loneliness and man's incapacity to com-municate with his fellow man, as well as man's joys and aspira-tions." Secrets that could not be breathed, things that could not be spoken, could not be sung, were revealed in dancing, the silent but eloquent communication of thought and feeling. Ailey had himself written his biography in dance, not only overtly, as in *Knoxville*, and in realistic works like *Blues Suite* and *Revelations*, but, ob-liquely, in metaphor and in myth, as in *Ariadne* and *Labyrinth*.

Alvin Ailey was one of the most intelligent and cultivated of American theatre artists. A university graduate, he was well read and possessed a reservoir of classical reference from poetry and lit-erature, music and painting. He conversed in several languages. He had the appetite for research, the sense of immortality, that make the historian.

His talents had been recognized and Ailey had been singled out for honors. He was the recipient of the Dance Magazine Award and the Capezio Award. In 1972 he received two honorary doctorates as Doctor of Fine Arts, one from Princeton University and the second from Cedar Crest College in Allentown, Pennsylvania. Well before the company's twenty-first anniversary, in 1979, Ailey had become a distinguished member of his national theatre.

The "business of being black," as Jamison spoke of it, obsessed Alvin Ailey. Paradoxically, he did not limit his capacity to love to the color of a person's skin. He could not have more sincerely mourned the death of Joyce Trisler had she been black instead of white.

Jamison had felt "pressures" exerted on her to capitalize on blackness, in part as a symbol for black Americans. She was not preoccupied by color, either through environment or from her own convictions. She insisted on being taken on her individual merits and not symbolically, as a useful fetish.

"I am aware of the fact that I am a black woman. That is what it is: a fact. It's not something that I have to think about. When I look in the mirror I see that Judith Jamison is a black woman.

"But it would be a lie if I said that I spent my life thinking about being black. The color of my skin had very little to do with the sort of person I was raised to be by my parents in Philadelphia. My brother Johnny and I went to white schools and there was never, that I can remember, any attempt at racial discrimination between students, either in grade school or in high school.

"Maybe I was protected from racial prejudice by being so much involved in dancing, but the only competitive thing I can remember from school was between me and another black girl—and it was on who could run faster.

"When I started dancing professionally I was not treated prejudicially by other dancers. It was just that—as I came to realize—dancers in the ballet were white, not black, or, *if* there were black dancers, they had light skins, that allowed them to "pass" for white. I was not among them. I was a tall, black girl who had been trained to dance.

"After spending fourteen years in the Ailey company, after traveling all around the world as a dancer, I still don't make the distinction between myself and other dancers by the color of skin. I don't think: Judi, you danced like a black dancer, one night; and, another night: Hey, girl, you know you danced—or nearly danced—like a white dancer tonight. I don't believe that John Neumeier choreographed Potiphar's Wife for me because I am black. I believe he did it as a role in *Josephslegende,* and he used me, the kind of dancer I am, to create the character."

That Potiphar's Wife was black added a grace note. The character was made exotic.

In the matter of *Cry,* "there Alvin had a specific viewpoint, about black women. It was dedicated to black women everywhere, and especially to his mother. When *Cry* is danced in America, it has a strictly relative meaning. But when *Cry* is performed somewhere like Romania, where a black woman is truly a romantic oddity, I get the same responses as in my own country."

Cry in such circumstances went beyond the specific, the black woman abased in white society, and became symbolic in a more universal sense. It was seen as evidence of the unquenchable human spirit, enduring, and rising to overcome unbearable oppression. People had whispered that *Cry* was "a revolutionary" dance.

If Jamison played Charades (the parlor game in which players try to guess the identity of one player by a few succinct clues) in the 1960s, she would have identified herself as *a: a dancer,* and *b: a female dancer,* and only if she were asked for her color would she have mentioned that she was black. Now, if she played Charades, she would alter the order of her clues, and give her identity as a woman; a woman who danced; and a woman dancer who happened to be black.

Alvin Ailey, meanwhile, was still in search of his identity, within the puzzling maze of his "black American" mythology. He had moved from his midtown Manhattan apartment and gone to live in Harlem.

TWENTY-SIX

Jamison rejoined the Ailey company for the 1979–80 seasons, which were to include fall and spring seasons at the New York City Center, a coast-to-coast tour of the United States, and appearances in the principal cities in Japan.

Jamison resumed her European engagements as Potiphar's Wife in *Josephslegende,* which was now being produced at the Vienna Staatsoper, in Munich, and by the Hamburg Ballet. In addition, Jamison was invited by Neumeier to dance for the Nijinsky Gala, a program staged in Hamburg in July.

There was more. Jamison signed a contract to appear in the lead of a Broadway show: *Sophisticated Ladies.*

Three years before, while Jamison was bound to the aborted musical, *The Only World in Town,* efforts had begun to obtain rights to produce a show with Duke Ellington's music. This had now materialized, as *Sophisticated Ladies,* named for one of Ellington's most popular compositions, *Sophisticated Lady.* Donald McKayle, who had been working with Ellington, at the time of the composer's death, on a television show, was engaged as the choreographer. There would be four principal roles other than Jamison's lead, and a cast of about a dozen singers and dancers, backed by a twenty-piece orchestra. *Sophisticated Ladies,* it was announced, would not be a conventional musical or a revue. Instead of a libretto, it would be based on sayings of Ellington, his own words, interwoven with dance and music.

Szilard was satisfied with the arrangements for Jamison's contract. There was every evidence that the show would be well organized; auguries for its Broadway success were good.

Budgeted at $1.5 million, *Sophisticated Ladies* had five producers, among them Ellington's publisher, Burton Litwin (whose company, Belwin Mills, lists two hundred and fourteen Ellington compositions in its catalogue). The show would have an out-of-town run, beginning in Philadelphia in December. It was scheduled for a Broadway premiere in February 1981.

Jamison started back to work at the Ailey Center, at first with a quaking consciousness that her left leg was fastened in the hip socket by four steel pins, reminder of the body's fragility. She soon put aside fears of this kind and accepted "the usual aches and pains" of dancing as "occupational." Besides her joyful anticipation of the year's work, diverse, and challenging in the new experience it offered her, Jamison was delighted that Ulysses Dove had choreographed a solo for her.

Dove had recently choreographed his first work for the Alvin Ailey Repertory Ensemble, as *I See the Moon . . . the Moon Sees Me*. The dance he made for Jamison was in five parts, a large work of its genre.[1] Music, by Robert Ruggieri, and poetry, by Robert Maurice Riley (read by Reuben Green), had been composed and written for the work. It had an enigmatical title: *Inside*. Jamison was to perform it on the domestic tour, in early 1980, and it would have its New York premiere during the spring season at City Center.

In the Los Angeles engagement of the Alvin Ailey American Dance Theater—at Royce Hall, on the University of California's Los Angeles campus, March 14–17, 1980—Jamison reminisced with a friend on her associations with the company. That autumn, she would have been with the Ailey for fifteen years. The Ailey itself was about to mark an anniversary, its twenty-second year of existence, on March 30. It was on March 30, 1958, that the twenty-seven-year-old dancer, Alvin Ailey, first presented a troupe of dancers under his aegis, in New York, and, he had often remarked, in so doing gave up "the happy, uncomplicated life" he had been living as a successful performer, then the most admired black male dancer in popular theatre in America.

The occasion of the company's twenty-second anniversary passed unnoted by the Alvin Ailey Dance Center on Broadway. The company was, officially, in its twenty-first season, until the new fall season began in 1980.

Spring that year was a season of gloom at the Ailey Center. On

[1] Ulysses Dove moved to Paris in 1981, on leave of absence from the Ailey company, to work with Jacques Garnier, director of Groupe de la Recherche Chorégraphique de l'Opéra Paris, as teacher, choreographer, and assistant director of the Groupe, which appears at the Théâtre de la Ville.

© JACK MITCHELL

Judith Jamison and Sarita Allen in THE MOOCHE,
choreographed by Alvin Ailey.

© JACK MITCHELL

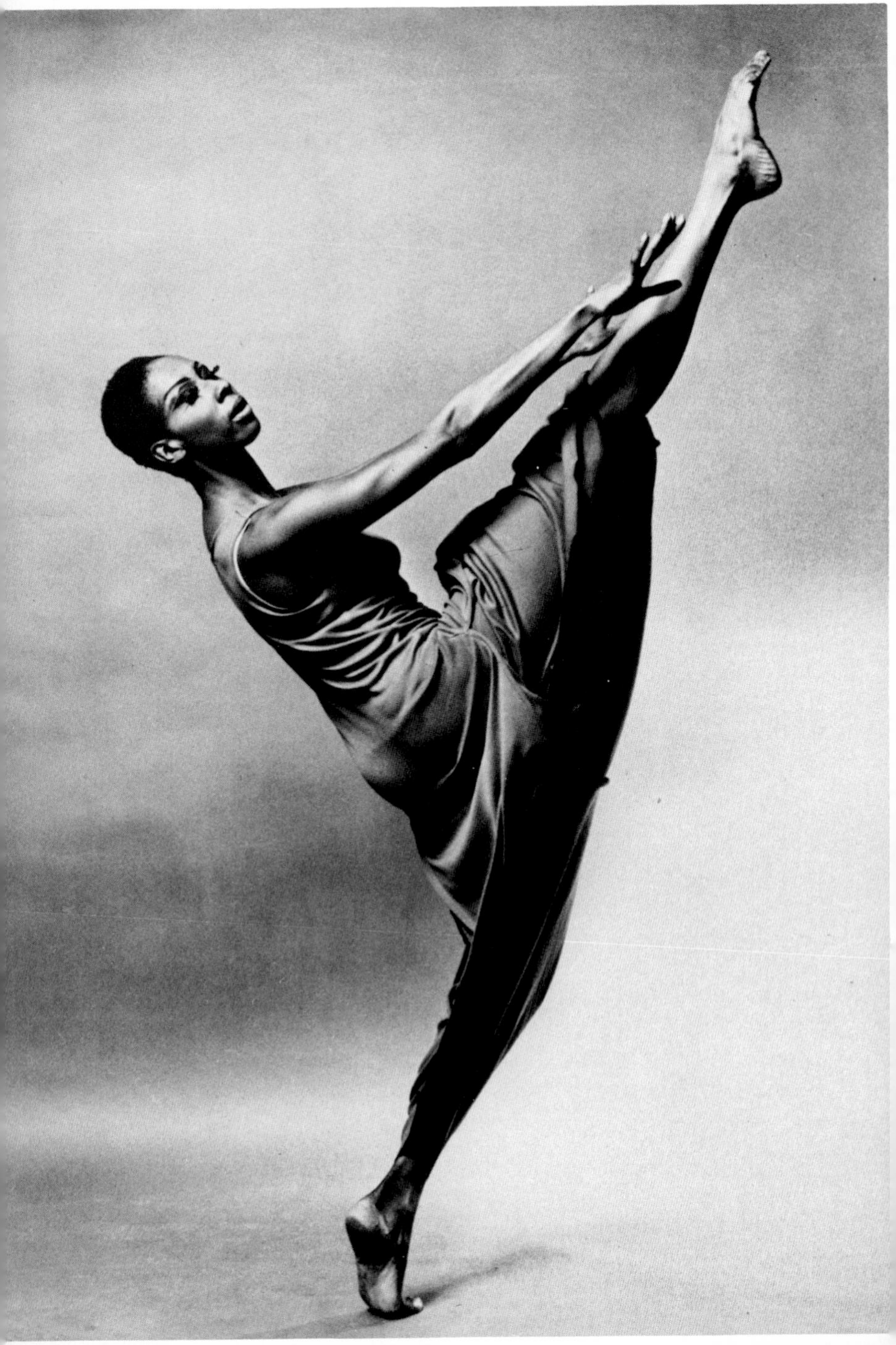

Judith Jamison...a body superbly balanced,
sublimely in command of space.

Judith Jamison and her manager, Paul Szilard,
in her dressing room at the Lunt-Fontanne Theatre
after the premiere of the musical
SOPHISTICATED LADIES, March 1, 1981.

Judith Jamison romping with her beloved dog, Emma.

in the "Sophisticated Lady" number of the
Broadway musical SOPHISTICATED LADIES.

Judith Jamison in SOPHISTICATED LADIES.
Costumes by Willa Kim.

March 7, Alvin Ailey had been arrested by police in New York and taken to Manhattan's Bellevue Hospital, where he was detained for psychiatric observation.

The news coursed like an electric shock through the dance world. Many were appalled by it and those who knew Ailey well marveled that such things could have happened to this good, kind, generous, and essentially gentle man. It was perhaps a relief to believe the tight-lipped anonymous statements made by Ailey's associates, that he had suffered "a complete nervous breakdown." Madness could excuse anything, even a sort of social suicide.

The charges brought against Ailey resulted from a fracas at International House, a student residence near Columbia University, and were of criminal trespass, harassment, disorderly conduct, and resisting arrest. Ailey was held at Bellevue (and charged $329 per day for being boarded and lodged there) for a few days, and released with the undertaking that he would seek psychiatric care.

Paul Szilard, Ailey's agent and manager, gave interviews to the press, explaining that Ailey was exhausted from overwork and worry. His choreographic commitments and his duties as the head of the Ailey Center had overtaxed him physically and mentally. The demented manner in which he had behaved on March 7 was caused, it was said, by temporary disorientation, suffered by Ailey as the result of a too strenuous dietetic regime. He had been on a liquid protein diet and had rapidly reduced his weight by almost fifty pounds.

Stanley Pleasant, Ailey's attorney (who, in the early 1970s, had been chairman of the board of trustees of the Ailey organization) obtained Ailey's release from Bellevue and, in statements to the press, announced that complainant charges against Ailey would be dropped at the court arraignment on April 15. Moreover, the record of arrest against Ailey would be "expunged."

Gossip, however, could not be quieted nor rumor stilled. Ailey's private affairs were made public. He had gone to International House in search of a protégé, a young Moroccan male for whom Ailey had arranged entry into the United States on a student visa.

Ailey and the Moroccan student met in Paris in the winter of 1979 and when the youth arrived in New York he went to live with Ailey in the latter's apartment. Then the young man had left Ailey and moved to International House, from where he returned to Paris. According to personnel of International House, Ailey had badgered them with telephone calls and harassed them with importunate visits in attempts to communicate with his friend. After the Moroccan student left, Ailey refused to believe that he had gone back to Paris, and continued to demand information on the young man's whereabouts. His insistence on gaining information (which Ailey later maintained was rudely refused him) culminated in the scandalous episode of March 7.

Upon his release from Bellevue, Ailey went to a sanatorium outside New York, for psychiatric treatment. Bulletins were reassuring and almost cheery on his progress. Ailey's condition, which had resulted in behavior so uncharacteristic of him as to be bizarre, was said to stem from depression. Ailey was not alone in suffering from what has come to be called the disease of the twentieth century: a state, often with physical symptoms, of morbidly excessive melancholy, with moods of hopelessness and feelings of inadequacy. Current statistics show a large and ever-growing percentage of Americans to be suffering from depression. It attacks people in all walks of life, and in surprisingly varied classifications of chronological age, religion, environment, and profession. Black persons, it is believed, are especially prone, from being compelled to endure more than an average degree of anxiety and frustration.

People in the arts are by no means immune. The episode on March 7 at International House was blown into a full-scale scandal in the press only because of the fame of the Ailey name. Ailey's company, more than any other dance company in the country, possessed a folkloric nature for the American public. Others, in American theatre, had before this been known to lose control of their urges and actions, to abandon grace and dignity under the influence of drugs, drink, or clinical madness. The sad news of their sufferings, and their crazed outbreaks, were hushed, kept, charitably, inside the world of the theatre. Ailey's troubles were blazoned in national newspapers and sent out by international news services around the world. The affair of March 7 at International House was baldly reported in dance periodicals and made the subject of feature articles in popular magazines.

Ailey's friends were troubled not so much by the arrest and the incarceration in Bellevue, as by the possible effects of the humiliating publicity. Ailey was described as "an intensely private man." He tried to keep his private and professional affairs divided, between "the thousands of people he knows as acquaintances and the few people he calls friends." There had been times when Ailey had been reluctant to give out his home address and telephone number. He lived, it seemed, a "mysterious" existence in Harlem, quite separate from that governed by the Alvin Ailey Dance Center on Broadway.

The noxious scandal would, Ailey's friends feared, "leave him without his dignity . . . and Alvin's dignity is more precious to him than gold." Ailey, however, was impregnable to gossip. At his arraignment on April 15, attended by dancers from the Ailey company, and some of his associates from the Ailey Center, he conducted himself with aplomb. Rather than being embarrassed at being seen in court, Ailey seemed to embarrass those who had come there to see him.

His recuperative powers were excellent. He left the sanatorium and resumed his duties at the Center, as calm and soft-voiced, as punctiliously polite as always. "Alvin," Jamison had remarked, "has never stopped being a Southern gentleman." Nor, despite the traumatic events of March 7, did Ailey appear in any way altered. He seemed "perfectly sane," and looked as he had looked for many years, since growing a moustache and short beard, at the 1980 Dance Magazine Awards on March 31.

Ailey liked African dress, and instead of a coat he wore a *dashiki,* a striped woolen cloak somewhat in the style of a poncho, which he had brought home from Africa. He collected African jewelry, massive bracelets and rings. Sometimes he wore a belt with a large buckle engraved with emblems of the American Indian. Having associated himself with his "black and brown brothers," and having so often referred to himself as "a black American," Ailey deeply shocked and wounded his friends by the use of the vituperative term "nigger," which he was reported to have used (as an epithet directed to the persons who subdued him) during the fracas at International House. This part of the incident, more than any other, convinced Ailey's friends that he had suffered a mental breakdown.

Although he seemed well at the Dance Magazine Awards, he told a friend that he was exhausted. "I am going to be fifty next January but I feel a hundred years old." It was not age that sapped his strength but a sense of futility. After twenty-one and more years of work, he said bitterly, he would like to feel—"as any normal man wants to feel"—that he had accomplished something. The Alvin

Ailey Dance Center, he was reminded, stood as a monument of his success. Ailey despondently replied: "Everything is ephemeral."

He was still obliged to beg for money, year after year, for the company's maintenance. "Every year I have to start all over again, to prove myself. The worries are bigger because the company has grown into this big organization. We need more money every year not because we are extravagant or impractical but because of inflation. It seems frivolous to be asking for money for dance while people are having trouble putting food on the table. But dancers have the same needs as other people. They want to make a living. I've made personal sacrifices for my work. I don't complain—I only wish I could feel that I've done something worthwhile.

"Dance has always been a very humanistic thing for me. But now this thing—the Ailey—is so big, it's so structured, that it's changed, and it's changing me.

"I have to behave like an autocrat to run it. Man, that's not the way I feel, the way I want to work with people."

He felt that his choreographic energy had been sapped by the rigid protocol of the new Ailey. Every work, in rehearsal and in production, had to fit into an annual budget, and it was required of Ailey that he plan at least a year ahead. So, he said, when he had an idea for a ballet, often the idea died, or he lost interest in it, long before it was possible to begin working on it in a studio, with his dancers.

He felt that his work was with the dancers but, in the midst of preparing for a new season, he would be required to work on applications for grants of funds, from administrations that demanded them at least a year—preferably, two or three years—in advance.

So Ailey had come to look on "the Ailey" as a monster, and to see himself as being devoured by it. The metaphorical conjunction of monster and sacrificial object gave Ailey's plaints an oddly impersonal tone, as though he were describing something out of myth rather than expressing feelings about himself. And in fact, the way in which Ailey conducted himself, the way in which he conversed, led people to think that, in the scant space of less than a month, he had wholly recovered from his *crise de nerfs*. The robustness of his physique, his benign, almost beaming expression, persuaded his friends into thinking that he was hale and hearty. But Ailey's discontent persisted and with it his feelings of inadequacy, almost of worthlessness.

He spoke of his friend, the blues singer Brother John Sellers, as an example of "integrity." Sellers and Ailey met in 1961, when the singer was performing at Folk City in Greenwich Village. Ailey at that time was looking for musical accompaniment for a pas de deux, for him and Carmen de Lavallade to dance at the 10th Annual Boston Arts Festival.

"I was into acting," Ailey recalled. He had just appeared at the Sheridan Street theatre in the play *Call Me by My Rightful Name*, "in the part of the black boy—the play was about two college boys, a black and a white, and one girl, who was white." Ailey was studying acting with Milton Katselas and the pas de deux (which for a week marked his temporary reunion with de Lavallade) seemed superficial to him. To Sellers, however, the undertaking was serious. He catechized Ailey, not only on the details of his life story but also on his philosophy, and only after he had satisfied himself on the sincerity of the young choreographer's purpose would Sellers consent to working with Ailey. "He had to believe in what he was doing," said Ailey of Sellers.

There was another episode with Sellers of which Ailey was even prouder. Appearing with the Ailey company in a London engagement a few years later, Sellers was required to sing the musical accompaniment to an Ailey work: *Been Here and Gone*. Ailey composed it as a suite of dances set to black folk ballads that he knew from the minstrel shows of his childhood in Texas. In London, Ailey added a song, "I Wonder as I Wander." This song Brother John Sellers would not sing, because it was a "white" song, and he did not understand it, could not feel it.

To Ailey, refusal to compromise was the core of integrity. *He* was obliged to compromise, not out of weakness or greed, but because of his responsibilities to scores of people who were now involved in the Ailey organization. "I lie awake at night," said Ailey, "wondering if I should quit. And in the morning I get up and go to work. I have to believe in what I am doing and it gets harder to believe every year."

He was, he complained, enslaved by a budget, "with a deficit hanging over my head." He was expected to treat the Ailey not as an artistic company but as a business undertaking, with profit and loss—deadening, Ailey protested, to the work of an artist. By giving up the administrative side of the company, he felt he had lost control "since 1968, when we spent more than we had," and had been called to accounting for grants of funds. Other artists preserved their independence, and their "integrity."

"Look at Donald McKayle. He went to Watts to start a school and company. I hear they promised him everything, even a theatre. They were going to have a *real* dance company in Los Angeles that would provide opportunities for talented black dancers on the West Coast.

"Things didn't work out as they were supposed to. So McKayle came back to New York, where he's better off. Instead of killing himself trying to get something going in Watts, he's free to work as he is doing on whatever job he wants to take and he's earning a lot more money free-lancing with musicals than he would have earned for working in Watts. It's only the dancers who lost out—and people in Watts. McKayle didn't have to give up his principles."

Ellington, said Ailey, "was cool, he did things in his own time, in his own way, or not at all." Ailey held up these paragons of integrity with which to mercilessly chastise himself. It was believed bad for his peace of mind to allow Ailey to dwell on thoughts of the dead, of Ellington and of Trisler, especially, following his breakdown. Ailey knew that if he ceased to mourn his beloved dead he would cease to be able to love the living. He had rashly taken on himself a punishing sense of responsibility for black dancers in America.

"Look at what Lester Horton did for me, when I was young and poor and didn't know much of anything except that I thought I might like to dance. He *heard* about me and Lester called me up and offered me a scholarship. I was a student at UCLA [the University of California at Los Angeles] but Lester arranged a schedule for me to take dance classes at his school. Lester had all the faith in the world that I would do what I wanted to do, if I worked hard enough.

"It hurts my heart that we have black kids at the school studying ballet and I know there is no chance of them getting into classical companies to dance. Nothing has changed.

"Arthur Mitchell's Dance Theatre of Harlem was supposed to prove that black dancers can dance in ballet—but that is just one, small company. And Mitchell's school and his company are ephemeral, too.

"When Mitchell left Balanchine's company, what other black dancer became a star at City Ballet? Who are the black dancers in the *New York City* Ballet, *the constituent of the New York City Center for Music and Drama!*

"There are maybe three black dancers in professional ballet [in the United States]. What is the ratio in the white and nonwhite population; and in terms of the ratio, what representation is there of black dancers in American ballet?[2]

"We teach ballet at the American Dance Center and we have lots

[2] The 1980 statistic: there are 25 million blacks in the country, a fact noted not only by dance artists but also by actors. Sidney Poitier, a highly respected film actor and director-producer, points out that, currently, only Richard Pryor and he represent blacks in Hollywood; that of the Latin-American populace, only Anthony Quinn and Ricardo Montalban are represented; and that from the Asian community there is no one. America is a multiracial society, said Poitier, but on the screen (as in ballet) it would be thought that no "minorities" existed. In 1981, the hundred-member New York City Ballet included one black dancer, Cynthia Lochard of the corps de ballet, who graduated into NYCB from its parent school, the School of American Ballet. Future opportunities for her appear to be limited, on the precedent of another black dancer, Deborah Austin, who remained in the NYCB corps for eight years (after which she left to join the Zürich Ballet in Switzerland). Two members of the all-black Dance Theatre of Harlem, Paul Russell and Ronald Perry, migrated into "white" companies. Russell was listed in 1980–81 on the roster of the San Francisco Ballet. Perry, a soloist, appeared in a featured role of *La Bayadère* (as an evil priest) and in Balanchine's *Theme and Variations*, with American Ballet Theatre. Besides Perry, ABT's ninety-member roster included another black dancer, Anna Benna Sims of the corps de ballet. Theoretically, Perry may expect to move into leading roles, such as Count Albrecht in *Giselle* and Prince Siegfried in *Swan Lake*. American ballet still suffers from a lack of male dancers, especially of the caliber required for the classical repertoire. Perry is a brilliant danseur and he is tall and handsome. However, in June 1981, another black classical dancer, Augustus Van Heerden (the only black dancer in the company), left the Boston Ballet, claiming that he had been discriminated against because of color. Violette Verdy and E. Virginia Williams, co-directors of the Boston Ballet, denied Van Heerden's charges but Henry Holth, president and general manager of the Dallas Ballet, admitted that "a matter of aesthetics" determines racist policies on casting dancers in ballets. The Dallas Ballet, a company of twenty, includes three "minority" members. It has engaged a Japanese-American dancer, Yoko Ichino, as guest artist. Dancers of Asiatic antecedents are more readily accepted into ballet companies than blacks. Ballet West of Salt Lake City has a fast-rising soloist of Oriental antecedents, Rhonda Lee. The Houston Ballet has engaged a danseur from China. At least one company has made efforts to integrate dancers in American ballet. The Philadelphia-based Pennsylvania Ballet in 1980 auditioned three hundred children from "inner city minority groups," admitting twenty-eight on scholarships to its school. However, there were no black dancers in the company. Even if Ailey's bitterness were to be dismissed as excessive, arithmetic would prove the truth of his statement that there is very little hope for a black dancer to make a professional career in ballet.

of black kids who show real talent, real affinity, for classical dancing. I have to tell them to concentrate on things like jazz if they
want to earn a living. There is no place for them in the white American ballet.

"It goes against my principles to have to say things like that. It
defeats my work, my whole life. I am going against everything I believe in, about the humanism of dance, and the relationships between people."

There was little or no hope of changing the situation, Ailey
thought, while Americans were, as he believed them to be, in-
herently prejudiced against nonwhite artists. When Ailey's statements on "racial issues" in dance appeared in print, they alarmed
and embarrassed his associates. Ailey's passionate feelings on the
inequities of prejudice were, however, admired when expressed as a
choreographer. *Masekela Langage,* revived at the New York City
Center in December 1977, was startlingly apropos as comment on
the current social conditions in South Africa.

Ailey spoke of Judith Jamison as a "phenomenon." She would, he
believed, become a successful entertainer providing she was given
the right roles. Her status as a dancer, in the international theatre,
was unlike that of any other living black dancer.

Jamison was about to begin working in musical theatre, reversing
the order in which Ailey had worked in New York. He was pleased
that she was going to realize the ambition of being the lead in a
Broadway show but he was glad that she had "made her way first as
a dancer."

"Judith is an extraordinary dancer. Like all great artists she is
unique. She brings some special elements to dancing.

"I respect her as a dancer because of her compassion and her
beauty. She has musicality, discipline, and taste—marvelous taste.
Above all, Judith is able to justify movement. That is what I ask
from a dancer, to justify movement. Judith does that."

He realized, Ailey said, that Jamison had not wished to be tied to
Cry, even though he had made the solo on her and for her. Jamison
now seldom danced *Cry;* it was more often performed by Donna
Woods. It had also been danced by Sara Yarborough, who, like
Woods, gave *Cry* a poignancy, whereas from Jamison the solo
derived "a raw, primal force."

He sympathized with Jamison's aversion to being typecast by *Cry,* tied to it as he, Ailey, was tied to *Revelations*. *Revelations,* Ailey said, had been intended as a full-length work, one to be performed in a single program—a highly innovative idea for a choreographer in 1959, when programming in American theatre, for ballet and for modern dance, was defined in three or more short works to a performance. Ailey longed to work now in multimedia theatre. He had no inclination to enlarge older works, nor even to choreograph purely dance works. He detested being asked to choreograph a "sequel" to *Revelations*.

"That would be good for business," he commented with a sneer, because audiences clamored for *Revelations* each time the Ailey appeared in a theatre. It had sometimes been necessary to encore parts of *Revelations* to avoid rioting by the public. Dance reviewers in New York and Los Angeles carped at the frequency with which the Ailey closed an evening's performance by dancing *Revelations,* while audiences never tired of the work.

"*Revelations* is how I felt, where my head was at, in the 1950s," said Ailey. He was now "into a whole new scene," one that he would reveal if only he could recapture his zest, summon the energy, to choreograph.

Jamison had many times heard second-hand of Ailey's admiring remarks about her as a dancer, and of his affectionate comments about her as a person. His generosity in releasing her from an obligation to *Cry* moved her. Told of what Ailey had said, by a friend, Jamison sat still and silent. The smoke from the cigarette held in a motionless hand rose in a thin plume, as the cigarette burned to ash. She put out the smoldering end and laid the long cigarette holder carefully on the table and then sat back, her arms folded under her breasts. She rocked herself gently.

Actors and dancers work from muscle memory, so much so that, in an access of real emotion, they behave as they have been directed to behave onstage. In 1977 Jamison had danced a solo, a modest work by Marleane Furtick, called *How Long Have It Been*. It began with Jamison seated but moving her body in an expression of anguish and yearning. Then, to the music of Lightnin' Hopkins, she arose in a wide-reaching, whirling dance. Now the friend watched as Jamison, transfixed by compassion for Ailey responded as though to keening music. "Poor Alvin!" she sighed.

The spring season had opened on May 7 at the New York City

Center, the seventeenth season of the Alvin Ailey Dance Theater in that house. Ailey, for the first time, was absent, as he had been absent on the domestic tour. A few days before the City Center opening Ailey had suffered another *crise,* an outburst of greater ferocity than that on March 7.

At three o'clock one morning, it was reported, Ailey had summoned a local fire station on a false alarm and then, apparently believing that the building was in flames, he had raced through the halls of his apartment house shouting the news to the tenants. It was alleged that when one woman opened the door of her apartment, Ailey had entered and physically assaulted her, although the woman was not seriously hurt. Police arrived and Ailey was seized and taken to St. Luke's Hospital for psychiatric examination.

Shortly after, Ailey was allowed to leave the hospital and thereupon committed himself to psychiatric care in a hospital outside New York. Prognosis this time was guarded as to his chances of complete recovery. Privately, some of Ailey's business associates voiced the belief that when he was sufficiently recovered Ailey might return to the Dance Center, but not in an administrative position. "This is a million-dollar business," said one of these business associates. "The dancers want to resist being treated as part of a business but they no longer have a choice. There is no state subsidy for theatre in this country and in these times [of severe economic stress and inflation] it is very hard to attract patronage, as donations. We have to treat the Ailey organization as what it is—a business organization, in the business of selling dance to audiences, who are consumers of entertainment. But popular as the company is, it cannot subsist on box office receipts. The only means of maintaining the Ailey company— of maintaining any dance company in the United States—is through funding. We have to work at getting grants from federal and state arts agencies, and from the industrial foundations. That's the only way the Ailey can hope to stay alive."

The day had come, as Ailey had foreseen, when a new breed in theatre, the fund-raisers, would become more necessary to the life of the company than the choreographer and the dancer.

Ailey's mother, Mrs. Lula Cooper, had neither the training nor the inclination to take over Ailey's administrative power. She could only fend off the curious press with optimistic statements, assuring those who inquired of her that her son's health would be restored and that he would choreograph again. Meanwhile, the company had to have a director under whom to function for the spring season at the New York City Center and during the tour of Japan. Judith Jamison was asked to take over the company. She consented, with the proviso that her title would be that of co-director to Alvin Ailey, and that her obligation would cease when Ailey returned to the company.

Jamison had also to fulfill her duties to the company as a dancer. She appeared in Dove's *Inside*—a work made possible in part by a grant from the New York State Council on the Arts—first in Los Angeles, during the March season of 1980, and later at the City Center in New York.

The program note was explicit:

INSIDE

(BETWEEN LOVE . . . AND LOVE)

I	Fear
II	Anger
III	I've Been Hurt Before
IV	Getting It All Out
V	Ready for Love

Wearing a red silk pajama suit designed by Judy Dearing, Jamison danced these transitions, these aspects and phases of a woman's feelings. The lighting, by Craig Miller, changed the color of her costume from red, through shades of orange, into purple. And Jamison once again was provided with a tour de force, of as great dramatic intensity as in *Facets,* except that while Butler's solo had been concerned with several women, Dove's was concerned with one.

"Chapter and verse," said Jamison of *Inside,* to a friend, "the story of a life."

Jamison went on tour with the Alvin Ailey American Dance Theater to Japan. When the company returned to America she went to Europe, to appear in scheduled performances of *Josephslegende,* and to dance in Hamburg, for the Nijinsky Gala.

Alvin Ailey, as his mother, Mrs. Lula Cooper, had said he would, and as Jamison had believed he would, returned to take the helm of his company, for the twenty-second year, during which the Ailey company would be presented December 3–21, 1980, and May 5–24, 1981, in seasons at the New York City Center. The company would again tour the United States and Canada. It would again have a season in Paris.[3]

From these appearances Jamison would be absent, on leave from the Ailey company. In late summer of 1980 she went into rehearsal for the Broadway musical *Sophisticated Ladies*.

These events occurred in the thirty-sixth year of Judith Jamison's life; her sixteenth, as a dancer.

Jamison, and those who had observed her career in dance, were reminded, this year, of the words spoken by Alvin Ailey in 1972, when, at the close of the Dance Magazine Awards ceremony (during which Awards for that year were given to Jamison and to The Royal Ballet's premier danseur Anthony Dowell), Ailey suddenly asked permission to speak. This is what he said:

"I'd like to say something about Judith, who is an extraordinary person in American dance, in the history of dance. Judith is a lady who came in 1965 to my company. A tall gangly girl with no hair. I always thought she was beautiful . . . Judith has developed, she has grown; she's a beautiful, extraordinary person. She must say something about the virtues of early training in our dancers. She was trained very young, and we must do something in our country about training all our dancers from an early age.

"We must learn the value of our artists. We must do something about getting the Government to subsidize the arts, so that our young people can get into what they are . . . We in the black dance have an extraordinary problem. We are involved, unfortunately, with a country which does not appreciate its artists, a country involved with racism, which I do not like. We are people as artists, as dancers, and we must learn to appreciate people for what they are, not for what their color is or for what they believe, but for what they have to give *as human beings*. I think that Judith has shown us this.

"We must train our dancers early, as I have said, and we must recognize and nurture their potential. We must do everything we can

---

[3] Alvin Ailey, seemingly fully recovered from his illness, was an even more mythic figure than he had been before. In 1981, the company, over which he remained as director, appeared more stable economically and, indisputably, strong enough to withstand defections. Ailey himself remained respected and admired in the international dance theatre. In 1981 he mounted a version of his *Memoria* for the Royal Danish Ballet.

for them. We, as artists, are the people of the world; we're the people who know; we're the people who believe; we're the spirit of the century; we're the people who came before; we're the people who have gone beyond . . .

"We must learn, however, to love one another. We must learn to appreciate; we must learn to live; we must learn to give. I salute Judith's grandmother and mother and father. I am only a messenger for the human message; I am only a messenger for what is real, for what is beautiful in mankind. And I think that Judith is a fine representative of that. I thank you all for giving her this wonderful tribute."[4]

[4] Reprinted with permission, courtesy of DANCE MAGAZINE, Danad Publishing Company, Inc., 1180 Avenue of the Americas, New York, N.Y. 10036.

LIVING

Gödel, a colleague of Einstein, conceived of time not as dimension per se but as enormous circles; as rings, the smallest radius of which was the radius of the universe. In a Gödel trajectory, there are curves strictly controlled by acceleration, in what we think of as space-time. Theoretically, if you have the same energy, you would return to the same event . . .

Physicists contend that, were that to happen, the person would suck her environment and everyone in it back with her into space-time.

Memory and the act of remembering have something of the nature of a Gödel trajectory, in the conscious purpose of living (and reliving) a life.

ONE

The baby born on May 10, 1944, in West Philadelphia, to John Jamison and his wife, Tessie Belle Jamison, née Brown, was a girl weighing six pounds, twelve ounces. Her long slender fingers and toes gave the infant an exquisite delicacy. Grandmother Annie Brown was a small woman and it was believed that the child, with her fragile bone structure, would also be petite.

At the age of fourteen, the child, Judith Jamison, had grown to five feet, eight inches; two years later, she reached her full height of five feet, ten. Though taller than the average for a woman, Jamison retained a delicacy. The ring finger of her left hand measures merely four and three quarters on a ring gage.

The dancer Judith Jamison combines fragility and force in a provocatively sensual way. Her limbs are almost too attenuated for the solid torso, in which the waist is scarcely more indented than that of a boy. She has small, high breasts and long lean thighs, sloping into powerful, slender legs.

Jamison's face is distinguished by pride and intelligence and, sometimes, an almost Oriental inscrutability. But she has a radiant, sweet smile, the truest indication of her warm and affectionate nature. She has the soft, dense, tightly crimped hair and the large luscious mouth, the lips curved in a double bow, characteristic of some African peoples. Other characteristics make her a black Nefertiti: the arched nose with flanged nostrils, the low broad forehead, the enormous dark eyes, set flush in their sockets, the whites as clear as those of a child. Her face, a pure oval, resembles the Gelede masks of the Yoruba, a great and ancient African people, whose kingdom encompassed cities of Egypt and of Arabia.

Jamison is unknowing and largely uncaring of the antecedents who have bred her. "My ancestry goes back only as far as a grandmother. Once, in school, my class was given a project, to make a 'family tree.' I went home and asked my mother to help me. She wrote her father's and her mother's names in one line; under it, she wrote her name and my father's name. Then she wrote mine. That was it. We have no past because no records were kept for us."

Three generations are sufficient to establish a dynasty and Jamison's heritage is more than that possessed by many Americans of her generation. Black people, leaving the South, jettisoned the past like sailors jumping ship: new identities were made in the future. The Jamisons are Philadelphians, every trace of an older heritage removed from the third generation, by chance or by intent. "My roots," says Judith Jamison, "are in the family photo albums; that is where I go to trace my family history.

"I know my mother's family, the Browns; Grandmother and Grandfather, Uncle Sam and Aunt Allie. My father came from Durham, North Carolina, but of his family I only know his sister, Aunt Henrietta. In the albums, I see my mother and Aunt Allie, and Henrietta. I see my parents when they were young, with my brother John, and with me. I see my whole life there, as I was growing up.

"I was shown one picture in the album and told: 'That is your father's mother.' And I was told: 'You take after her.' I never knew her; she is a stranger, this woman who is part of my past.

"I don't remember asking my dad questions about his mother but I think the photo haunted me. It was eerie—this unknown woman, her blood, through my father, flowed in my veins.

"In our family we never talked about where we came from. We were very close, we were affectionate to each other, but we did not discuss feelings or try to analyze things. I suppose you could say that in our family we deal more with reality than with the abstract."

The Jamison children, a boy, John, and the girl, Judith, grew up within boundaries, ample and resilient, in which there were steadfast compass points: home, with the parents; Grandfather and Grandmother's houses, one in town, one in the country; school, throughout the primary and secondary Philadelphia educational system; recreation—the Judimar School of the Dance, Marian Cuyjet's academy, for Judith; and Bethel Church where the Jamisons worshipped. The permanency of this existence, its unfaltering rhythms, bore the Jamison children through childhood into adolescence. For Judith Jamison, the rhythms remained almost unaltered into the year she was twenty-one. It is in this familiar geography and history that Jamison reviews her past.

The earliest memory she has of herself is at the age of four, "going on five," sitting at the back of her father's big truck, holding the family cat in her lap, looking back at the house in which she had been born. The Jamisons were moving to Germantown, to the house in which they still live, and where Jamison grew up.

"There was nothing heavy in it for me, leaving the house in West Philadelphia. It was nothing traumatic. If I felt anything it was glad, to be riding in the back of my daddy's truck, which was always a big treat. And I was busy trying to hold the cat, Kit-wit, from jumping out of the truck. I looked back at the old house and went away from it, to the new house in Germantown, which was right next door to my grandmother's house—my mother's mother's house.

"Before we left West Philadelphia, I had a bad dream. I dreamed our house was on wheels, and it started rolling, rolling, so fast that I couldn't catch it. It went rolling down a hill. I know why I dreamed that dream. In Philadelphia, the milk was delivered by horse-drawn wagons. I knew the sound of the wooden wheels on the cobbly street. Then the sound changed, when the wagon changed from wooden wheels to rubber tires. The milk came in glass bottles—the bottle had a little seal that you had to flip up.

"When we moved to Germantown, my dad loaded up his truck every day and we drove over to the new house, about a forty-five-minute ride from West Philadelphia. The old house got emptier and emptier but we came back to it, to sleep, every night, until everything was moved out. It was during that time that I had my nightmare—about the house rolling away on wheels. I thought: I've had a bad dream. I didn't know anything about nightmares until later, when I read about them in a book.

"Before I was five, I did not really know my grandmother, except to think of her as a warm, soft lady. My first impression of her was the softness of her skin—like marshmallows. In Germantown, we lived right next door and she would come to visit, or I would go visit her and my grandfather, and my Uncle Sam, who lived with them. I made up a code, to talk to them, through the wall: two knocks for Grannie, one knock for Uncle Sam. The walls of those houses are tremendously thick, so I would have to bang on them with all my might. It nearly drove my mother crazy, but my grandmother didn't mind. Nothing that my brother and I did upset our grandparents. They had raised three children . . .

"In summers, the grandparents took care of Johnnie and me. My grandfather had a lot of land, and he built a house in the country, where we used to stay. It had a big garden, with corn and water-melon.

"I was always aware of the beauty of my family. My grandmother had been a beauty as a girl—petite, with an hourglass figure. She passed on her beauty to her daughters, Tessie Belle, my mother, and Aunt Allie. All three have beautifully proportioned legs. The knee is small, the calf long, the thigh is exquisitely tapered, the leg is almost hyperextended.

"I related to my family through the family photo albums. Mom and Aunt Allie, and my father's sister, Aunt Henrietta, used to have their picture taken together. Mom was very pretty and Aunt Allie was spectacular!—big eyes, high cheekbones; she looked something like Carmen Macrae. Aunt Allie was very chic. She was the dresser in the family. She used to look as though she had stepped out of the pages of *Vogue*. Aunt Allie was the first in my family to get a col-lege degree. She went to the University of Chicago and became a law-yer—a government lawyer—in Chicago. Aunt Allie was also the first woman to smoke in the family.

"The sisters are quite different. Mom is ladylike and demure. Aunt Allie had great gusto. It's from her that I get my sense of humor.

"My mom is the rock on which our family is built. We all clung to her. While Johnnie and I were children, even after we were grown up, she stayed home. Her one care was for the family. She never had a life of her own until recently, when she began teaching creative drama to children. I remember her, from my childhood, as always being at home, the queen of our home. My father was the king.

"The impression I carry of my father and mother is one of radi-ance. Mom was very pretty and my father was magnificent. I thought all men had to look like him: deep-chested, broad-shouldered, long-legged. Both my parents are short-waisted, with very long legs. I take after my father, with long legs, slender, with high calves, and I'm broad-shouldered as he is.

"What a gorgeous couple my parents made when they were young! There is a photo of us: Mom and Dad, Johnnie—in a suit—and me—in a Sunday-go-to-church dress—but I don't have to look at it to remember the scene. I can still *see* in my head that room, just how it looked—the purple sofa, the dining table. I as clearly remember the beauty of my parents. Mom was then in her late twenties, Dad a little older.

"I admired the beauty of the Browns, my mother's side of the family, so much that I used to wish I resembled them instead of my father's mother. The picture they showed me, of Dad's mother, was of a woman who looked nothing at all like the women in my mom's family. Because her face seemed so strange to me, I thought, as a child: What a weird-looking woman! And I thought: If I look like her I must be weird-looking too.

"I don't remember that anyone ever commented, in a derogatory way, on my looks, except that people, of course, were always telling me I was tall. A fourteen-year-old girl of five feet eight is as tall as —maybe taller than—a boy her own age. But I didn't have to go through any adolescent troubles, wanting boys to admire me. I was too busy competing with boys at sports, that is, when I wasn't dancing. So I was spared the kind of misery you hear about adolescence. Nobody ever came along and told me: 'Listen, you are a teenager'— meaning, I was going to come in for a lot of problems. Boys did not seem mysterious, and glamorous, to me. I had a brother and I knew him and his friends. Boys were boys, girls were girls, and some girls went to ballet school.

"It was a very healthy, uncomplicated outlook on life, and on growing up. I may have seemed overprotected and too innocent but I did not feel deprived by the sort of life my parents gave us. At home I always had a room of my own. I never lacked for privacy, a thing that is very important to me. I used to stay in my room with a pile of books, and records going on the phonograph. I think my parents realized that children do a lot of growing up when they are alone. Children are terribly selfish and self-centered, and they are possessive. You never think of your parents as real people—a man and a woman and not just 'parents.' It is only later, when you leave home and look back, that you begin to wonder who they really are, *as persons*. But then there is never again time enough, and the perfect opportunity, to find out.

"I wonder a lot now about my parents. My father, who has such a gift for music, and so much love of music—why did he not have a career as a musician? My father has a beautiful baritone voice. He wanted to be a concert singer. What turned him away from that goal, what made him become, instead, a sheet-metal mechanic? My father has a good and honorable profession—in which he earned a good living for his family—but my father is a singer. The first memory I have of Dad is singing me to sleep. The first time I remember feeling proud was because my father was singing in our church.

"Some day I want to ask him, what made you choose your life; why did you do so-and-so, instead of this-and-that? I want to know about this man who is my father. I want to know everything about everybody, so that I can know everything about myself.

"For a long time my mother was my second self. In our family, my mother is the crown. She is a woman of very strong character, and she is the pivot of this family. That is no exaggeration . . .

"Once, my mother went out shopping and was taken ill but when the police brought her home, I pretended that there was nothing wrong. Instead of screaming and crying, I began laughing, and teasing her, refusing to accept that there was something seriously the matter. *I would not let myself believe . . .*

"My mother had had a cerebral hemorrhage and was near death. They put her to bed and sent for my father, to come home from work. The world was coming apart, everyone was in a state of panic, except me. I stayed calm, while the iron rule I lived under lay in a snoring coma in the other room.

"I knew my mother was not going to die, and she didn't. She made a complete recovery and it did not surprise me. If I had believed, for a single moment, that my mother would die that day, I would have died too. It wasn't hysteria that I felt; it was that this was my anchor, and that I could not let it go.

"What is it like to be a woman like my mother? A true matriarch, who is the foundation for other people's lives . . . My mother has a fine mind, she has great capabilities, but she seemed satisfied, as her mother was, with being a wife and a mother. Aunt Allie had a career. Did my mother envy Allie her independence, did she want a career for herself?

"These are questions that, even now, I would hesitate to ask my mother for fear that she would misunderstand, and imagine that I felt she could have made more of herself, in a career outside the home. It's not that, at all. What I long to know is whether *she* made the choice, or if it was fate that decided her life for her.

"My grandmother, to whom I have always been close, is another mystery to me. What was she like as a girl? Was she much different from me? Times change but do people really change? The things that I need, because I am a woman, are they any different from the things my mother, and her mother, needed as women? And men, as men, with their needs, are they much changed between my father's generation and my brother's? My brother has a son. When he is a man, what will *he* be like? Families, people closest to each other, remain mysteries. Is it out of loneliness that people fall in love?"

Jamison is proud but almost entirely without vanity. She speaks of herself without embarrassment and without aggressiveness. She recapitulates events in her life without apologies or excuses. Jamison, in that respect, is like a Trobriand Islander, in whose language there are no words that mean *because* or *why*. She has a curious detachment: "Judith Jamison, as I see her, is a dancer who is a woman, who happens to be black. I guess these three things: dancing, femininity, and blackness, make up who and what I am. I have never tried to separate them because if I did I would be fragmented, maybe shattered. I try to know myself, not because I am on an ego trip but because it helps to see yourself as you go from one phase to another; if you've changed, and the ways in which changes affect you."

Child of the theatre, Jamison unconsciously looks at herself, the performer, in perspective, turning various aspects to the view. The "phases" of her life are like scenes on which the curtain rises, the curtain falls, and rises yet again.

TWO

For European audiences, Judith Jamison is the black Venus. Her size, her blackness, her beauty are as bewitching as her dancing. As an American performer, she is an enigma to them. Europeans do not know how she was formed, they understand little of the environment in which she grew up as a child in Philadelphia. It is inconceivable to many Europeans that Judith Jamison is a product of middle-class society and that, until she went to New York in 1965, her existence was almost as circumscribed, and she almost as sheltered, as any carefully brought-up European miss.

To American audiences, Jamison is hardly analogous to the popular and romanticized concept of the black performer. She did not rise, miraculously, from the ghetto. There are no rank and bitter memories of childhood. Rebellion against an unhappy destiny was not the goad that spurred her to the heights.

Jamison was reared within a family whose influences on her development remain constant and of which she remains conscious. Her sense of family is almost like a sense of God. For Jamison, her family is her root and anchor, the source of her self-identification.

"I started school when I was five," Jamison said. "At that time, it was usual to start when you were six and you graduated at eighteen. Nowadays there are labels for everything, but back then, if you were a bright child, that was enough—people didn't classify you as 'gifted.' I was bright enough to start to school at five and I finished high school at seventeen.

"There was a progression, where we lived, for schooling. We began at Henry School and studied there until the sixth grade. Then you went to Houston [Junior High], seventh to ninth grades. By the time I got to Houston, the system had changed, and Houston stopped at eighth grade, so I had to take my ninth year at Lee, which was the biggest school I ever attended. After that, I went to Germantown High.

"I got a super education. Classes at Henry School were about fourteen students; it was the equivalent of going to private school. Even at Lee, which seemed so big to me, there were only about three thousand students. These were white schools. At Lee there were two black students, and it was all Jewish. We got all the Jewish holidays . . .

"I don't recall that there was ever a feeling of being different than the children I knew in school. Blackness and whiteness did not become issues for us at Henry School, nor at Lee. They were neighborhood schools and the progression was natural. You moved up into higher grades with the same kids you had started with in first grade.

"I do remember, though only hazily, one incident, when I was still at Henry School. We had started having 'best friends' and mine was Murray Mald; he was M.M. and I was J.J. One day he invited me to his house for lunch and I went and afterwards my mother told me I was not to go again. That was all that was said. I don't think I asked my mom why, although now, as I look back, I suppose she was trying to protect me from being hurt. Parents lay down rules for their children, and it is usually to protect them. But this was a situation that was introduced to me, not one that I had to meet on my own. I thought, at the time, that my mom wanted me to come home for lunch, but not: *M.M. is white.*

"The school was a good twelve blocks from home and Johnnie and I walked them four times a day. Johnnie went to another school after a while, and I continued at Henry School. A few years ago, while I was at home, I decided to walk the way to school again, to reminisce. A lovely walk but I don't know how I did it four times a day every school day when I was a kid! There and back, morning, afternoon, and lunchtime. Mom always had Campbell's soup and sandwiches waiting for us. I never went back to M.M.'s house.

"I need to tell you [O.M.] something about the social structure. Germantown was at the bottom of a class strata. It was mainly white families, with maybe two or three black families, in an area of about twenty blocks. The whites were considered to be people who could not afford to move to Mount Airy, which was higher in the class strata. Airy had professional people, white-collar workers, as compared to the blue-collar workers in Germantown. There were black families in Mount Airy, the families of professional men who were lawyers or doctors.

"The division was not so much between black and white as it was between professional men and the laboring class. Of course, there was a certain amount of prejudice. It was difficult for a black family to move into one of those fifty- to a hundred-thousand-dollar homes on Mount Airy. Above that was Chestnut Hill, with its huge mansions, and *no* black people lived there—*regardless*—even if they happened to be presidents of banks!

"In the schools, the students were from all the class strata, black and white, rich and poor. The social structure was lower-middle class and upper-middle class, with Chestnut Hill the most posh.

"Other lines were drawn, among black people, for color. At that time we were not black people, we were Negroes, and this was before 'black is beautiful.' Either you were a professional, a lawyer or doctor or a big business executive, or you were of a lower class. And you fell into another sort of class, depending on if you were light brown or dark brown. When a black man was a success, he married a light-skinned woman, as light-skinned as he could find, because that was a status symbol.

"Light and dark skins were normal in our family. Part of it was dark brown, part of it was light brown. My grandparents' name is Brown, Brown was my mother's maiden name. Mom is dark brown in color and my Aunt Allie has a skin the color of honey. Their brother, Uncle Sam, was a shade in between. Grannie is light brown and my grandfather was black—the most beautiful shade of red-black I have ever seen.

"I have always been fascinated by the varieties that exist in 'black' skins, and in my family we tend to have rich red-black skins, or black skin with a tinge of green. Never ashy black. Ash-black can be very beautiful. I saw ash-black skins in Africa; a coal black, with a grayish tinge.

"My grandfather was the darkest-skinned of the family. My father is a beautiful rich brown color and Johnnie is darker, but not as dark as our grandfather. Johnnie married a girl with light skin. Bo [the pet name of Chloe Jean Jamison, Judith Jamison's sister-in-law] is very fair, with red hair.

"Aside from color—what shade you were [in the range that is

characterized by mulatto, quadroon, and octoroon]—there was the thing with hair. A lot of black people were very much into hair. This was before the Afro became stylish, and the longer you grew your hair, the better. I had my hair straightened in the years I was at Fisk, where I went to a hairdresser every week. She was marvelous and my hair has never been in better condition. The trick to making hair like mine grow, even into an Afro, is to straighten it from the root, about two inches, and let it grow naturally after that. As a child, my hair was much longer than it is now. My mother used to tie bows in my hair. She dressed me in pink, with bows to match. Johnnie and I were always well dressed—never overdressed—and we had to meet Mom's standards of what *her* children should look like . . .

"My mother's standards for the family were very high but, here again, there was no trauma attached to being a child in my family. I accepted everything as natural and normal. If I had thought about it, I would have believed that the way we lived was the way everybody lived.

"I never analyzed myself until now [during our conversations] but I don't feel that I was rebellious, unless quitting college was rebelling. All the time that I was growing up I was busy. My time was taken up with school, and dance lessons. When I had time to myself, I listened to my records, or read books. You [O.M.] asked me if I was a child who loved solitude. My mother would describe that as: 'Why do you stay in your room? Why are you closing the door?' She would say to me: 'You can't stay in your room all the time, playing your record player, and never taking your nose out of a book.' She would say: 'So-and-so is giving a party and you are invited. Don't you want to go?' I was happy, up in my room, with the record player and my records, and the books. The thing I said most often, when my Mom asked me: 'Where have you been?' was: 'To the library.'

"Being in my room was all that I wanted. Summers, I used to stay up there, reading and listening to music, only coming down for meals. My mom would tell me I had to go out and get some fresh air, I had to go and play. I cannot describe myself as a lonely child, or a solitary child. I was a child who was happiest when I was by myself.

"I was happy dancing but dancing was just something that I had always done. I don't remember when I learned to read, when I realized that I liked listening to music, or when I first danced—all these things were natural in my life, from the time I can think of myself as alive, and me.

"It's hard to go back into the past and relive your experiences in childhood. The child you were is another person that you have to examine, like a stranger. I am trying [in these talks] to separate what I truly remember—what I know I experienced—from memories that have accumulated about me as a child. Your parents relate you little episodes, tell you things you did, things that happened, when you were little, and if you hear these stories often enough you begin to picture yourself, as though you were actually *remembering*.

"I know that I remember some things because when I think about them the experience is *there*. I can still feel them. I see myself in the situations. Things like: cutting my foot and breaking an arm. They are clear, true memories, like walking home from school, and the episode of going to lunch at M.M.'s house. Those, and other things, happened to *me*, and not to another soul in the world.

"I wish I could say that I started to dance as some sort of great revelation. The truth is, dance came to me like reading, or listening to music—as pleasure, for joy. I remember starting with Miss Cuyjet and I remember, in every detail, my first performance. I could dance the dance Miss Cuyjet made for me to 'I'm an Old Cowhand'—step, *piqué;* step, *piqué;* turn. I know the actual steps. I remember the feelings I had when I did that dance. I suppose you would call them feelings of excitement, a thrill. But I was dumb. My mom asked me if I felt nervous and all I could say was 'Umm.' I pressed my lips together and I wouldn't talk. Other little girls bubble over when they are excited. My mom had to realize that *her* little girl clammed up. The thing was too big to talk about. I guess what I felt was a sensation of terrific power, dancing for an audience.

"I know that from very early in my life I enjoyed the sense of power, which, for me, is the sense of control. Supreme, exquisite control! I liked being the source of that power.

"You could say, my power-thrill thing was almost religious. You could say, it exalted me.

"Religion, to me, was music and power—the music of people singing, the music of the voice of the minister preaching, and the power that this music had on me, and on the congregation.

"Our church is Mother Bethel, African Methodist Episcopal, the first black church in the United States.[1] It was established by a black man, Richard Allen. When I was a child, Sunday was the high point in the week. At the start of services, ten choirs would progress down the aisles. I loved church. My father sang in the adult choir; I sang in the young people's choir.

"Best of all, I liked listening to the sermons. We had preachers of great dynamism. Most of them had really splendid presence, and speaking voices. They say children get restless in church. I never did. I would be riveted with attention during the one-and-a-half-hour-long sermon, never taking my eyes off the minister. I watched how he held the whole congregation in his hand—spellbound—until he chose to let it go. It was my first understanding of power.

"I often imagined myself in situations where I had great power, where I had absolute control. I pictured myself driving the longest train in the world. I could feel the mass of the train, the power in it, and myself at the controls. I saw myself piloting an enormous airplane, flying through the skies." She had a sense of illimitable space and the sensation of moving through it with incredible speed. Always, she was aware of her own identity, of herself as "the force in control."

But Jamison was also moved, by emotions whose nature she could not fathom, to a state of exaltation. "Our church is what is called 'old-time religion,' in which the minister and the congregation share very personal communication with God, and in a very direct way. When I joined the Ailey company and danced in *Revelations*, I knew exactly what Alvin wanted to say, because, in my childhood, in our church, I saw, over and over, how the minister would inspire the people, and how we would get the Spirit in us. Get the Spirit in direct communication."

She began to perceive another kind of power, beyond that of the physical, the power of communication and of revelation. At such times, the child Judith Jamison would be flooded with glorious sensations, her body seeming to become as light as air, and as powerful. It was this early perception of her body, of space, and of the thrill of

[1] The church referred to by Jamison as "Mother Bethel" is Bethel Church in Philadelphia, built under the leadership of Richard Allen and dedicated, in 1793, by Bishop Asbury. See Mabel M. Smythe, ed., *The Black American Reference Book*, Englewood Cliffs, N.J.: Prentice-Hall, 1976.

a powerful communication, that made Jamison a dancer before she ever stepped on a professional stage.

"I have to say, looking back, that dancing was the most important thing in my life. It must have been, because it is the thing that has lasted. I loved to run, but I did not ever plan on going in for the Olympics. I loved to dance and I *did* become a dancer.

"Oh, there was nothing too heavy about the thing. I drifted into dancing the way little girls do, because their moms send them to dancing school. I may have had more facility than the average child. I may perhaps have liked *learning* to dance, the routine classwork, more than most children do. So I assimilated what I was taught and I found joy in dancing. But there has to be more to it than that, for you to dedicate your whole life to dancing. Little girls get sidetracked by other interests. They begin by liking to dance and they go off into a thing about, say, horses; they take up horseback riding. Or skating, figure skating. Or swimming—and go out for the Olympics, maybe. All these are very physical, very stimulating activities that make terrific demands on the child, as dancing does.

"There is the whole bit of growing up. Some little girls want to become nurses—the compassionate feminine instinct that is part of the maternal instinct, I guess. They want to grow up and get married. When you are little, you don't think of it in steps like falling in love with a man and getting married. You make the jump: grow up, get married, with the love part left out, because it's the state of being married that you are thinking about. The state of being a mother, of having your own family, your own home—more examples of power, and of control.

"Instead, for me, dancing went from the class in the studio to the performing on the stage, in a direct line. I was sidetracked only once, when I went to college. That part of my life is in parentheses —a paragraph, not a whole chapter.

"I don't want to give the impression that I was religious in my dedication to dancing. Far from that. Dancing was as natural, almost, as breathing for me. It was not a compartment in my life; it was a normal aspect of life for me. This, I know, was because there were no pressures on me, from my parents or from my teachers, to prove myself. I was already an overachiever at anything I wanted to do, because, as I've said, I was brought up to do a thing well, or not do it at all.

"Dancing, in my childhood, was not as serious for others as it was for me. There were aspects about it that were just 'fun things,' or so they seemed at the time. Like dancing at Convention Hall [in Philadelphia] for the Christmas Cotillion. The last time I danced in the Cotillion, I received an Award of Merit, which was presented to me by Joan Crawford.

"In class, things were taken seriously by the teachers and the students. Of my teachers, I recall Dolores Brown, John Jones, Melvin Brooms, and John Hines. Then, there were the guest teachers, the stars, we studied with, like Maria Swoboda and Vincenzo Celli. Miss Cuyjet was always very emphatic about our going to work with the guest teachers.

"I studied with Antony Tudor in Frankfurt, a suburb of Philadelphia, where he gave master classes on weekends. And to take class with Mme. Swoboda I went to the YMCA—I can still smell the chlorine in the bathrooms!

"I had eleven years with Marian Cuyjet and the impression she left on me is the one I carried into performing. In those eleven years, dance was choosing me, more than I was, actively, choosing to become a dancer.

"Later, when I transferred from Fisk to the Philadelphia Dance Academy, my ballet instructors, as I recall, were Nadia Chilkovsky, James Jamieson (whose name was pronounced the way people keep trying, wrongly, to pronounce *Jam*-ison), and Juri Gottschalk. I also took what you could call a 'blend' of modern dance classes at the Academy. Not any one method—like Graham's, or Limón's, or Horton's, but an amalgam of several modern dance styles—the rudiments, we may say, of modern dance movements. I can truthfully say that I had not studied modern dance when I began dancing. I was primarily trained in ballet. I learned something of the Horton techniques with Joan Kerr.

"At the Academy, we studied dance history, which I loved, because, at the same time, we were studying art. I have a very graphic sense of history, maybe because of being a dancer. I like to picture the personalities, to feel that they were real human beings, and then I see them moving, in three dimensions, in the history book.

"Also at the Academy, where the education in dance arts was very thorough, I studied composition and Labanotation. It was a college-oriented study of dance arts, with dance in the studio a principal, not a peripheral activity.

"That's where I met Agnes de Mille—or, to be more accurate, where Agnes *found* me . . .

"What seemed like several phases was really one phase: growing up. Throughout those years, there was a steady rhythm. The rhythms altered, just a little, from phase to phase: one rhythm for my childhood, another for my adolescence."

THREE

In Vienna, during the UNITEL filming of *Josephslegende,* Jamison went one day to the Flea Market, where she bought an old watch. It was of dull silver, the color of pewter, heavily chased. When a spring was touched, the case flew open, revealing the face.

Jamison took a childlike pleasure in manipulating the spring, until the watch fell apart, disgorging its works. At her hotel, she deftly fitted them back in the case and found that the antique timepiece kept perfect time, but her enjoyment of its purchase was soured by the discovery that, while the watch had been sold to her as something of more than a hundred years old, its mainspring was patently of modern manufacture.

Friends assured her that she had not been gypped at the Flea Market. It was because of its great age that the watch had needed a new mainspring. "It's not that I worry over being taken," said Jamison, "it's that, when something like this happens, I ask myself: 'Are things ever what they seem to be?' "

The need for stability, for order in her work and for trust in her relationships, is of overwhelming importance to Judith Jamison. She is uneasy with the ambiguous and dismayed by subterfuge. She has never been able to suffer deceit, even in fun.

"When I was little, I believed everything people told me. I mean, I accepted it as gospel truth. My brother John was three years older and I adored him. Anything he did, I had to try to do. Whatever he said, I believed. He was 'it,' the original wise man.

"Johnnie told me that Arabian steeds were different from other horses because, while other horses had ordinary bones, the bones of Arabian horses were made of ivory. It made good sense to me, because Arabian steeds were special.

"Taking what Johnnie said as gospel, I would give out this kind of information, and my mom and dad would nearly die laughing. Then my feelings would be hurt; I would be crushed. My mom would tell me not to believe everything I heard and that I had to stand teasing, if I was so foolish . . . At the same time, my mom, who wanted me to love the truth and never tell lies, would herself fib, to protect me.

"There was a big house nearby, and somehow it fascinated me. I wanted to know who lived in it. My mom was very evasive; she warned me not to hang about the place. It took years for me to understand that certain 'ladies' lived in that house, that it was a high-class brothel . . . or, at least, that it had that reputation. But I went past that house, often, wondering what was so strange about it. Children can smell a mystery, somehow.

"I was a very serious, seeking little girl. It took my mom a long time to find out that I was going through an ultrasensitive phase. I was so intense, about everything, especially dancing . . .

"In class, I was completely knitted, tuned up, like a real 'ballerina.' I did not go to Judimar to play but to dance. I loved to dance, but I took it seriously. I see myself: the leotards, the tights, the slippers; and my bun. When I danced, my hair was gathered back, the two braids tucked under, into a chignon. But, I was too shy to express my feelings about dancing.

"What brought me out of myself was the pleasure of competing, first with Johnnie. I started out by trying to do what he did, to emulate him, and after a while it was to prove that what he could do, I could do, also. I guess it was when I got to be eleven, and twelve, that my instinct to compete got the most intense.

"I used to play dodge ball with the guys: with Johnnie and his friends, and I was a whiz at it—give me a dodge ball and I could kill you! Dodge ball for girls is usually a tame affair; it's different when boys play, and I wanted only to play it with the boys. You stand in a sort of a square and where, in volleyball, there is supposed to be a net becomes the dividing line. You try to strike other people out with the ball; the game is on how you throw, and fake, and so on. You try to aim low, so you don't hurt the other person, but when you play with the guys, you have to be ready for dirty pool. They aim, really, to knock the other person off his feet.

"By that time, I could palm a ball, as Johnnie could, and though I was a skinny kid, I had good balance—incredibly good balance. Even so, I got knocked down, often; that's how I got most of the scars I still have on my knees, falling and cutting them on the cement. I was a little ruffian!

"Of course, Johnnie and I did other things, like building model airplanes. I liked that because after all the work, you had something, something beautiful, for your pains.

"Best of all, I liked to run. At Henry, I was the fastest runner in the school, among boys and girls. At recess we used to run races and I always came in first. I was another Wilma Rudolph!

"Then a new girl, a black girl, named Anne Byrne, came to Henry and she was as good a runner as I was, maybe better. Anne was taller than I was and I remember how that upset me. But I figured that, because she was taller, she would be slower. The first race we ran, she won. I nearly died.

"That went on for two or three days, with Anne beating me. I said to myself, this will never do, I have to be number one! Of course, I didn't say it out loud, or confide it to anyone . . . The next day, we began to race, and I told myself: *This is it!* I began running, so hard, that I left Anne behind. I looked back, to see if she was gaining on me, and I forgot to gauge the distance to the wall. When I looked around, I was on it, with no time to slow down, or even to put my hands up. I hit the wall and broke both arms. The left, I cracked, the right had a compound fracture. There was no pain, right then. Not even shock. All I remember feeling was: *I won!*

"It was just a race, so nobody went: Yeah! or made a fuss. Recess was over, and I started to go back into class, when suddenly I was on my knees. I couldn't figure out what was happening but I couldn't walk. I sat down and some kids came and asked me if I was okay. I must have looked funny, because they ran and got the school nurse. She took me to Germantown Hospital, where my arms were put in casts, the right one to above the elbow. On the way over, I was fascinated to see a thing like an egg come up on my right arm. The two doctors—they must have been interns—had a terrible time getting the casts on. They slopped the plaster in the buckets all over themselves, the floor, everywhere. Meanwhile, it was coming on for four o'clock and I was due home from school. I kept thinking of what my mom would do when she saw me.

"The nurse was very sensible. She called from the hospital so that it was not too much of a shock when we got home. Mom opened the door and said something like: Ahhh . . . but I could see *she* was being very calm, so *I* would keep calm. We were both trying not to excite each other.

"Mom tells me that the time I really freaked her out was when I was still a kid-kid, before we moved to Germantown, and I fell downstairs. She says she picked me up and ran with me to the hospital but I, of course, don't remember anything of that incident. I used to think, though, it was just as well I fell down in the old house, which was two-storied, and not in the Germantown house, which has three stories.

"I wore the casts on my arms for six weeks—the left came off a little earlier, I think. I rode the trolley car to school and it was a relief, having the casts off. I put my arms around the pole in the trolley car, because they felt so light—as though they might float away. It took me awhile to get used to my arms again; they had this strange, strange buoyancy, as if they had been given a life of their own—independent of my control. I remember the sensation—they kept *writhing*.

"Of course, it was the reaction of the muscles, and the nerves, after being taken out of those heavy casts—in those days, the plaster of Paris casts weighed tons. But what I remember is my *feeling,* the strange sensations I had in my arms, and my own feeling about what was happening to them. It was eerie—like having a pair of serpents attached to your shoulders, with minds of their own. It took me awhile to get accustomed to my arms again—or, as I should say, for them to get accustomed to me.

"I was lucky. I've never had arthritis, or rheumatism, or anything of that sort in my arms and wrists. The breaks healed completely; they must have been clean breaks. And although I was a string bean, I was very healthy, very strong for my age, so there were no bad repercussions. And, I did win the race!

"If I had 'childhood illnesses' they were mild, because I have no memory of being ill, excepting one time, when I was about eleven or twelve—when *everything* happened to me!—and I came down, suddenly, with something that must have been a kind of influenza. I was at home, luckily, and I felt funny: hot and cold, and hot-hot, burning up. I must have said: 'Mom, I feel funny,' because, I remember, she put me to lie down and she and my dad were opening drawers, getting sheets and blankets to cover me, because I kept telling them I was cold.

"It was as though I were far, far in the background, and all this activity was going on, way beyond me, but it bothered me. I told them not to slam the drawers, to stop making all that noise, but it was as if everything around me was getting more and more remote. Maybe this is how you feel when you are dying.

"That is the only experience I really remember, other than breaking my arms. I was not accident prone and, *knock wood!* I've not had many injuries, dancing.

"Other than running, I did not go in for many sports—you can't call dodge ball sport, the way I played it with the guys; that was mayhem! Johnnie and I used to ride our bikes but after I once rode mine into a tree, I didn't much care about it. I never liked sledding —tobogganing. I think I loved to run because of the sense of freedom you have, when you run—the glorious feeling when you let yourself out, to the fullest extent. There is the exhilaration of speed, of course, but, I think, more than that is the thrill of the power in the body, the instrument.

"I don't have the words to express what running meant to me, as a child. It was not the joy of movement per se, any more than I loved dancing as movement per se. Running was one thing; dancing was another thing. Each, in its own way, allowed me to express very deep feelings, feelings that a child could not explain, that were secret but very real to me.

"When I was not running, or dancing, I was so shy that you could not get two words out of me outside my home. With strangers, I clammed up. I had very intense feelings about the people who made up my world: my parents, and Johnnie; the grandparents; the aunts; Uncle Sam. My world extended to other people, who were not looked on as strangers but as sort of part of the family. Like Dr. George.

"He was our family doctor but he seemed another grandfather, he was so kind. Very patient, very gentle—and very handsome. He was elegant, in a starched white coat, with immense dignity. I went to Dr. George for years and years. He died, and I've never had a regular doctor, what you could call a 'family' doctor, again. I don't have a doctor in New York. It's just as well I don't often get sick . . .

"Johnnie and I were going to be doctors. We planned on going to college to study medicine. I was going to be a neurosurgeon. Nobody put this into our heads, it was our idea. I suppose I picked neurosurgery because that is about as delicate, and as difficult, as surgery can get. I was always fascinated by the mystery of what was inside the human body, the mystery under the skin.

"We used to go to Gustine Lake, a public swimming pool. I loved swimming but hated diving. One time, I cut the sole of my foot on a broken cola bottle at the bottom of the pool—some vandal had dropped the bottle into the water. It was a deep gash but it did not bleed a lot, so I could see inside the cut. I was amazed to see little grains. I had never imagined that these globules were inside my foot. I don't remember pain, or being frightened; I only remember my amazement at seeing what was inside the foot.

"I belonged in high school to Future Nurses of America and I used to watch operations in the hospital amphitheatre. I was fascinated by the incredible skill, the incredible control of the surgeons. I saw a Caesarean, appendectomies, the operation to remove cataracts from the eye. I thought I was just cut out to do that kind of work. My fascination was with the way the human hand could handle the knife.

"The fascination was, too, with the mystery of the body; what made it move, what made it go, what made it alive. I suppose this old fascination I felt as a child, about the secrets of the physical body, has in some ways carried over into my work in dancing—in the meaning of dance, and, when I dance a characterization, the meaning of the role in its inner self.

"I went to college but I did not study to become a neurological surgeon. Johnnie did not study for a profession either. He got married and he became a man with responsibilities, to a wife and to a child. He drives a huge bus, cross-country, just as I used to dream of driving a huge train. We find the sources of our powers. Johnnie has the lives of all the people who ride his bus in his hands. I am responsible for my own life."

FOUR

"I had no desire to go to college," said Jamison. "When I graduated from high school I was happy to be able to read all day, listen to music all day, and go to ballet class every day. I think I could have spent my whole life just doing these things. My mom had other ideas. She and Dad wanted me to go to college. My grades were so good, the teachers said, there was no reason I would not do well in college.

"They gave me applications to fill in, from my junior year. After graduation, my mom began asking me what plans I had made for college. I had to admit I had made none. So I got more applications and some I filled in, but I never sent them. I would stuff the application forms under my mattress and pretend I had mailed them. There must have been a pile under the mattress, by the time I got round to admitting to Mom that I had sent not a one.

"Mom didn't make a fuss. She just said: 'Okay, if you don't want to go to college, you've got to get a job.' She could not see me lying around the house all day, only going out to the library, and [dance] class. She was firm about that.

"So I began job-hunting. It was hilarious, I had no idea what to do, nor what I *could* do, to earn money. Mom sent me to an employment agency. The woman gave me forms to fill out. She asked me for my Social Security number. *My what?* I didn't know what she was talking about. It was as if I had gone to a foreign country and they were talking a language I did not understand. You can be that unprepared for life, after going through twelve years of the best education in America!

"The woman in the employment agency explained how I had to apply for a Social Security number. She told me to take a business course. Learn shorthand, typing. Bookkeeping would be good too. Could I file? Oh, I felt so dumb . . .

"I left the house every day with my mom thinking I had gone job-hunting. I went to the library and read all morning. In the afternoon, I went to the movies. That's how I spent the summer after graduation.

"Just before fall, a woman we knew came up with the idea that I should go to Fisk. I didn't even have to worry about money, they said, I'd be admitted on a Physical Education scholarship. I'd be teaching dance to P.E. students, as a part of the scholarship arrangement. So I went to Fisk but not as a Physical Education major. My major was psychology. If I was not going to become a neurological surgeon I guess the next most fascinating thing I could think of being was a psychologist—that way, I'd be finding out what made people tick. The mysteries of the mind were, at the least, as exciting as the mysteries of the body underneath the skin.

"Fisk was the first big trauma of my life. Fisk University, Nashville, Tennessee. Going there from Philadelphia was really going into a new world, a new culture."

Founded in 1865 by the American Missionary Association, and historically associated with the Congregational Church, Fisk University was predominantly for black students. Although it encouraged enrollment nationwide, and made no religious demands of the students, it was primarily a Southern educational institution.

"Fisk was the first place where I understood what prejudice was," says Jamison. "Not color prejudice, between black and white, but class prejudice. I went into a social situation that I had no warning about—a totally new experience for me.

"When I got ready to go to Fisk, my Aunt Allie bought me a trunkful of new clothes. She took me to Bonwit Teller, which was *the* store in Philadelphia, and we went on a shopping spree on her charge account, to outfit me for Fisk. As a treat, we had lunch at Bookbinders, which was also *the* restaurant for lunch in Philadelphia. I was treated as though I was going to make my debut.

"But, when I got to Fisk, with my trunk of new clothes, I found that I was an oddity—every other girl at Fisk had at least *five trunks* full of clothes, and everyone was competing in the best-dressed campaign. When the girls went home on vacation, they must have just junked all their clothes because when they came back to Fisk the five trunks were always full of more new clothes, in the latest fashion.

"I bowed out of the competition. After the first semester I never wore anything except jeans and a sweat shirt.

"It was not only the clothes that made a difference between me and the girls at Fisk, it was the whole attitude about life. Fisk was full of the daughters of rich men; I was the daughter of a blue-collar worker in Philadelphia. Their values and my values were not the same. The things they took seriously—like clothes, beaus, parties—I found boring.

"I spent almost all my time in the P.E. gym but it was not a success for me, teaching people at Fisk to dance. Dance—the way I wanted them to dance—was hard work instead of a fun thing for them. Anyone who was serious about dancing had to be weird. When I wasn't dancing by myself, I was listening to jazz. I discovered jazz music at Fisk, through a man who used to play jazz as seriously as I danced. Until then, I had mostly listened to classical music, and to pop music of my time, of course, but at Fisk I learned to appreciate the beauty of jazz.

"I also spent a lot of my time playing bid whist. That was my education at Fisk: jazz, and bid whist. I studied Psychology but I didn't major in that or anything else. Fisk and I parted company in mutual indifference. I left Fisk and transferred to the Philadelphia Dance Academy, where I got a real education, similar to what I would have got going to the Juilliard School in New York. Best of all for me at the Philadelphia Dance Academy, I learned that I was not cut out to teach dance—I wanted to *be* a dancer.

"I was twenty years old when Agnes de Mille brought me to New York but I have to laugh at myself now, comparing Judi Jamison at twenty with girls of thirteen today. Girls even younger than thirteen, as young as ten, if we are to believe what's in print about the youth culture of the 1980s. I was innocent and ignorant. The conditions depend on each other.

"I'm glad that I was so green because it meant that I was wide open to new experiences. Not jaded, not careful. So I really *experienced,* I really and truly lived my life, year by year, episode by episode. It's still, for me, the best way of growing. I feel I received influences—from Carmen [de Lavallade] when we were dancing in *The Four Marys,* and from everyone else that I came in contact with, that I was impressed by as having greatness. I couldn't have been influenced by these artists if I had been closed to experience, if I had already formed opinions about dancing, about myself as a dancer.

"When I say that I was 'influenced' I do not mean that I saw and imitated other dancers. I have never imitated another dancer in my life. The influences I am talking about were learning processes, understanding what dancing was at its highest standards. You have to *see* great dance to recognize what it is . . .

"At the beginning, I was a demon on technique. Technique was my god. That was the phase where I worked with Pat Wilde at Harkness and it was a phase I lived in for a very long time. Later, I realized that technique is only the bare bones of dancing. When you are *a dancer* you go beyond technique.

"Technique is the only important thing for American dancers nowadays. A lot of the young dancers think—*have been made to think*—that they are the greatest technicians who have ever lived and that they are superior to all the dancers before them. They still have a lot to learn—as I learned, by looking at dancers like Carmen de Lavallade, and like Consuelo Atlas and some others in the old Ailey company.

"I am glad I came up in that era, and that I had the chance of looking at and learning from some great, great dancers. We were not in dance as a business, and, God knows, not to make our fame and fortune. Those one-night stands were survival of the fittest. It was a wonder any of us survived, dancing in conditions you wouldn't expect a dog to perform in. Either the stages were so slick that you fell down, or so bad that you picked the splinters out of your feet and your behind when the curtain closed. They would wax and polish the floors of the gyms where we performed, under the mistaken impression that we wanted a shiny, slippery floor! Even in the colleges with dance departments, they knew next to nothing.

"When we worked the college dance circuit it meant that we taught college students in huge classes, and rehearsed, and that night performed—all as part of the same job. Years went by like this. The company was just about to fold, or had folded, or was getting back together again.

"There was the time I spent at Harkness, that I remember chiefly for breaking my ankle—and for my first Scandinavian, Tim Harum. He was really named Avind Harum and he was six feet, five inches

tall—a Norwegian and, I thought, a fabulous dancer. I loved dancing with him and he was so much fun to work with. He and I
laughed all the time—probably the only two dancers at the Harkness
who were laughing.

"I remember being at the Harkness in Alvin's *Ariadne*. I had to
wear a skirt ten feet wide. I posed on top of a ladder, and I danced
there, chiefly with port de bras, while I gave birth to Avind.

"Funny, but though I remember these episodes, I cannot remember what I felt like at those times—what I was thinking about
myself, about the people I was working with, about dancing. I wish
I could remember emotions as easily as incidents. Even incidents
sometimes blur and you find yourself mixing up things like dates.
Though, never for me, people—I always remember people very
clearly.

"A lot from the very early days has come back to me, through
having to remember and to analyze things, as I have been doing in
these talks [the conversations with O.M.]. I couldn't remember a
thing about that crazy film I made in Paris, except that I worked
with two men—and now I *see* myself as I worked in that film:
dressed in a silver metallic costume, with a miniskirt. I was twenty-
two years old and it was the adventure of my life! We, the two men
and I, were all over Paris—we nearly got arrested on the Champs-
Élysées. I ate omelettes and salads, and had nips of champagne for
breakfast. It was wild. And they paid me $125 a day, the most
money anyone had ever paid me up to then.

"Something else that has just come back to me is that I used to
like flying but I learned to hate it after one time, flying back from
Ghana, we ran into a terrible thunderstorm. There were ten of us in
the company, including Alvin, and we were all scared for our lives.
The plane was dashed about so much that our seat belts tore. When
we landed, the pilot got out and went down on hands and knees and
kissed the ground. I've been nervous about flying ever since.

"I was all of twenty-eight before people began paying notice to
me. Before that I was just the tall girl with the umbrella in *Revelations*. I felt I had had important roles in other things—*Blues Suite,*
and, especially, the role I danced [in premiere] in *Masekela Langage*. But it was only when Clive Barnes wrote a review about me
[May 5, 1971, in the New York *Times*] that you could say I had
'arrived' somewhere. That review was one of the most important

things in my life. I remember how it began: 'For years it has been obvious that Judith Jamison is no ordinary dancer . . .' I don't clip reviews but I will always remember that one, of Clive's, for *Cry*.

"No doubt about it, *Cry* made the big difference for me. I've got to count the years as "before *Cry*" and "after *Cry*," because there's that much of a division.

"I knew that there was a difference by the way the company behaved. Until then, I had never been given any publicity whatsoever. Suddenly, there were interviews, and people, including Alvin, were making statements about me as a dancer. They really knew I was there—people were really looking at me. Box office has a lot to do with the publicity a dancer gets from her company. If you're good box office, then you get pushed into big roles. It's a fact of life.

"Dancers make their names in different ways. The Russians defect and they are on television, in the newspapers; they become 'news.' So the public rushes to see them dance and that's bound to be good box office. American dancers find other ways to get publicity. Some of us do it by dancing.

"If it was only for the publicity, no one in his or her right mind would be dancing. There are better and easier ways of becoming a celebrity than by being a dancer. But without the right kind of push, the right kind of presentation in a company, a dancer hardly has a chance of ever emerging out of the background. You remain one of the crowd.

"I understand why I got no publicity in the Ailey company. Alvin has always said he wanted an ensemble, no stars, for a repertory company. And when I went into the Ailey it was a man's company, not a woman's company. Alvin had stopped dancing just awhile before, but there were several important male dancers: Jimmy Truitte, Kelvin Rotardier, Dudley Williams. The same year I joined the Ailey, there was Miguel Godreau. People in the company were still talking—and went on talking for years—about Alvin as a dancer. I had a fever, from wanting to have seen Alvin in his *Creation of the World,* something he performed before I had even heard about the Ailey company but that people seemed to remember as having happened yesterday.

"The Ailey was a patriarchal company for a long time. It was hard for Alvin to accept a woman as the star of the company, which is what critics started calling Judith Jamison after *Cry*.

"I think that the best thing that could have happened, for me, for the company, was what did happen—I began to work outside the Ailey, and to appear with other companies as a guest artist. Then, when I danced in the Ailey, it was easier to accept me as being in a different category than I had been before *Cry*.

"Transitions are not easy and though I liked making the transition from being anonymous to being recognized, I suffered because I lost the feeling of closeness, of being part of a family, that you have when you are a child at home—and when you are a young, unknown dancer in a company like the Ailey. You go away and when you come back things have changed, you've put a space between yourself and others, and you've got to accept each other on new and different terms.

"The transition was made harder for me and easier for me by all the changes inside the company. Year to year, it changed. Some of the changes were forced on Alvin but they were administrational ones, changes to do with the way the company was run, the way money was spent. The commencement of the budget. The deficit. All the operational things about the company that we, the dancers, didn't know about and, to tell the truth, didn't want to hear about, because our work was dancing.

"Some of the changes Alvin invited; some he forced on the company. For a while, we didn't know what we were: a ballet company? a modern dance company? an ethnic company?

"Alvin went through his classical phase and it lasted a long time. The company had a series of ballet masters: there was Ramón Segarra, who gave two hour-long classes, after which the dancers' legs felt like wet noodles. We had the ballet mistress Fiorella Keene, until she left us to go to ABT—where she died, poor thing. For a while, Ali Pourfarrokh was not only ballet master but Alvin's assistant, until Ali went back to Teheran to become the director of the Iranian Ballet. Alvin's inspiration was Sara Yarborough.

"Some of the dancers from the old Ailey lost heart and left. Others were let go. It was a very disoriented period when nobody seemed to know just what direction the company was going in. All the time, Alvin was saying that he intended to maintain the 'true' nature of the Ailey company.

"A dancer could go mad, trying to find out what a company director wants, or means. I don't feel that is the business, the responsibility of the dancers, but you have to look out for yourself. You're a fool if you don't. I was lucky to have Paul to look after my interests, in and outside the Ailey company. And, as I say, from the time I began working as a guest artist, my status changed. I could come and go in the Ailey without having to undergo any of the big traumas that were worrying other people.

"I accept the Ailey for what it is. It is called an eclectic company, because it combines all the theatrical dance styles in the rep. I think it is best described as a nonclassical dance company. It's the rep that makes the Ailey unique. That's its real character. Dancers come and go, and good dancers contribute a lot to the company, but I believe that the company itself has a strong character, and that it is in the repertory, the multiple styles of our dancing.

"Belonging to a company in America is a lot different from belonging to one in Europe. European dancers have a stability and a security we do not. There are drawbacks to both systems. European dancers—like the Russian defectors—complain that they don't get enough opportunities to dance because, in ballet in the opera houses, the seasons are fewer than in big American companies. American dancers complain that they are worked to death, that they never have enough rehearsal, and that they are 'used' instead of 'developed' by companies. Here, the dancers work on contract for one season at a time. It's up to the company director to decide if you are going to be engaged for another season, or let go at the end of the current season. American dancers belong to a union but our companies don't have responsibility for the dancers. The system is much different in the European theatres, where the dancers and singers are like Civil Service employees, eligible for pensions after they have worked for a certain length of time. The theatres are under a ministry, part of the national government. Here, a company exists on its own, under its founder-director, and it's up to him to raise the funds for the company to subsist on.

"European ballet is bureaucratic and in America the choreographer has perfect freedom to do as he wishes. There is really no basis of comparison on which to say this system is good, this one is bad. What most affects American dancers is the instability of their work. They never know if they are going to be hired for more than one season. When you are not rehired, you go out looking for another job. It's not always easy to find the kind of job you want in dance. Most out-of-work dancers fall back on teaching. A lot of dancers teach and dance, at the same time. I taught my share at the Ailey, in the residencies—when we worked in colleges—and in the school. There are dancers in the Ailey now to whom I gave their first class.

"I don't want to teach while I am dancing. In these next years I mean to concentrate on dancing as much as possible, and in as many different media as I have the opportunity for. I love dancing in Europe and I hope I get many more chances to do so. I want to keep on dancing with the Ailey, because it's my 'home' company and I am very close to it. But I also want to try my luck on Broadway, in musical theatre—as a different kind of dancer than the one I have been, so far.

"I would be dishonest if I said I was not interested in money. Earning enough money to be independent is very important to me. When I began dancing I used to think it was wonderful that people would pay me for doing what I wanted to do more than anything else in the world. I still feel that but, without being cynical, you stop being naïve. I appreciate the money I earn and the good I can do with it for the people I love.

"Love doesn't change. My parents still live in Philadelphia and though I manage to get them to New York or Washington for a premiere, I can't persuade them to leave home as much as I wish they would, to visit me.

"I love my family very, very much, but I have come to feel about them almost as though I am the parent and they the children. I feel protective. I wish I could do everything to make life easy and happy for them. The joke is: *they* are happy, with each other. They protect and cherish each other.

"I must seem very changed to my family, from when I was a child, and a girl growing up. Parents have to learn to accept their children as persons, just as children have to learn to recognize that their parents are real people, *a man* and *a woman,* not extensions of yourself. I don't think I've changed, basically, from Judi Jamison from Philadelphia. I still find myself reacting in ways I did as a child. Like making a 'nest,' wherever I am, as I made a nest for myself in my room at home. I still build 'walls' of music around me and retreat into my nest, alone.

"I retreat into my nest for nourishment. That's how I find out where my head is, how I solve my problems. It makes me sound selfish, but I don't need people with me at those times. I'd rather be alone. The only creature I ever wanted in my nest was Emma.

"It's impossible for me to think of Emma without feeling grief. Before I had Emma, I tended to look on people with pets as eccentrics. You have to form a relationship with an animal like Emma before you can understand what it means.

"One of the happiest times of my life was lived in the years after I got Emma. I bought her for seven hundred and fifty dollars, cheap at the price, because she was the runt of a litter, from aristocratic parents. I had to borrow some of the money to pay for Emma, but I'd have paid twice as much for her.

"At that time, I lived on Third [Avenue] and Ninth [Street]. It was a very bad neighborhood, but the rent was all I could afford. Emma and I used to walk the streets at all hours of the day and night. There were bums lying on the sidewalks, and all sorts of odd characters hanging around—they used to get fed from a mission, St. John the Divine. I never felt scared, once Emma was with me. No one ever said or did anything to me. I guess Emma was pretty intimidating to look at.

"Later, I moved in with Miguel, on Twentieth [Street] and Ninth [Avenue], and Emma and I still walked the streets without a single worry. She was a perfect city dog. Then, one weekend, I was invited, with Tom Ellis and Robert Livingston—who is Molly Parnis' son—to the country and Emma went with me. She, me, and those two big men, all jammed into a little car all the way to upstate New York, to Peter Shaffer's house. That was the weekend I discovered *Equus,* which I had never heard of, although the play was such a big hit on Broadway: Peter's famous play. I heard people talking about it and I was fascinated, and Peter said: 'You want to see the play?' And when I got back to New York he sent me tickets, and Tom Hudspeth and I went to see *Equus,* sitting in Peter's seats, fifth row, dead center.

"While I was discovering *Equus,* Emma was discovering what it was like to run through the woods. It was a beautiful place, in a forest, with a brook, and Emma nearly went mad with excitement. She and I ran for what must have been miles and she saw her first deer. She did not know what it was. Maybe a dog with horns? She barked herself hoarse and I laughed so much I nearly cried.

"That's how my memories of Emma are, all mixed up with memories of people—like Peter Shaffer—because to me Emma was never just a dog, she was part of my life as I was part of hers.

"Well, when you analyze this, what sort of a person am I? I like to hole up in my nest; I had a dog I loved as much as I have ever loved a living creature. Do these things say something about Judi Jamison?

"It's easier for me to talk about myself as a dancer. When I am asked to describe how I work at dancing I always think of what Marian Cuyjet used to tell her pupils, at the Judimar School. She used to say: 'Dance, even if you are in a corner, as though you are in the middle of the stage.'

"By that she wanted us to know that the size of the role was not the important thing about dancing. It was *how* you danced. Some dancers 'save' themselves for special occasions, as though they have only so much to give and they need to apportion it. On the contrary, I had to learn to pace myself in rehearsals. When I came to New York, I was accustomed to dancing full out. That's how I like to dance all the time because it takes an effort of will to hold back, to hold in. It's my instinct to dance always full out. With my whole heart and my whole mind. Sometimes, with my soul.

"One night, at Avignon, where we performed in an open-air theatre, in *Carmina Burana,* I came as near as I have ever been to a religious experience. Under that open sky, with the moon shining, and birds passing overhead, I felt as though I was dancing on the earth, not for myself, not for the audience, but for God."

FIVE

"When I analyze my life," said Jamison, "I realize how much of it has been motivated by men.

"I am sure that my ideas about men were formed through my father. He is still my ideal of what a man should be: strong enough to be gentle. This is a very important element in a man for me: gentleness. But so few men feel that they can afford it. There is still the belief that to be a strong man you need to be a hard person. In my experience, men are usually trying to prove how tough they are.

"One day, a long time after I had left home, I was walking with my parents in the street and I noticed how my father's hand found my mother's elbow, cupping it so lovingly, so protectively, as they crossed from one sidewalk to the other. I saw in that gesture what my father feels about my mother, what my mother means to my father.

"In my position—I accept that I have come to occupy a position —I am often asked about my opinions on women today. Usually the interviewer wants to know what I think about the status of black women. In terms of relationships between men and women, in terms of women loving men, I don't see any great distinction between white women and black women. I believe we feel the same, and that our circumstances are the same.

"I know I am a woman. I like being female. I have ideas about femininity, some of them, I admit, coming out of my environment. I am still enough my mother's daughter, and my grandmother Annie's granddaughter, to believe that a woman is naturally a nurturing and a compassionate person—as a man is a protective, cherishing person.

"It would have been nice if I had been able to fall in love and marry a man and live a good life with him, as my grandmother Annie and my grandfather Timothy did. I would like to have a marriage as good as the one my parents have. That's why I don't have a marriage. I'm still not ready to settle for second or third best, after knowing what the real thing can be.

"I don't apologize for feeling these things, although I know they are out of style for many people. I don't apologize for the way I live, or for what I choose to do. I have reached the stage of life where I believe I am entitled to make a choice about where I work, how I live, who I love. These are what I consider to be my freedoms—my personal freedoms.

"The feeling of being free to make my choices came to me very gradually. Part of it came from being independent, economically independent. I am by no means rich but I work hard to afford my lifestyle, to afford the choices I want to make. A few years ago, I became—on good advice—a corporation. I got an accountant to take care of my money, because I am an impulsive spender. I can go for weeks or months without spending a cent, and suddenly I become a spending fool because I want to buy something, for me, for someone else, that gives pleasure. You can't know what a thrill it is, to be able to spend money on something you want to buy, unless you've had no money—hardly enough money to pay the rent and buy enough food to hold you together while you're working. *That* was the way I lived for a long time. It's the way a lot of dancers live in America.

"Speaking of the men in my life, I've got to count those in my life as *dancing,* and in the part of my life I still think of as *living,* as one, because, to tell the truth, it's the men from my life in *dancing* who have made the most effect on me, and on my life.

"There's Alvin, to begin with. There's Dudley and a few other male dancers. Miguel Godreau belonged to both aspects of Judi Jamison, as dancing and as living, but in analysis I've got to count him more on one side than the other because Miguel's true effect on me was *as a dancer*—that burning dancer that I will never forget.

"When I admit this, do I make myself less of a woman and too much Judith Jamison the dancer? I don't know and no one can tell me. I'll have to live my whole life through before I'm ready to answer that question.

"Alvin's great influences on me are as a choreographer and as the director of the company to which I belong. I'm still an Ailey dancer, no matter how much I perform outside the company. Alvin helped to form me, just as Miss Cuyjet's school did. I've worked with other choreographers than Alvin Ailey and they have helped to form me too. I am always aware of the dancer's debt to the choreographer, as I am equally aware of what the choreographer owes to the dancer.

"This awareness was brought home to me very strongly when I began working with John Neumeier. *Josephslegende* is a very important part of my life. I prefer to say 'life' to 'career' because 'career' sounds so cold, so organized. It's all right to refer to a 'business career,' but dancing is too personal, too personally involved, to be thought of in the same way.

"Working with John in Hamburg opened a new dimension to me. I love the role of Potiphar's Wife because it came to me when I was old enough to understand how to dance it. A lot of my life story went into Potiphar's Wife. John wanted me to dance as a woman hungry for love, a woman who would not accept love—the kind that dear old Kingy offered her—on any terms except her own. I understood that woman.

"Potiphar's Wife, in John's ballet, is also a woman who has to feel rejected and rebuked. I understood that about her too. By then I knew what passion can do to people, how it can tear you apart. I knew what passion was.

"I am a passionate person by nature. This is part of my female sexuality but it is more than that: it is my nature as a human being, regardless of sex. In the theatre, I know when I am dancing for passionate people in the audience. It comes to me, like a deep vibration. That is when I dance at my best, in response to the passionate communication.

"I am drawn to passionate people and I understand that it is dangerous to feel passion. That's an element of dancing too—the danger. I have to balance passion, I have to control it, in my dancing and in myself. The same element of passion, and of danger, that I feel in dancing, I feel in personal relationships.

"I seem to have been luckier in dancing than in living. Part of the problem in living, for me—for any woman who is successful at what she does for a living—is that people expect me to go on performing offstage. I know when I am onstage and when I am off. The trouble comes when other people—like the man I'm with—get confused about my identity.

"You know the old story of the rich girl and her lover: 'Does he love me for myself or for my money?' Women who are successful eventually have to ask themselves the question: 'Is he with me because he loves *me*, Judi? Or is he with *the* Judith Jamison?'

"At first, you don't want to ask that question because you're scared it's going to make you into an egomaniac. After a while, out of the instinct for preservation, you have to ask the question—but only of yourself. It's not easy to answer it. One way, then you're really an egomaniac. The other way, you've lost your illusions about the lover, and sometimes about love.

"All women in positions comparable to mine have the problems I have, about relationships in love. I realize that I have additional problems, that I share with other black women.

"For all that we hear about the 'new morality' and 'militant feminism,' things have not really changed, to the extent where relationships, deep down, have been changed between men and women. Men still feel that their masculinity is being challenged, being threatened, by women who are what is called 'successful.' It's accepted that to be successful you've got to be tough. God knows, it's true. Without toughness no one would survive and grow. But being tough is a good thing—trees are tough. It's being hard that's bad, and being too hard means being brittle, and that's when you are most breakable. But toughness is not something everybody understands and respects in a woman. It's still believed that you are less feminine for being tough.

"When you are a black woman you've got two strikes against you as a successful black woman. You're 'uppity' as they say, as a woman, and it's double trouble to be an 'uppity *black* woman.'

"I'm not an authority on black women in love, I have no statistics to prove this, but I believe that it's much harder for a successful woman who is black to have what is called a successful love relationship, than it is for successful women who are white. More is demanded of us as black women. We are the 'mother' images of our time.

"I don't conform to any image that others want to superimpose on me. I am a woman, and I don't decide to fall in love with a man because the color of his skin is black like mine, or because it is white. I don't decide to fall in love—it happens to me, like an act of God. It would be the happiest thing in the world for me if I could fall in love with a man, and he with me, forever and ever. I still want to believe this can happen, even if it sounds like a fairy tale from long ago.

"In my position, you come to terms with being lonely. You are especially lonely in love if you are a successful black woman. It's not only in a love relationship, a sexual relationship, that you sense this loneliness. You feel it in professional relationships. I've never met a man, however intelligent and sympathetic he might be, who was actually able to treat a woman seriously. It's always as though, however serious a woman's purpose may be, it's something frivolous, because she is a woman.

"While I was involved in the off-Broadway project, Paul [Szilard, Jamison's manager] went along with it and arranged my guest engagements to suit, but I knew Paul didn't take me seriously—didn't take as serious *my* serious commitment to the off-Broadway project, which was truly a serious commitment to me. He was patient, and agreeable, but I know he didn't understand.

"Men will humor women they love, but do men ever really understand us when we are serious? Do they treat us, as they would treat another man, with respect over the things *we* consider to be serious? I think that most men fail to understand that a woman can be serious about anything, especially something that she wants to do.

"Successful women can afford to become serious about their work, and anything else they choose to take seriously, but even then men think the women have whims and fancies—that will pass. I have earned the right to be serious when I want to be, but at a cost. You have a lot of loving friends and a few friendly lovers, on your terms.

"Up to just a few years ago I was still very much my parents' child. After *The Mooche,* when my picture was in the papers and in magazines, and I was being called 'a red-hot dancer,' all I could think was: What is Daddy going to say? That's not the kind of dancer I was supposed to be, when I was studying at the Judimar School—in those days, I was a ballet dancer.

"It pleases me that I am now dancing with the Vienna State Ballet and with the Hamburg Ballet. I've appeared with a ballet company in America but only as a novelty—a black dancer in *The Four Marys,* and the black part of the black-and-white *Pas de "Duke"* for American Ballet Theatre. I could never have become a ballet dancer in my own country. I was born black and I grew up tall. Lucia Chase did not want me for her company, but then neither did Arthur Mitchell ask me to join the black classical company he formed as Dance Theatre of Harlem.

"I don't like it, that the conditions that were in effect when I began dancing are still the same for black dancers in ballet. The excuse was that I was too tall, as well as that I was too black. That was supposed to be the reason why I could not be taken, permanently, into American Ballet Theatre. It was not that I was not talented enough, nor that I was not properly trained, to be a classical dancer.

"Well, sixteen years later, as Alvin says, there are no black dancers in American ballet and it's not because there are no talented and well-trained black ballet dancers, *or* that *all* these talented, trained black ballet dancers are over five feet, four inches tall.

"Alvin makes enemies when he talks about the racial issue in dance, but who better than Alvin knows the extent of that bigotry? Who better than the black dancers who are considered to have made successful careers in the American theatre?

"The thing is, by becoming a successful black dancer in our country, you are forced to explain—even, to apologize—for having achieved success, while so many other black dancers have not. You carry a responsibility you never wanted, never asked to take on. It's a responsibility that can crush you, if you're not strong enough to stand up under it and say that you can be responsible only for yourself. Doing your best is the best you can do.

"That's why it's so dangerous to let people make you into an example, to point you out as one of a kind. It's the thing I'm most scared of in my work—being made into an example.

"You are then expected to produce the formula for success. No one can give a pattern to anyone else, not as a dancer. You have to find yourself, find your way, through means that apply only to you. I had to learn this lesson. It's a lesson every dancer learns. For the black dancer, it's a hard lesson, harder, I think, than for the white dancer in America.

"Alvin has nearly killed himself, carrying the responsibility he took on himself. I feel just as strongly about things as Alvin does but I am not the dreamer Alvin is. I know that I cannot change things, no matter what I may do to try and change them. What could

I do? Refuse to dance? That would be like cutting off the head to save the body.

"I dance because that's what I do best, know best to do. And I am sometimes made into a token. Once, I was elected to the NEA—its committee for dance. I was the token black. But, on the other hand, being black has not been made an issue for me. The only time I felt insulted was once, in Chicago, after I had danced at a gala, in *Facets,* and at the reception following the performance I was introduced to the boxer Muhammad Ali, who said he didn't like the way I had danced, because it wasn't 'black.' I told him that if I was chartreuse, I'd still dance the way I do.

"That was a terrible night for me, all round. Misha [Baryshnikov] and I had been such good friends, from the time we did *Pas de "Duke,"* and especially after we danced it again in Vienna. While we were at the Staatsoper so was Gelsey Kirkland, and she and Misha had some sort of row. Anyway, on the plane going home, Gelsey sat by herself in coach, and Misha and I were together in first class. He talked to me all the way. I felt I really knew him. Then, when we met in Chicago for the Gala program, where we were *not* dancing *Pas de "Duke,"* he was in a funny mood. He barely acknowledged my greeting when I went up to him, grinning, so happy to see him. I was crushed but I thought: Maybe he's nervous about dancing. After the performance he was just as cold. He snubbed me and everybody else. He got up from the table and left the party. I was hurt *at the time,* but I did not take it as a personal insult. Misha might have been going through a bad time nobody knew about. You can get so low that you forget everything else except the thing that is eating you. Times like that, you are hardly responsible for what you do, how you act. I did not stop loving Misha. And when we met again, other times, he was just as sweet to me as he had been before Chicago. But in Chicago, that same evening, I was insulted, really insulted, in the worst, most personal way.

"I went to say goodbye to the hostess at the reception and she did an awful thing. She pushed her hand up under my dress and said: 'Where are those great legs? Why are you hiding those great legs?' I was horrified. I had never met anyone so rude in my life.

"Barring Mohammed Ali, those bad things don't happen to me because I am black. They happen because for people like that woman in Chicago I am a dancer—and dancers are not really human.[1] If I counted my hurts from being black, I'd say that ABT did not want me in the company because of my color. But, neither did Arthur Mitchell want me in his . . .

"Occasionally, you are treated in such a way that you know what it means to be a 'star.' You get invited to dine at the White House. It's one thing to be asked to dance at the White House; it's another to be asked to eat, as a guest, with the President of the United States and his wife.

"A time that I really felt I was being treated as a star was when I flew from Los Angeles to Texas, to the LBJ ranch as the weekend guest of the President and Mrs. Lyndon Johnson. My plane was more than two hours late but there was this big limousine at the airport, and people waiting to drive me out to the ranch. When we got there, to my amazement, everybody was waiting for me. There was this huge crowd of people from the White House, people from Washington, theatre celebrities, and probably half the politicians in the state of Texas, all waiting for Judi Jamison to arrive, because President Johnson and Ladybird had said, 'Let's wait for her'—*for me*. It was fantastic! I'll remember that barbecue as long as I live.

"Times like that one, you feel happy and proud. It's more than merely an ego trip, it's real happiness, a rush of love, because the Johnsons didn't have to do what they did. They did it because they wanted to . . .

"It was a courtesy to Judith Jamison. And, if they paid me the courtesy because I'm black, I'm pleased and proud about that too.

"I've had some wonderful experiences, as a dancer, and not all of them spectacular, like having the President of the United States hold up a party to wait for me to arrive.

"On my first guest artist engagement, with the San Francisco Ballet, I stayed in the home of [the company's co-director] Michael Smuin and his wife, Paula. They were so nice to me and Paula took me shopping. We went to I. Magnin and I spent more money on a

---

[1] Some members of the audience show a distressing insensitivity which confirms Jamison's belief that the performer is not thought of as human. Jamison is not alone in suffering affront. An English ballet historian, asked to speak at a charity "Benefit" for a ballet company, was invited, after the lecture-performance, to dine with the "Friends" of the troupe. One of them, a man, suddenly thrust the lecturer's lips apart, asking if her teeth were false. He had heard that the English lose their teeth at an early age. The lecturer, incidentally, is white.

leather coat than I had ever before spent on something to put on my back. I suddenly had some money to buy something I wanted.

"One evening, after performance, the Smuins took me to supper at a famous restaurant in the city: Bali's, where they serve the best rack of lamb in America. It's owned and run by Armin Bali and her son and daughter, and I hear that people fly their private planes into San Francisco to eat at Bali's. Madame Bali is famous for something else—she is the mother of ballet in San Francisco, especially of the Russian dancers. The restaurant walls are plastered with Rudolf Nureyev, ten times bigger than life. Armin introduced Natasha Makarova to her husband, Edward Karkar. She is mother, matchmaker, banker, everything you like, to the Russian ballet dancers.

"Well, we had this great meal, and Armin Bali came and sat with us and after a while she took a huge green cabochon ring off her hand and put it on my finger, and she said: 'This is for you, to thank you for dancing as you dance.'

"*That* was an experience I won't ever forget, this lady making such a gesture, in such a calm and sweet way, as though she was giving me a bead, instead of something that was worth a small fortune. The ring is priceless to me, not only for its own value but for the value I set on it as the gift it was. This was not a politician making a nice gesture, this was not somebody doing something that would make a good story in the newspapers, if you want to be bitchy and think that those were the reasons the Lyndon B. Johnsons were so nice to me . . . Nobody but me, the Smuins, and Armin Bali, knew about this incident. And, afterwards, I found out that the ring was one Armin had brought from Armenia and treasured for its sentimental value—which, of course, made her giving it to me all the more wonderful.

"In this incident, the gift, the compliment, was to Judith Jamison, dancer. Armin Bali had seen me dance *Cry* and she admired the way I danced. Her gift, of that beautiful ring, was a gift to an artist. *She* didn't care if I was black, white, or chartreuse."

SIX

"I am proud of being an American," said Judith Jamison. "Wherever I dance, I dance as an American dancer. I'm proud of that too. And from dancing outside this country I've learned enough to be able to compare conditions between American dancers and European dancers.

"Whether we are black or white dancers, we in this country work under much different conditions than dancers do in the European opera houses. I am not going to get into the argument, pro and con, on the subject of state subsidy for theatre, but the facts are that other countries accept theatre and the arts as part of life and here, in our country, we do not. The dancer is still a curio, something outside 'normal' life.

"The seriousness of working as a dancer is something the public does not understand and I think it is not the obligation of the dancers but of educators to inform people about the values of the arts to our society.

"The difference in attitudes, between Americans and Europeans, is something you feel as soon as you dance for a European company, after dancing in an American company.

"When I began working in Hamburg, and then in Vienna, in *Josephslegende,* it was different from any previous experience. I had been dancing on overseas tours for years before that but in the Ailey company. Now, I was dancing as part of a European company.

"It was not only the fact that I had a dresser, that I was treated with respect backstage as well as by the audience. It was the sensation that this was a different world from that of my home theatre—theatre in America.

"Things had a sense of permanency, something very important to me. It's not that I resist change—I accept and sometimes I invite change but I need a basis of stability in my own life and in my work. The anxieties I felt working in European theatre were all artistic anxieties; good pressures, necessary pressures. They were not the anxieties we felt for so many years in the Ailey company, not knowing if we would finish a season, far less start another season. I've lived most of my life as a dancer in a state of dread, with a sense of impermanency.

"I realize that my pleasure in dancing in Vienna came from several different things. I was working, for the first time, in a full-length ballet, and one in which I had the female leading role. I was working with a full company, something I had always wanted to do, instead of so often dancing solo, as I was doing after *Cry*. I was working with people, especially John Neumeier and Kevin Haigen, who respected my work, who respected *me,* as much as I respected them. I was taking on a role different from any I had danced before, but a role in which I felt very much at home, in a ballet that linked my childhood, when I went to Sunday School at Mother Bethel, with my grown-up existence. And not least of all, I was performing in a famous old opera house, the Vienna Staatsoper.

"I knew all these things but I was unprepared for the emotion that I felt on opening night. I was in the wings, waiting to go on, and I listened to the orchestra. A swell of music lifted me, and suddenly the tears were pouring down my face, because this—this wonderful experience—was happening to me in a foreign country instead of in my own country.

"I wanted, at that moment, for it to be happening to me at home —in New York at the Met or at the State Theater. In Washington at Kennedy Center. In Los Angeles at the Music Center. Somewhere, some place, that was home.

"For a while I couldn't stop crying. My dresser stood next to me, carefully blotting the tears as they ran down my cheeks onto my neck. She smiled and smiled at me, and I just stood there, bawling like a baby. She was just able to blot me dry before I had to go onstage.

"That experience taught me something about myself and what it means to me to be an American dancer. Now, that's a responsibility I take very seriously, wherever I happen to be dancing. I feel that I represent something of my country, of my people, to the audiences who come to look at Judith Jamison dance.

"Alvin has this missionary zeal, and he is a lot more articulate about it than I could ever be. Alvin used to talk about making an odyssey, like a pilgrimage, when we went to Africa. Everywhere the company danced, it was, as far as Alvin was concerned, dancing as an *American* company. In all the tours we went on, sponsored by the U. S. State Department, we were seriously working as American ambassadors of dance.

"In many ways, Alvin and I feel the same about dancing, and about being black American dance artists. The difference between us is that Alvin romanticizes things, and I am more of a pragmatist.

"Alvin and I have this love-hate thing, a relationship that I think we both appreciate, if neither of us truly understands it. I've tried to analyze the relationship between us.

"Sometimes I think that what we feel about each other is the way twins feel. It's not a brother-and-sister relationship, because I had one with Johnnie, and this is nothing like it.

"When I went into the company there were only two ways that people, men and women, looked at Alvin. He was a father image to some. To me he was not; I already had a father image, formed on my dad. And Alvin had an attraction, for men and women, of a kind I had never known and that is hard to believe—it was so obsessive, so possessive.

"I think that, consciously or subconsciously, Alvin encouraged these attitudes. For some he was the father; for others, the lover. There was never anything sexual between Alvin and me. He did not attract me that way, I did not attract him. But I believe we understood a lot about each other. Sometimes, we could read each other's minds. That did not always make for a frank and happy relationship, if one of us disapproved of something the other one was doing—or not doing, as the case might be.

"I guess that what I am trying to say is that there was a strong empathy between me and Alvin and I've always believed that if only I had been a man, I would have been Alvin's best friend. There is something about Alvin, about Alvin's sense of his masculinity, that will always prevent him from accepting a woman as his equal, as his friend. But I was, I am, Alvin Ailey's friend, all the same.

"People—mostly men—who think they know Alvin best, still say that Alvin is enigmatic, that he is mysterious. I think that Alvin likes mystery, likes being secretive, as much for the sensations of power they give him as for the privacy he needs. I think that the ways in which Alvin thinks and acts are the ways of a creative artist. And

that the ways in which I think and act are the ways of the performing artist. There is a gulf between and I understand that gulf, even if
I cannot cross it.

"Another gulf, as I've said, is the matter of sex. Alvin is very pa-
ternalistic and he's what I call an old-fashioned 'Suthun' gentleman
in his attitude towards women, the weaker sex. I am not maternalis-
tic. I don't fit Alvin's image of a woman, of a black woman—even
though, as I have read lately, I am supposed now to be the 'mother
figure' in the Alvin Ailey company.

"*Cry* was as close as Alvin and I ever got to each other. I've said
this many times. Alvin thinks that in *Lark* I was farthest from him,
from his intentions for me, than I have ever been. *Lark* came at a
time when I was still into technique, never mind that I was praised
for 'characterization' in *Cry*. I didn't begin to really use a dramatic
sense, consciously, until *Facets*. In *Cry,* I did what Alvin told me to
do, and if, as critics have written, the audience could not tell where
the choreography ended and where the dancing began, then that's as
much a triumph for Alvin as it was for Jamison.

"I have a nature that allows me to take pleasure in something I do
well. I love perfection, I admire what is flawless, in myself, *if* I
achieve it, and in other dancers. Alvin has done so much to feel
pleased and proud about but he can't let himself feel pride and
pleasure. It's something about his nature, or, maybe, about the way
he was brought up. We both had strict upbringings, Alvin and I, in
the home, and in religion, but of the two I think, from what I know
of his story, that Alvin had a freer, easier time in childhood with his
mother than I had with mine. Still, it's Alvin who has the bigger
bump of responsibility.

"Alvin and I are both worriers. The difference is that I will let
worry eat at me only so long and then I turn it off. The funny thing
is: I learned this trick from Alvin, only he doesn't practice it
anymore. He lets things push him too hard, too far. I believe that I
am the type who will always stop short of the brink.

"I wish Alvin would allow himself to be happier than he is. Happiness is a condition you make for yourself. No one can give it to
you, although, if you let them, people can reduce your happiness,
can take it all away. Alvin needs to really believe that he has done
great things, that he—more than anyone else—has done great things
for black dance in America.

"I so much admire Alvin for what he has achieved. I admire Arthur Mitchell for what he has managed to do with the Harlem ballet. These two men, and many other black dancers, are making big contributions to American dance. Some of them believe in all-black dance for black dancers. Others, like Alvin, understand that there is good in the mixture of dancers, from the different racial strata of American life. Each one is entitled to his own opinion, his own philosophy.

"You can't just apply your ideas and expect them to stick. I went to Philadelphia schools where the student body was predominantly white. I wanted a first-class college prep school for John Charles, my nephew, and that happened to be a white school, but it did not suit John Charles. His grades fell, he was unhappy. So he moved to an integrated school, primarily black students, where he is happier. What worked for me will not necessarily work for someone else.

"I fully understand what black pride is. I identify with it because I am black. I only wish that in my education—in the education of black American children—there was more emphasis on being black, on the black tradition.

"When Alvin choreographed *Ariadne,* I knew what the ballet was about. In school, I had learned Greek mythology. But when Alvin choreographed *Yemanja,* it meant nothing to me. Nobody I knew had ever heard of a black goddess by that name, a goddess—as I found out—who was the black Venus.

"Why couldn't I have learned about black gods and goddesses, and black heroes, at the same time I was learning about Greek ones? There should be literature for black children, just as there is for white children—something to grow on, legends and folklore to identify ourselves with, the way the educational system provides for white children to do.

"The business of being black in a white society is something that takes up so much time, takes so much heart, that it can become a lifelong occupation. I want to say to people: 'Look, here is who I am. I am Judith Jamison. I am a woman who dances; a woman dancer who is black.'"

So let it be written of her: She is the sum of various parts; of a family whose nobility lies in its quiet, calm sense of dynasty; of Marian Cuyjet and all the teachers who taught her what it means to dance; of all the fellow dancers who have inspired and helped her, and of all the choreographers whose silent, secret images have been clothed in her form and made living in her movement. She is the exalted child of "Mother Bethel" and its "revelations," and she is the little dancer of Philadelphia's Town Hall. She is the matriarch of Alvin Ailey's *Cry* and the swivel-hipped vamp of *The Mooche,* as she is Potiphar's Wife in *Josephslegende* and the multifaceted Women-in-love of Butler's *Facets.* She is the woman who lives through the five stages of Ulysses Dove's *Inside (Between Love . . . and Love).* She is the sister of every black, and every woman, and every dancer. And more, she is their cause.

INDEX